Reforming Education

Ambitious programs of education reform have been introduced by many governments around the world. *Reforming Education* is an important study of large-scale education reform in five different settings: England, New Zealand, the Canadian provinces of Alberta and Manitoba and the US state of Minnesota. The book looks at a variety of reforms, covering:

- school choice;
- charter schools;
- increased testing of students;
- stricter curriculum guidelines;
- local school management.

Drawing from theoretical and empirical work in education, political theory, organizational theory and public administration, *Reforming Education* provides a clearly developed conceptual framework for analyzing reform programs. The author reviews the political origins of the reforms, the process of adoption into law, the implementation processes used to support the reforms, and the results of the reforms for students, schools and communities.

The explicit political and comparative orientation of *Reforming Education* enables readers to look at reforms across different settings and to make judgements about the assumptions, processes and outcomes in large-scale reforms. It will be of interest to those working in education policy or public policy.

Benjamin Levin is Deputy Minister of Education and Training for the Province of Manitoba. He is also a Professor of Educational Administration at the University of Manitoba. His research interests are in education policy, politics and economics.

Educational Change and Development

Series editors: Andy Hargreaves
Ontario Institute for Studies in Education, Canada

Ivor F. Goodson
Centre for Applied Research in Education, University of East Anglia, Norwich, UK, and Warner Graduate School, University of Rochester, New York, USA

Reforming Education

From origins to outcomes

Benjamin Levin

London and New York

First published 2001
by RoutledgeFalmer
11 New Fetter Lane, London EC4P 4EE

Simultaneously published in the USA and Canada
by RoutledgeFalmer
29 West 35th Street, New York, NY 10001

RoutledgeFalmer is an imprint of the Taylor & Francis Group

© 2001 Benjamin Levin

Typeset in Garamond by Taylor & Francis Books Ltd
Printed and bound in Great Britain by TJ International Ltd,
Padstow, Cornwall

British Library Cataloguing in Publication Data
A catalogue record for this book is available from the British
Library

Library of Congress Cataloging in Publication Data
A catalog record has been requested for this title

ISBN 0–750–70982–0 (hbk)
ISBN 0–750–70981–2 (pbk)

Contents

Acknowledgments

I acknowledge gratefully the financial support of the Social Sciences and Humanities Research Council of Canada in the conduct of this research. All findings and opinions are solely my own.

Intellectual work always has an important collaborative element. Many people have contributed to this book in important ways. My friend and colleague Jonathan Young has worked with me throughout this project, always trying to guard against my tendencies to glib generalizations and hasty conclusions. He has steadfastly declined to share authorship, which I took as an indication of his modesty but which should perhaps be a warning that the book does not meet his standards!

Colleagues around the world helped me think about the issues and read versions of this work. In particular I want to thank Stephen Ball, John Beresford, Mike Bottery, Bill Boyd, Carol-Anne Browning, Jim Cibulka, Marian Court, Scott Davies, Yehezkel Dror, Lorna Earl, John Fitz, Frances Fowler, Sharon Gewirtz, Ron Glatter, David Halpin, Andy Hargreaves, David Hargreaves, Mark Holmes, David Hopkins, Heather Hunter, Joce Jesson, Reynold Macpherson, Hanne Mawhinncy, Michael Mintrom, Frank Peters, Sally Power, Tony Riffel, Nancy Roberts, Heather-jane Robertson, Jan Robertson, Viviane Robinson, Jane Strachan, Martin Thrupp, Geoff Walford, Darrell Ward, Mel West, Geoff Whitty, John Wiens, Phil Woods and Cathy Wylie. At the same time, it should be clear that the interpretations are my own. I know that at least some of the colleagues mentioned above would disagree with parts of the argument developed in the book.

A number of colleagues in New Zealand were especially helpful in helping me understand developments in that country and in arranging meetings with key people during my visit there. The School of Education at the University of Cambridge in England offered me a home away from home on two extended occasions, for which I am very grateful to Donald MacIntyre, Gill Morley and Mel West. James Aryee provided tireless research assistance, and Yolande Choiselat and Mary Franceschet assisted in the late stages of the work. I thank all those who agreed to be interviewed for this study, and all those who provided reports, documents, data and other information.

Acknowledgements

I changed jobs twice during this project. Shortly after it began I was appointed Dean of the Continuing Education Division at the University of Manitoba. My colleagues there – as fine a group as anyone could hope to work with – were endlessly tolerant of my taking time away from them for this research. In the last year of the work I became Deputy Minister of Education and Training for the Province of Manitoba, and had excellent support from my new colleagues in the Manitoba Department of Education and Training. I want especially to thank the Minister of Education and Training, Drew Caldwell, for his understanding and support of my academic work in a world where there are always far more pressing matters than writing a book!

A full and satisfying home life makes writing possible and, much more importantly, life worth living. My boundless thanks to my wife, Barbara Wiktorowicz, my three daughters, Clare, Anna and Ruth, and my extended family. Their combination of tolerance, support, pressure and criticism is exemplary.

Introduction

In recent years education has been a major focus of government policy in many countries. Governments have legislated or otherwise attempted changes in many aspects of education provision, including curriculum, testing, governance, finance, teaching methods and teacher training.

This book examines changing education policy in five settings in industrialized, English-speaking countries. It looks at national policy in New Zealand and England, at the US state of Minnesota, and at the Canadian provinces of Alberta and Manitoba. Each case examines a program of reform that occurred over a period of years – in some cases over the term of more than one government. The book focuses on the sources of reforms, the politics of their adoption and implementation, and on their outcomes in an attempt to examine the possibilities and limits of education reform.

The book is about both the process and substance of education policy. It describes and analyzes actual policy developments in these five settings, explaining what was done and why. At the same time, the book is a discussion of the process of policy development, looking in a more general way at the forces that shape education policy and its implementation.

Many of these reforms have been controversial. While proponents claim they will improve standards and outcomes, and will help countries to be successful socially and economically, opponents attack reforms as increasing inequity, demoralizing teachers, and destroying a proud tradition of success in public schooling. Education reform in the 1980s and 1990s has been politically contentious in a way that the enormous expansion of the 1960s was not.

Another important feature of recent reform projects has been their cross-national element. In a world of global exchange, states are increasingly interested in learning about what other states are doing in similar policy fields. Reforms are influenced by "the spirit of the times," which increasingly has an international flavor to it.

Yet everything we know about the process of policy change and implementation leads to caution about the impact of reform. It is very difficult to change well-established institutions in a lasting and meaningful way. And the consequences of reforms are not always those that were anticipated, by either proponents or opponents.

In many respects the discussion of education reform has generated more heat than light. There is a great deal of polemical literature, claiming that particular policies will bring the promised land or, alternatively, will destroy everything we value. Careful empirical work looking at the nature and consequences of reforms in various settings is much harder to find.

In all the discussion of reform, of course, it is vital to remember that policies impact on real people in substantive ways. At the level of national analysis, whether by governments or by academics, one can easily lose sight of the ways in which individual lives and collective practices are changed and shaped by distant decisions. One cannot avoid this impact – as Peter Berger (1976, p. 150) has written, "At the foundation of every historical society there are vast piles of corpses ... There is no getting away from this fact, and there is nothing to be done about it. It is an inevitable burden of the human condition." But one should try to remember it.

Howlett and Ramesh contend that "how analysts explain public policy and the aspects they emphasize depends on their frames of reference, which in turn depends on their interests, ideologies and experiences" (1995, p. 7). My own views about public policy in education have been shaped by a number of vital experiences – my work while still in high school in trying to organize a high school students' union, my election at age 19 as a member of a school board, many years of activity in a political party, seven years as a senior government official responsible for education policy, a senior management role in a university, and many years as an educational researcher trying to shape policy and practice in the light of available empirical evidence as well as strong value commitments. I started as – and continue to be in many ways – critical of much of what is done in schools. I see many institutions, public and private, as being insufficiently responsive to changing social and economic conditions (Levin and Riffel, 1997). But I am also a strong believer in public institutions and social action that tries to make our society fairer and less unequal.

Although these views undoubtedly color this book, I have also tried to be as dispassionate as possible, and to look carefully at the available evidence. In the best of all worlds, public policy would draw extensively on carefully developed evidence to assess its effects. Unfortunately there is no educational equivalent to the now-standard idea in health care of "evidence-based decision-making," the presumption that we ought to try to find out what effects our interventions have. Indeed, policy-making in education often seems to fly in the face of what research tells us is effective. Social policy will always be shaped by multiple forces, but surely one role of researchers is to try to inject more and better empirical evidence into the debate.

In thinking about education reform, whether one believes that schools are better or worse than they used to be is not the point. There is every reason to think that schools will be under continuing pressure to change as other aspects of society change. There is benefit in looking as directly as we can at what has been done in the name of change and how it has worked. If this book has a bias, it is that all aspects of reform are likely to be less straightforward than is often assumed by enthusiasts of any political stripe. The right reasons may sometimes yield the wrong results, and vice versa. My hope is that this examination will contribute to a more thoughtful discussion of the important issues around education policy.

The Study

This study was designed in 1995–6. The design was guided, as is usual in research, both by a conceptual framework and by pragmatic questions of time and resources. Comparative studies are difficult undertakings because researchers need to develop enough understanding of each setting to be able to avoid hasty generalization or inaccurate comparisons. Given my interest in the importance of history, culture and political context, the requirement for such sensitivity has been a vital concern. And the more jurisdictions one adds to the comparison, the greater the difficulties become.

The five jurisdictions in the study were chosen for varied reasons. A first restriction was to include only countries where the primary source material was in English. In some senses this is a problematic restriction, since other countries in Europe and Asia appear to have had quite different experiences. However, it was a practical necessity. England and New Zealand were included as the two English-speaking countries that had experienced the most dramatic changes in education policy. Australia might have been included, but because it is a federal state it would have been much more complicated to study than a unitary state such as New Zealand. As a Canadian I wanted to look at my own country, which has a rather sparse literature on education policy. Education is a provincial responsibility in Canada, so it was necessary to select a limited number of provinces. At the time the plan for this study was developed Alberta had had the most comprehensive and contentious set of education reforms in the country, although that honor – if honor it be – has probably now shifted to Ontario. I also thought it important to include my own home province of Manitoba, where reforms were less extreme than in some other provinces, though still quite contentious.

It was important to include a United States jurisdiction in the study for many reasons. The US is still the largest source of and market for educational research. It is an exciting, fast-moving policy arena because it is so decentralized at both the state and district level. The US also has an impressive policy research capacity in education to draw on. And the US political system provides an important counter-instance to the parliamentary systems in the other settings. I considered several US possibilities, including

Kentucky and Chicago, both of which have been the subject of extensive research. At one time I hoped to include more than one US setting, but limitations of time and resources precluded this. I eventually chose Minnesota as the US case because it was the first state to adopt two important reforms – school choice and charter schools – because there was some good scholarly work to draw on, and because it is proximate to me, making the logistics of research easier.

The research plan for the study involved five data elements: scholarly literature, original documents and source materials, contact with other researchers doing related work, secondary analysis of existing data, and collection of new data primarily through interviewing. A brief word can be said about each of these.

Most good research begins with careful study of existing work. In this case a large body of work already existed in regard to England, and fewer but nonetheless valuable sources were available on New Zealand and Minnesota. The weakest literature was in regard to Canada, and especially in Manitoba. Because a considerable amount of the relevant literature is unpublished, contact with researchers in other countries has been an important part of the process of locating as much work as possible.

The study gives considerable weight to original documents, with particular attention to political debates in parliaments and legislatures, and to official documents on education reform issued by governments, their related organizations and other interest groups. Many of these sources are now available directly via the Internet, vastly improving research access to them. Organizations in each country – departments of education, teacher organizations and others – were very helpful in making documents available. Academic colleagues in the other jurisdictions also proved very helpful in pointing to important documentary sources.

Given the scope of the study and the considerable amount of related work that had been done in some of the jurisdictions of interest, taking advantage of the knowledge and work of others was a cost-effective strategy. However, the main value of contact with colleagues in other countries has been the dialogue on understandings and findings. I have shared materials from this study with other researchers quite extensively and benefited greatly from their feedback. The Internet has facilitated this sharing, and has changed dramatically both the possibilities and the practicalities of international research. Colleagues have noted errors of fact in some cases, but even more importantly helped me understand the nuances of the different settings. Debates over papers from this project at conferences and seminars in many different places as well as via e-mail made a very material contribution to the analysis.

Part of the study plan was to try to make use of data put together by colleagues elsewhere doing related work, such as interview transcripts from earlier studies. In the event I made less use of this data source than anticipated. In some cases other researchers have been prepared to share data, especially where these were clearly in the public domain already. In other cases colleagues felt that their ethical undertakings to those they interviewed or to other sources of data prevented these from being shared.

Finally, the study plan recognized that there would be gaps in the other data sources that would require some original data collection, especially in Alberta and Manitoba, where there is very little published literature. Visits were made to all the jurisdictions in the study. A small number of formal interviews and a much larger number of informal discussions took place during those visits and on other occasions. These involved not only people who had played a key role in the events under study, but also people who had been careful observers of the reform process rather than participants. Respondents were uniformly helpful and willing to share their time and knowledge.

In total the project accumulated a very large body of evidence, with dozens of feet of shelf space of papers, documents, newspaper clippings, and other evidence, many tapes of interviews and discussions, and another large amount of material stored electronically. As is the case in most research, what is reported in this book is but a small portion of the evidence. Selection of material to include was based on the conceptual framework and four central research questions outlined in Chapter 2. The book includes several extended excerpts from relevant sources in the form of "boxes" which are intended to give a fuller flavor of the evidence than can be done in most of the text.

Organization of the Book

The book is in eight chapters. The first two chapters provide background. Chapter 1 examines changes in the international context for education reform since World War II and especially the last ten or fifteen years. It looks at the way in which larger social forces have been changing with consequent implications for the substance and process of education policy. Chapter 2 outlines the four-part conceptual model and central research questions for the study and this book.

Chapter 3 provides a brief overview of the five settings and a description of the reforms in education that were made in each. The bulk of the analysis in later chapters is thematic rather than geographical, so it is important for readers to have an initial grasp of events in each setting. Since each of these reforms could easily be the subject of an entire book, the account here is necessarily highly condensed. Timelines of the reforms are provided in Appendix 2, and readers are also referred to more extensive sources should they wish more detail.

Chapters 4 through 7 examine the four main aspects of reform identified in the underlying framework for the study – their origins; the process of adoption; the process of implementation; and their outcomes. Each chapter outlines a conceptual approach to the issues and then looks at evidence from the five settings. Because the time periods, scope and basis of evidence vary quite a bit among the settings, the descriptions are inevitably uneven, with some places and events getting more attention than others.

Chapter 8 draws together the main findings and implications of the study, and makes, perhaps immodestly, some recommendations both for research and for practice.

A Note About References and the Literature

This book draws extensively on the available literature on reforms in each of the jurisdictions. Main sources are cited in the text. However, I have sought to avoid too frequent text citations that are distracting to the reader. At the same time, textual citations do not do adequate justice to the secondary materials. Accordingly, readers will find a discussion of the main sources in Appendix 1.

1   The Changing Nature of Education Policy

The Context for Education Reform

Any discussion of education policy should begin by providing a historical and social context, since education cannot be understood independently of more general developments in society over time. Education is intended to serve other social purposes, so ideas about education will change as ideas about those other purposes change. Education is also an important part of the public sector or state apparatus, so ideas about education will also be shaped by changing views of the role of the state.

To understand recent changes in education policy, we need to go back about fifty years – to the end of World War II. For more than thirty years after World War II, education policy in the English-speaking industrialized countries (Britain, the United States, Canada, Australia, New Zealand) was marked by powerful common features. Perhaps most importantly, the number of young people increased substantially due to the very large cohort of births after the war – the Baby Boom. Governments invested heavily in expansion of the system, and over thirty or more years the system grew dramatically in every way. Many new schools were built, and standards of accommodation changed so that almost all schools had proper gymnasia and libraries. Secondary education became practically universal (though always with some significant number of students not completing), and vocational forms of secondary education were developed. Provision for music and physical education improved. Tertiary education also expanded dramatically. Whole new types of institutions of higher education were created. In short, what was in 1945 still a relatively modest and selective system became, by 1975, a very large system with participation rates at all levels that were much higher than had ever been seen before.

Demographics were not the only factor pushing expansion. Human capital theory provided a strong argument for more education as a key factor in fuelling economic growth. Education was also seen in all these countries as a means of addressing, if not solving, many long-standing social problems. Not only were there more students, but the role of the school was

7

extended as well. Schools were increasingly asked to try to reduce crime and discrimination, to teach children to avoid habits such as smoking or drinking, and to integrate a larger and larger range of disabilities. As the role of schooling expanded beyond the narrowly academic, new programs and services were added at all levels, such as special education, guidance and counseling. Class sizes dropped steadily and significantly. Spending rose rapidly in real terms and, after enrolments stopped growing in the 1970s, spending continued to rise in per pupil terms. Yet costs to students were either reduced (in many areas of tertiary education) or in some cases eliminated altogether.

The expansion was supported not only by increasing numbers of students and by great belief in what education could accomplish, but also by a long period of rapid economic growth. Governments were able to balance their budgets, keep tax increases to modest levels and still fund many new ventures. As has historically been the case, economic expansion fed optimism. A large proportion of the population had a very direct interest in the expansion and enrichment of public education.

In all these respects education was typical of state services in general. The same expansion of public activity that occurred in relation to schools also took place in other sectors such as health care and transportation. Whole new sectors of state activity opened up, such as the environment, recreation and culture. A buoyant economy allowed governments to increase taxation and to increase substantially their share of total economic activity. By the 1970s all of these were at levels that had previously only been recorded in times of war.

In the 1970s, however, the atmosphere began to change. All of the drivers of the expansion of education, and of the public sector generally, altered. As the Baby Boomers moved through the school system, not only did enrolments shrink but the proportion of the population with children in school began to shrink, and other social policy concerns, particularly health care, grew in importance. Expectations for schools had been built to enormously high levels, and an inevitable disenchantment began to set in when it became evident that more schooling would not itself lead to less poverty, less crime or lower unemployment. It became clear that we did not know how to – or could not – educate all students to high levels of competence. A similar reaction was occurring to other social programs of the 1960s that did not seem to be leading to the promised nirvana. In fact, some social problems, such as crime rates and unemployment rates, seemed to be getting worse even as formal education was expanding.

Bovens and t'Hart argue that the decline in confidence in governments is also linked to changing expectations, in particular the reduced public willingness to accept any kind of risk. As they put it:

At one level, we have grown more disappointed with government as the great societal problem solver. At the same time, however, our expectations concerning a life free from acts of God, nature's capriciousness and other random forces beyond institutional control have continued to rise. As a result, the tragic dimensions of public life, not so long ago still accepted as an important feature of statecraft and governance, have faded from both popular discourse about politics and from the evaluation designs of policy analysts. Since we no longer accept misfortune as a cause of social ills, someone has to be blamed for them.

(1994, p. 147)

At the same time, governments began to face serious fiscal problems. The public share of GNP had risen steadily in most countries, and governments became less and less able or willing to tax at the levels required to sustain their operations. Deficits grew larger and larger. The 1970s witnessed periods of high inflation, and when a major recession hit many countries in the early 1980s, government spending and debt became very important political issues. Maintaining existing programs became problematic, and continued expansion vanished from the agenda.

During the period of expansion, thinking about education and social policy had been dominated by ideas about the importance of the state. In economics, Keynesian ideas held sway, and in social policy ideas of public investment to support growth were prominent. But these, too, began to change in the 1970s. New ideas that supported proposals for a smaller state sector and the importance of markets gained in prominence. Public choice theory stressed the inevitable self-interest of economic and social actors, and the consequent need to restrain them. Arguments for moving authority away from public organizations to individuals and families became more powerful.

Growing doubt about the efficacy of programs coupled with less ability to finance them and less political support for them were part of what led to the rising success of conservative political movements that were committed to less government, less public sector spending and lower taxation. The 1980s witnessed the triumph of conservative governments in Britain, the United States and Canada, and the increasing hegemony in many countries of the ideas promoted by conservatives of a smaller state, lower taxation and a greater emphasis on individual and family self-reliance. Ironically, criticism of state sectors made by those who saw them as inadequate responses to inequality were used to support the arguments of people who wanted a smaller state altogether. Those who were most advantaged organized to defend the arrangements that supported their advantages, whether those involved low levels of taxation, the creation of new areas open to profit-making activity, or state support for private schooling. A variety of measures were taken in various countries to promote this new political agenda.

9

However, the election of so many conservative governments suggests that the new conservative message also captured strong populist sentiments about the state of society and remedies for problems (Apple, 1996).

Even this broad sketch, in the view of some, fails to do justice to the scope of the change that is occurring in many societies. A number of commentators argue that we are actually undergoing a transformation in basic ideas about the organization of society. This change has been described variously as postmodernism, post-Fordism or the information society. Its manifestations are held to encompass fundamental changes in the economy, in social relations, in the role of the state, and in how individuals think about themselves and others. To cite just a few examples, Giddens (1994) writes about the need for a new approach to social policy in light of the rise of reflexivity and the need for individuals to reinvent themselves continuously. Hargreaves (1994) points out the importance of changes in conceptions of time, intensification of experience, increasing individualism and diminished certainty. Many of these arguments are linked to the need for changes in institutions, including schools, to meet new social conditions.

Others are much more critical of recent changes. Ball (1998) focuses on the increasing influence of commercial and market forces on public services in many countries. Others (e.g. Apple, 1996; Dale, 1989; Barlow and Robertson, 1994; Berliner and Biddle, 1995) have also argued that recent years have seen a deliberate effort by the affluent and powerful to reorganize society to their own benefit.

History is a combination of continuity and change, with an ever-shifting balance between the two. However, caution should generally be exercised in evaluating claims of major social transformations. One's own historical period always looks full of uncertainty precisely because we do not know how things will turn out; we cannot see the future. What looks like great change to those living in it can look much more like stability from a longer-term perspective. The middle ages, for example, are now considered a time of great social stability, yet to those who lived through them they seemed as full of upheavals and unexpected developments as our time does to us (Tuchman, 1978). As Beniger (1986) points out, allegations of transformation in society are frequent while transformations are uncommon by definition. At the same time, powerful large-scale shifts in societies are often virtually undetectable to those living in them because they take place over many years.

Whatever one's views about the historical scale and reasons for change, there can be no doubt that important changes have taken place in the social policy context in recent years. The collision between an education system used to growth and governments committed to the opposite led to a period of ferment in education policy in many countries during the 1980s. A long period of rapid growth in the provision of education, fueled by a rapidly expanding economy and great faith that education could be the means of resolving many enduring social and economic problems, came to an end. In its place, we entered a period marked by stagnant or declining funding and considerable dissatisfaction, at least among elites, with what schools were seen to have achieved. Governments struggled to develop new education policies that would, they hoped, be both less costly and more effective.

Changes in the substance of education policy were accompanied by important changes in political processes as well. Policy-making in education had tended to occur through discussion and eventual consensus among the key internal participants, such as government ministries, teacher organizations and administrator groups. As governments became more interventionist and as education increasingly became a political priority, the relatively slow processes of negotiation and accommodation disappeared. Instead, governments adopted top-down change strategies, rapidly implemented. Groups within the system, such as teachers and administrators, were quite often identified by politicians as a part of the problem, thus legitimizing their exclusion from policy-making. Education policy became much less consensual, more a matter of conflict and more overtly driven by the political agendas of particular governments (Macpherson, 1996; Mazzoni, 1991).

While educators were losing influence in the policy process, business groups were gaining influence (Whitty, 1989; Borman *et al.*, 1993; Manzer, 1994). The rising influence of big business can be seen both as cause and consequence of changes in government policy, since corporate executives tend to be much more critical of schools and supportive of reforms such as reduced spending than are other social groups (Livingstone and Hart, 1998). Business leaders occupied an important place in the official policy-making process. They chaired commissions on education (such as Brian Picot in New Zealand) and issued influential reports (such as the Minnesota Business Partnership or the Conference Board of Canada). A recent United States summit meeting on education involved political and business leaders, but almost no representatives of the educational community (Good, 1997). The increasing emphasis on private sector practices also meant that business methods were frequently held up as examples for schools to emulate. Ideas such as Total Quality Management were exported to the schools sector. Private sector approaches such as contracting out were also advocated. An increasing amount of the commentary on public policy drew on business models and analogies, in all of which ideas of deregulation and market mechanisms were often held up as ideals for the public sector as well.

Also given a more important role, though in a less direct way than business, were parents. Much of the education rhetoric of the 1980s was concerned with giving parents a greater voice in the education of their children. Governments sought ways of involving parents in policy formation. For example, much more use was made of commissions and public hearings in formulating policy than had previously been the case. In some cases governments provided financial and organizational support to various organizations of parents. However, as parents are generally not politically organized, especially beyond the individual schools their children attend, finding a serious role for parents in the policy process has proved difficult. Public hearings tended to be dominated by organized groups, which in many cases in education meant existing educational or business groups.

Again, these trends in education mirrored those in other sectors. Over the last twenty years all areas of public activity have witnessed reductions in funding, concerns about value for money in public services, more confrontational political processes, a greater emphasis on private sector models, and attempts to increase the role of consumers in public services. Bottery (1998) points out the commonalities in the way that the British government approached policy in such diverse fields as schools, health care and policing. Ball argues that

> during the last fifteen years we have witnessed in the UK, and indeed in most other Western and many developing societies, a major *transformation* in the organising principles of social provision right across the public sector. That is to say, the forms of employment, organisational structures, cultures and values, systems of funding, management roles and styles, social relationships and pay and conditions of public welfare organisations, have been subject to generic changes.
>
> (1997, p. 258, emphasis in original)

I take up later in this book the question of the extent to which it is useful to think about these reforms as part of an international pattern. However, it is clear that there are some commonalities in education policy shifts in the English-speaking industrialized countries. Four common contextual elements of reform as well as three common elements of reform in the countries studied seem to be particularly important.

Commonalities of Context

In terms of context, it is important to draw attention to the dominance of economic rationales for change, the overall climate of criticism of schools, the absence of additional funding to support change, and the growing importance of diversity in thinking about education policy.

First, the need for change in education is now everywhere cast largely in economic terms, and particularly in relation to preparation of a workforce and competition with other countries (but see Merson, 1995, for a discussion of the ways in which this argument was itself gradually reshaped in Britain during the Conservative period). Education is described as being a key component of countries' ability to improve, or often even to maintain, their economic welfare. This brief excerpt from an OECD report is an illustration of a line of reasoning that can be found in many, many reports of governments and other organizations in almost every country.

Only a well-trained and highly adaptable labour force can provide the capacity to adjust to structural change and seize new employment opportunities created by technological progress. Achieving this will in many cases entail a re-examination, perhaps radical, of the economic treatment of human resources and education.

(OECD, 1993, p. 9)

We hear so much of this rhetoric now that it may seem self-evident, but the main rationales for education policy change thirty or forty years ago were quite different, having much more to do with social mobility and individual welfare. The current emphasis on the allegedly apocalyptic consequences of failure in education were largely absent in that last great period of education reform. Economic rationales are not, to be sure, the only reasons being advanced today for educational reform. Equity goals are still cited, as are individual social mobility and citizenship, but the balance has clearly changed in the direction of an economic emphasis. A sense of fear seems to have replaced the sense of possibility as a driver of change in education. In the classic phrase of the US report *A Nation at Risk*, the problems of education are "an act of unilateral educational disarmament." Moreover, there has been increasing emphasis on individual responsibility for life outcomes; what Giddens (1994) has called "the self as a reflexive project."

Second, education change is occurring in the context of criticism of schools. Government policy documents typically take the view that school systems have failed to deliver what is required. International achievement tests have become a particularly important part of this critique. Insofar as these rank countries in order of achievement, a large number of countries will inevitably see their own performance as inadequate. The specifics of the criticisms of schools differ across settings, but among the main allegations are that the so-called progressivism of the 1960s damaged achievement, that teachers are overpaid and often do not work very hard, that school systems have become too bureaucratic, with a consequent reduction in creativity, and that schools are excessively dominated by wrong-headed theory instead of by solid traditional practice. Critics often argue that the alleged failures of schools are especially lamentable in view of the high level of spending on education. The efficiency of the system is seen to have declined greatly as per pupil costs rose significantly while outcomes as measured by tests and exams are held to be unsatisfactory. In short, the general tone underlying much reform is negative – an effort to undo damage.

Education reform is always motivated by criticism, of course. Indeed, many of the criticisms of the 1980s were also being advanced in the 1950s (Levin, 1998b). What is interesting about the current criticism is that it is most strongly expressed by certain groups or sectors, and is not widely shared, it appears, by parents. For example, a series of Canadian opinion polls (Livingstone and Hart, 1998) has shown that the only group strongly supporting the typical reform agenda as defined below is corporate executives. All other groups are more supportive of schools and less interested in large-scale reform. Livingstone (1998) also cites polling data from the US and UK as well as Canada showing that public confidence in schools continues to be higher than that expressed for government or business. The efforts to convince people generally that education is in a state of crisis seem not to have been generally accepted, but remain a strong part of official rhetoric nonetheless.

Third, large-scale change is no longer accompanied by substantially increased financial commitments to schools by governments. The funding picture varies quite a bit around the world, with some jurisdictions making real cuts and others modest increases, but in every setting in this study governments have largely decoupled reform from funding. However, public support for stable levels of social services, including education, remains quite high in the countries of study, and there continues to be significant support for stable or increased education funding, even at the price of higher taxes (Livingstone and Hart, 1998). Although there is much rhetoric about education as an investment, especially when post-secondary students are being asked to pay higher tuition fees, governments still more often treat education as a cost than as an investment. The line about money not solving problems is now heard so often that it has become widely accepted, but that should not blind us to its novelty. It is hard to think of any other major reform in education that was not accompanied by injections of large quantities of money. The attempt to move the gears of education without the grease of financing produced some very loud noises from the machinery.

Finally, nations have become increasingly sensitive to issues of diversity in managing public policy. Differences within nations in ethnicity, language and religion have become vital policy issues almost everywhere. Minority groups, whether ethnic, religious or linguistic, have grown increasingly assertive about what they consider to be their rights, and education has been one of the main areas of conflict. Both legal and political systems have changed in response, with legal institutions in particular often delivering vital support to the claims of minorities. Canada has one of the most complex sets of minority concerns (Riffel *et al.*, 1996). The country's two primary linguistic groups, Anglophones and Francophones, each have constitutional rights in education. So do religious minority groups in some cases. Aboriginal people have reclaimed increasing control over their own institutions, and immigrant ethnic minority groups have also been vociferous in arguing for educational entitlements. But similar issues exist in most other countries as well. Relations between Blacks and Whites – and latterly also Hispanics – have been a central issue in education policy in the United States. Although the US Constitution prohibits a religious establishment, debates about the place of religion in schools are probably more heated today than they have been for a hundred years, thanks in part to the rapid growth and political influence of fundamentalist religious groups. The place of the indigenous Maori and migrants from a number of other Pacific islands has been equally at the forefront of policy in New Zealand. In Britain the issues are somewhat more muted, but there have certainly been important debates about regional devolution (to Scotland and Wales) and about the role of religion and minority languages in schools. Ideas vary greatly on how best to cope with issues of diversity, but the importance of the issues is evident to all, including those who wish diversity would just go away.

Commonalities of Strategy

Turning to the kinds of strategies governments have adopted, it is important to recognize that the components of reform programs do vary in important ways across countries and, in federal countries such as Canada and the United States, between provinces or states. Nonetheless, three kinds of proposals are a key part of many reform packages:

1   decentralization of operating authority to schools and the creation of school or parent councils to share in that authority;
2   increased achievement testing with publication of results and its corollary, more centralized curriculum;
3   various forms of choice or other market-like mechanisms.

One of the strongest trends in education reform across national boundaries has been the move to shift authority to the level of the local school. The first steps in this direction in the US and Canada involved largely an administrative decentralization (Brown, 1990), in which school administrators were given more authority over staffing and budgets to improve efficiency. More recently emphasis has also been given to political decentralization, which gives an increased role in governing schools to parents, and in some cases to other community members. This movement has perhaps more to do with effectiveness – questions of purposes and strategies – than with efficiency. The logic of decentralization assumes that changes in governance are key to improved performance of schools; that local bodies are in the best position to define and make necessary changes; and that parents especially have important knowledge about how the educational enterprise should best be carried on for their children. Unhappiness with the perceived bureaucratic character of large school systems has been an important part of the rationale for decentralization. The case for parental governance of schools is also linked by some proponents to issues of rights, arguing that parents ought to be able to influence substantially, if not determine, the nature of the schooling of their children.

The degree of control shifted to local schools, usually at the expense of regional authorities such as school districts, has varied but has in many cases been quite substantial. In Canada and most of the United States, parent councils remain advisory, but in England and New Zealand as well as some places in the US (such as Chicago and Kentucky) school governing bodies – which are made up of parents and other community members – have very substantial authority over the schools.

The second strategic element involves more testing of students on a standard curriculum or set of learning objectives, with results being made public. Testing is seen by advocates as important in moving towards a market-like system. Since test results are regarded as the main basis for choosing a school, achievement testing needs to have public results. As well, a logic of testing leads to a prescribed curriculum so that all students can both have the opportunity to learn and be tested on the skills and knowledge that are regarded as most important. Jurisdictions have taken different approaches to both these issues, but more state control of curriculum and more assessment of students has been a common factor in many places.

Increasing national assessment is complemented by more and more international assessment, and these results are also used more overtly for public comparisons (Cibulka, 1991). Countries now proudly hold up their rankings on the latest international achievement study as a badge of honor, just as schools may cite their exam results (published in the newspapers in Britain) or test scores and college-entrance rates (US) as evidence of the quality of their work. A new education literature is burgeoning on themes of assessment and accountability (e.g. Cuttance, 1994; Macpherson, 1996, McEwen, 1995).

A third reform proposal being implemented in many settings involves increasing the influence of parents over schools by giving them the right to choose the schools their children attend. Advocates of choice policies work from one or both of two beliefs. Some proponents urge the creation of systems that try to mimic the characteristics of economic markets based on the belief that market systems are inevitably more effective and efficient than state systems, so that market-like mechanisms will necessarily bring improvement in schooling through the rigors of competition.

A second, more complex line of argument rests on the belief that parents can make the best choice of school for their children, and ought by right to be able to make such choices even if they are not popular ones. These proponents of choice may have no particular liking for the capitalist economic system. Some are quite conservative (such as those who defend choice as a way of recognizing religious beliefs in schools – e.g. Holmes, 1998). Others regard the existing system as highly stratified and see choice as a way for those with less economic or political clout to have more influence over schooling (e.g. Nathan, 1996).

A less flattering picture of the tendency to favor market solutions is provided by Plank and Boyd (1994), who term it "the flight from democracy." They see in the advocacy of private sector models a deep-seated distrust of democratic politics.

> The two most striking features of American school politics in the past decade have been an obsessive concern with the multiple "failures" of the educational system and a propensity to embark on a flight from democracy in the search for solutions. The consequence has been the growth of an *antipolitics* of education, in which disagreements about educational policy and practice are increasingly likely to be addressed in conflict over the institutions of educational governance rather than in open debate on the merits of alternative goals and strategies ... in the hope that new institutions will place braver, wiser, and nobler persons in charge of children's schooling.
>
> (1994, pp. 264–5)

Reforms advocating school choice have been among the most controversial of all in recent years. They are often seen by detractors as a fundamental challenge to public education. Aspin and Chapman write:

> It is clear that over the past decade, the social, political and ethical foundations upon which systems of public education were developed have been subjected to radical scrutiny in many places ... The new view ... rests upon the notion that education is to be conceived of less as a public good or a form of welfare agency and much more as a *commodity*, the selection of which is a matter of private choice and hence dependent upon personal provision and the norms of the market place.
>
> (1994, p. 5, emphasis in original)

Various vehicles have been employed to make education more market-like, including allowing or even requiring parental choice of schools, tying school funding to enrolments, various restricted versions of voucher plans, and charter schools. However, in every case schools resemble a market in only a limited sense. No jurisdiction has a system yet that involves a direct payment between family and school except in the case of private schools, and there the trend has been to reduce direct costs to families through higher public subsidies. Also, in general there has been more attention to the demand side of the equation than to changing the supply side by providing a significantly more diverse range of schools. In fact, market mechanisms have been constrained by other simultaneous reforms, such as testing and inspection, that have tended to push schools to be more homogeneous.

As a set, these reform agendas are driven by what may be called a managerialist focus, a belief that the central problems of education can be remedied through changing the organization and management of the system in accord with a set of theoretical principles that can be applied regardless of context. The reforms embody an important if sometimes unstated set of assumptions about how schools work and what will result in change. They have in common the belief that educators cannot be trusted to deliver appropriate education because of their self-interest. Reform must therefore come primarily from outside pressures. Schools tend to be seen in this model as production enterprises, with students as the objects, curriculum as the vehicle, and management structures as the key variables of change. The reform strategies seem to imply that if schools are threatened with public disclosure of poor results, if enrolment and financing are dependent on academic success, if different people have control over decision-making, then the right decisions will be made and student achievement will improve.

These assumptions seem paradoxically out of step with the conventional wisdom about improving organizational outcomes in other sectors. There is little in these reform programs, for example, that mirrors the popularity of such private sector trends as quality management, learning organizations, focus on customer service, or constant development and innovation. Whereas schooling reforms focus on outside pressures and less autonomy for educators, the business literature is full of calls for more autonomy for workers, a stronger focus on teams, and the importance of an internally directed search for improvement. Whether such developments are actually occurring in the private sector is another question entirely (Lowe, 2000). Still, it seems ironic that education changes supported by business executives and intended to improve economic performance are moving in a different direction than the most touted reforms in the business sector.

Conclusion

This chapter has provided a brief overview of the background and context for the reform programs to be considered in this book. Although recent reforms involve some sharp discontinuities with earlier policies and practices, they also grow out of the past and need to be understood in that light. The reform efforts of the 1980s and 1990s are clearly responses to what went before, and are partly reactions to what came to be seen as earlier failures or excesses. It is also important to recognize the extent to which changes in education policy are influenced by larger social and economic developments. The analysis draws us back clearly to political questions as lying at the heart of education policy, which is, after all, about the choices that governments make. The next chapter lays out an approach to thinking about the development and implementation of political reform in education.

2 Conceptualizing Education Reform

The word "reform" often has a positive normative character, implying something desirable. In this book the term is used to refer to programs of educational change that are government-directed and initiated based on an overtly political analysis. The changes examined are driven primarily by the political apparatus of government rather than by educators or bureaucrats, and justified on the basis of the need for a very substantial break from current practice. In other words, for our purposes here, reforms are those changes in education governments have undertaken to make. I do not claim that these reforms are necessarily desirable. This definition of reform also stresses the political element in education reform in contrast, for example, to reforms that may emanate from within the school system itself.

The Four-Element Model

This book tries to address the entire reform process, from its inception to the point where some judgements can be made about its results. The main theoretical frame for the study is a stage theory of policy. There are many of these (a good overview can be found in Howlett and Ramesh, 1995), all of which involve some series of stages moving from the identification of a problem through the identification or adoption of particular strategies to issues of implementation and impact. To an extent, any specific delimitation of stages is arbitrary and a matter of personal preference. For this study I define four elements or phases of the reform process – origins, adoption, implementation and outcomes.

1 Origins. The focus here is on the sources of reforms as initially proposed by governments, the role of various actors and forces in originating reforms, and the assumptions about education and reform (explicit or implicit) contained in these proposals. Where did particular proposals come from? How did they become part of the government agenda, when so many ideas do not?
2 Adoption. Here the interest is in what happened to reforms between their initial proposal and their actual passage into law or regulation in each

jurisdiction. Policies as finally adopted or made into law often differ from those originally proposed. I wanted to examine the politics of the reforms, and the factors that led to any changes between proposals and approval.

3   Implementation. A considerable body of research in education and other policy fields lays out the difficulties of moving from policy to practice. My interest was in the model of implementation, if any, that governments used to move their reforms into practice. What steps were taken to implement reforms? What "policy levers" were used? What model of implementation, if any, informed the reform process in each setting?

4   Outcomes. Interest here is on the available evidence as to the effects of reforms. Any political action may have a number of results, some which were intended by policy-makers and others which were not. Because the reforms under study are about education, I wanted to give particular attention to what may be known about how the reforms have affected student outcomes and learning processes in schools.

There is nothing inevitable about this particular organizational frame. Other schemes have been defined in the literature. Ball (1990) developed an approach that looks at reforms from economic, political and ideological perspectives while focusing also on structural, interactional and discursive elements. Bowe *et al.* (1992) develop their analysis in terms of three elements – influence, text production and practice. Taylor *et al.* (1997) use a similar structure focusing on elements of context, text and consequence. Each categorization scheme draws attention to somewhat different aspects of reform, and each can be useful.

Though I find a four-part categorization useful for analytic purposes, and though the categories are discussed separately in the following sections and chapters, they are in practice overlapping and interactive. In political analysis, discrete categories and periods are devices of the analyst, not the experience of those directly involved. An adequate account of policy must, however, deal with all the elements. Policy intentions are important, but must be seen in the light of political practicalities that may substantially change preferences, and in light of the actual consequences that are provoked by any given policy. On the other hand, one cannot simply read back from outcomes to intentions. Some policies may be substantially rhetorical, with little thought given to actual outcomes. In other cases outcomes are not those that were anticipated, especially in complex policy systems such as education. If policy intentions are resisted, then outcomes are likely to be shaped by the resistance as well as the intentions. No one element of the process is necessarily predominant.

Planning and Contingency in Policy Thinking

The common view of reform tends to assume that a given political or ideological analysis leads to a reform program that in turn leads to changes in practice leading to particular outcomes. A great deal of the work on policy in education and in political studies embodies this kind of means–ends analysis. Some work embodying these assumptions operates at a high level of abstraction, concerned with such matters as the changing role of the state and the impact of globalization as determining forces in political events (e.g. Taylor *et al.*, 1997; Carter and O'Neil, 1995). Education reform in these works is often treated as the implementation of a set of well-defined political views arising from a belief in the reduced role of the state or the primacy of markets over public provision. This approach can be found in many of the analyses and critiques of such recent policies as school choice (e.g. Lauder *et al.*, 1999).

These analyses are important and rightly draw our attention to the links between education policy and broader issues of power and social policy. However, few would now uncritically accept a model that posits analysis leading to choice leading to action leading to results as a complete formulation of how the political world works. More than thirty years ago, Allison's account of the Cuban Missile Crisis (1971) showed how much more was actually going on during a critical political episode than the narrow models suggest, and much work since then, reviewed elsewhere in this book, has supported his analysis. Political action may be characterized, by both proponents and opponents, as the result of careful thinking and well-laid plans, but such analysis may overstate the logical and understate other aspects of the political world. Politics is intentional, but it is also frequently provisional and ad hoc, and may be shaped as much by the vicissitudes of the moment as by well-defined intentions. One finds a high level of ambiguity and contingency in every aspect of the political process. At every step, multiple and conflicting influences come to bear, purposes change or are worn down by existing structures and processes, and circumstances change in ways that require modification of plans and actions. As Ball puts it:

> National policy making is inevitably a process of bricolage: a matter of borrowing and copying bits and pieces of ideas from elsewhere, drawing upon and amending locally tried and tested approaches, cannibalising theories, research, trends and fashions and not infrequently flailing around for anything at all that looks as though it might work. Most policies are ramshackle, compromise, hit and miss affairs, that are reworked, tinkered with, nuanced and inflected through complex process of influence, text production, dissemination and, ultimately, re-creation in contexts of practice.
>
> (1998, p. 126)

Thus the view, often expressed, of politics as an irrational activity.

Yet an account that places too much stress on the contingent risks understating the importance of power and the significance of longer-term changes in institutional structures, organizational roles and power relationships. Neither the importance of means–ends rationality nor the underlying contingency of life can be ignored – both must be accommodated in an adequate theoretical account. This difficulty is precisely why careful empirical work with a clearly articulated conceptual framework is important. As Whitty and Edwards (1994, p. 30) write, "the detail is fascinating and important and only in the detail is it possible to glimpse the complexity of power in its various manifestations."

The approach used in this book values both a means–ends rationality and a sense of the chaotic – rather like a mathematics formula in which the value of each term is initially unknown. Reform is driven in some important ways by a kind of linear calculus. This is the numerator in the equation. If there were no sense that an action would produce particular consequences there would be no reason to undertake the action. In politics, careful calculation of consequences is of absolutely central importance, although the consequences that are of interest certainly include personal, partisan and symbolic outcomes as well as substantive policy consequences. However, this numerator is modified by a denominator that contains all the contingent elements. Sometimes the numerator is larger and policy is driven by careful strategy. Other times the denominator is larger and policy is primarily the result of the accidental and unforeseeable.

Coming to grips with these issues is not easy. After all, one is essentially trying to give a coherent account of something that can look pretty much like incoherence. As Ball puts it, a good account should

> capture the messy realities of influence, pressure, dogma, expediency, conflict, compromise, intransigence, resistance, error, opposition and pragmatism in the policy process. It is easy to be simple, neat and superficial and to gloss over these awkward realities. It is difficult to retain messiness and complexity and still be penetrating.
>
> (Ball, 1990, p. 9)

Alternative Perspectives on Policy Formation

How can one make sense of something that is as elusive as Ball's formulation suggests? Literature from several disciplines suggests that an adequate account of policy-making should take account of the following points:

- Political decisions are shaped by many considerations, including the requirements of staying in office and the vicissitudes of the moment as well as the beliefs and commitments of policy-makers and their advisors.
- Politics is substantially shaped by symbolic considerations that may have little to do with the real effects of policies.

- Human abilities to understand problems and generate appropriate solutions are limited and often inadequate to the complexity of the problems. The entire process of policy development and implementation takes place in a context that is constantly changing, multi-faceted, and very difficult to read.
- Strategies for reform may focus on elements that are politically salient but that cannot produce the kinds of changes we really want or, to put it another way, the focus may be on what can be done instead of on what might really make a difference.
- Institutions such as schools or governments possess considerable ability to resist or alter policies to fit their own dynamics.
- History and culture are very powerful influences on policy and practice.

A number of these themes will recur in later chapters in the more detailed discussion of reform programs. However, some of the underlying complexities can be illustrated through a brief discussion of some of the important work in these fields.

What shapes political decisions?

Just as an understanding of policy requires attention both to rationality and contingency, so government generates both people's deepest hopes and aspirations and their highest levels of cynicism. Any understanding of large-scale education reform should be rooted in a sense of how government actually works. Unfortunately, the policy literature in education is often only weakly connected to the political science literature on government, and as a result often underestimates the political and contingent aspects of government.

Many accounts of policy-making in education seem to assume that politics is primarily about policy – that governments are there primarily to define and implement a program. Especially among critics of policies, governments are often viewed as being fundamentally interested in particular policy outcomes based on a priori ideological commitments. Of course, policy is important in government, but the evidence would certainly seem to indicate that it is only one factor, and often not the pre-eminent one. Governments are also fundamentally about politics, and politics involves getting elected and staying in office as well as accomplishing goals while there. The requirements of electoral work are clear enough. Governments and individual politicians must please enough voters and supporters to be able to maintain themselves. This leads, as is well known, to all kinds of devices designed both to assess and to influence public opinion and especially the views of key supporters.

To complicate matters still further, governments are subject to all the internal politics of any organization – currying favor, trying to increase one's own power, jockeying for future rewards, pleasing one's own constituency, and so on. Colleagues in a government may dislike each other intensely, for example, while still having to work together closely and put on a public face of collegiality and mutual support. One has only to read any political auto-biography to see just how important factors other than policy are in the politician's life.

Politicians also change positions frequently. Even when there are not changes in government via elections, ministers move from one portfolio to another every few years, making it difficult to sustain a political program.

In the world of politicians and those who work closely with them, every-thing occurs in an atmosphere that is extremely intense and fast-paced. There are a huge number of pressures and very little time, so that almost everything is done more quickly than might be wished. Senior politicians and staff have to deal with an enormous range of policy issues, so they can never be very knowledgeable about most of what is on their agenda. Issues crowd in on one another, each one requiring attention and analysis but with key decision-makers not having time to give enough attention to any of them. Politicians also have little or no respite from political work. Ministers and senior officials typically work very long hours trying to cope with all this, with the result that people are often tired or almost overwhelmed by the set of issues facing them. Moreover, days at the office are usually followed by evenings and weekends of political events and discussions. The boundary between work and life seems to dissolve, such that one's whole life is taken up with politics in one way or another. In this atmosphere, time for planning or reflection is at a premium.

Another fundamental reality of government is that unexpected events occur frequently, divert attention, and change political priorities. Whatever one's plans and intentions may have been, crises emerge that require atten-tion. An event halfway across a country or around the world can completely rearrange the priorities of a government for days or weeks. A storm or flood, a sudden price hike or bankruptcy, a popular protest, the emergence of a scandal can all divert a government's attention. The day's media reports can easily displace all sorts of other, more important issues. Much of political life is a struggle between having an agenda that one tries to move forward and simply responding to all the things that end up on government's plate. Politicians are also often under intense pressure from competing interests. Little wonder, then, that issues sometimes get short shrift, that attention moves rapidly from one thing to another, and that the moods and events of the day often dominate long-term agendas.

Symbolic politics

Murray Edelman is a political scientist who was among the first to argue the view that politics should be understood as being as much a symbolic activity as a practical one. In other words, political talk and action are intended to shape and to respond to people's ideas as much as to their practical interests. In two books, *The Symbolic Uses of Politics* (1964) and *Constructing the Political Spectacle* (1988), Edelman develops the idea of politics as being largely a symbolic activity in which actions are intended to have psychological consequences.

> Practically every political act that is controversial or regarded as really important is bound to serve in part as a condensation symbol. It evokes a quiescent or an aroused mass response because it symbolizes a threat or reassurance. Because the meaning of the act in these cases depends only partly or not at all upon its objective consequences, which the mass public cannot know, the meaning can only come from the psychological needs of the respondents; and it can only be known from their responses.
>
> (1964, p. 7)

In his second book Edelman puts the issue even more starkly.

> Accounts of political issues ... become devices for creating disparate assumptions and beliefs about the social and political world rather than factual statements. The very concept of "fact" becomes irrelevant because every meaningful political object and person is an interpretation that reflects and perpetuates an ideology. Taken together, they comprise ... a meaning machine; a generator of points of view and therefore of perceptions, anxieties, aspirations and strategies.
>
> (1988, p. 10)

In this view of politics, words and other symbolic activities are of critical importance, but not in any straightforward sense. Instead, they are designed to achieve emotional and symbolic purposes as much as anything else. "The propagandist whose verbalizations are most intensely embraced is the one who finds a formulation that evokes and synthesizes a large number of the experiences of concern to this audience" (1964, p. 124). When this is done, language "is in no sense descriptive, but only evocative" (1964, p. 125). Specificity of meaning is not necessarily desirable. Words are intended to be ambiguous as a way of allowing a range of people to project their own feelings and opinions on to what has been said. At the same time, "the most astute and effective use of this language style conceals emotional appeal under the guise of defining issues" (1964, p. 137). Emotion is officially deplored as a means of invoking emotion, such as a sense of self-righteousness. Or, as Edelman put it in his later book, "Ideological argument through a dramaturgy of objective description may be the most common gambit in political language usage" (1988, p. 115).

Edelman also argues that politicians use symbolic responses as a substitute for dealing with real interests "which permits the organized to pursue their interests effectively" while others are being satisfied with what is largely rhetoric (1964, p. 40). In other words, the political spectacle is also used to hide policies and actions that do have material advantages for some groups over others.

In symbolic politics, events are used to create legitimations for political actions. As Edelman puts it, "A crisis, like all news developments, is a creation of the language used to depict it; the appearance of a crisis is a political act, not a recognition of a fact or of a rare situation" (1988, p. 31).

Edelman's analysis of politics may strike the reader as particularly cynical. However, similar views on politics have been expressed by a number of other theorists. Deborah Stone, in *Policy Paradox and Political Reason* (1988), describes problem definition as the strategic representation of situations: strategic in shaping a course of action, and representational because the representation of problems necessarily relies on interpretation by both speakers and listeners. Another important aspect of problem representation concerns the attributed causes of problems. Stone distinguishes between explanations of problems that embody mechanical, intentional, inadvertent or accidental causes as being most important (p. 149). However, in politics accident is less and less acceptable as an explanation of events people don't like (Bovens and t'Hart, 1994). As the lawyer in the recent movie *The Sweet Hereafter* says in trying to convince a bereaved parent to sue over an accident in which her son was killed, "There is no such thing as an accident. Someone has to be at fault."

Stone also provides a fascinating discussion of some of the vehicles that are used to create particular representations of problems, including stories (that are told as if they are typical), synecdoche (again assuming that one instance stands for many), metaphors (such as the highly emotive expression about "throwing money at problems"), as well as insightful comments on the selective use of data to support a particular point of view. She stresses the importance of ambiguity in allowing people to see what they need in a given commitment or event, thereby making it possible to build political support or coalitions (1988, p. 123).

The limits of capacity – fuzzy gambling

Political imperatives are not the only source of limits on government capacity to create and sustain reform. Human capacities to understand and solve problems are also limited. Israeli political scientist Yehezkel Dror has spent many years thinking about the nature of governance in the contemporary world. Dror's book, *Policymaking Under Adversity* (1986), provides a thorough and thoughtful account of both the potential and the limits of government action. Dror describes what he calls "policy adversities," or the factors that make policy-making difficult. Policy issues themselves can be very complex, may include many interacting and dynamic factors, often seem to be highly intractable, may be outside the sphere of government, and can involve inherent contradictions (1986, pp. 38–45). But these are not the only difficulties. Human problem-analysis and problem-solving capacities are themselves limited in important ways. For example, people tend to overestimate the influence of immediate or visible causal agents, to give credence to the obvious instead of the important. We tend not to see the importance of subtle and long-term changes, to infer causality when events are connected only fortuitously, to give too much weight to what we have seen or been told most recently, and to be powerfully influenced by preconceptions and stereotypes (Kiesler and Sproull, 1982). Edelman's argument regarding the powerful effects of symbols can itself be read as a form of human incapacity.

The result, Dror argues, is that policy-making may best be viewed as what he calls "fuzzy gambling," a situation in which not just the odds but the rules themselves change as the activity progresses. Moreover, Dror contends, there is "at any given moment a high probability of low probability events occurring. In other words, surprise dominates" (1986, p. 186). In such a context, policy is far from a straightforward matter of calculating costs and benefits.

Dror is not, it should be added, a pessimist about governance. He has many suggestions about ways to improve policy-making, including better training and support for both politicians and policy advisors. However, he is unflinchingly a realist in looking at what he calls "policy-making incapacities," and recognizing that there is no easy way to remedy them.

Focusing on the wrong issues

Another critique of policy-making in education has been based on the claim that reform does not address what really matters, partly because it is so hard to change what really matters. US researchers Richard Elmore and David Cohen have addressed this problem extensively.

Cohen (1995) points out that changes in student performance, which is surely what most education reform at least purports to care about, depend fundamentally on what teachers and students do in classrooms. Yet many reforms, including those described in this book, are not primarily aimed at teaching and learning, but focus instead on school organization, governance, finance, curriculum and assessment. Reform advocates make the assumption that changes in the latter will result in changes in the former. However, Elmore is one of many who have noted that "Changes in structure are weakly related to changes in teaching practice, and therefore structural change does not necessarily lead to changes in teaching, learning and student performance" (1995, p. 25).

Or, as James March (1978, p. 219) put it more colorfully, "Changing the schools by changing school administration is like trying to change the course of the Mississippi river by spitting in the Allegheny river."

However, focusing on changing teaching and learning is easier said than done. Governance or curriculum changes can be put in place through legislation and can be pointed to as real changes. Altering teaching and learning practices is much more difficult because these depend on the decisions of so many individuals and are so difficult to alter.

Yet even if the focus is on the right policy variables, policy-makers may well overestimate their influence.

> policy-makers frame solutions to problems by acting as if policies were the main determinants of the outcomes they're trying to produce, but we know that this is never the case.
>
> In fact, the influence of policy is at the margin of choice ... the range of public objectives and their effects on choices are always less coherent and consistent than the rhetoric of policy-making implies.
>
> (Elmore, 1987, p. 165)

The nature of institutions

Policy changes inevitably have to work their way through institutions. Governments, school systems, political parties, labor markets – all are institutional structures with a history and sets of understandings that may affect the way in which policy takes shape. Neo-institutionalism is a subset of organization theory that has provided a renewed focus on the important role institutional structures and processes play in shaping and containing policy. Neo-institutionalists (e.g. March and Olson, 1989; Crowson *et al.*, 1996) argue that characteristics of institutions and institutional systems have strong effects on organization functioning independent of rational analysis or self-interest.

A substantial body of theoretical work deals with the ways that organizations try to cope with external pressures and demands (see Levin, 1993, and Levin and Riffel, 1997, for extensive reviews). Although organizations of all kinds are strongly affected by changing external conditions, the dominant view among researchers is that organizations try wherever possible to maintain the status quo and to avoid changing in response to external demands. Kaufman writes that organizations have two main responses to uncertainty: "incorporation of the source of the uncertainty within the organization – that is, expanding the boundaries to include it – thereby making it subject to the norms and controls of the system" and "reduction of exchanges across boundaries in an effort to satisfy most needs internally – withdrawal from the source of uncertainty as it were" (1985, p. 43).

Organizations try to manage uncertainty by creating standard ways of thinking about and acting on issues and problems. These standard practices come to shape what people see as possible or desirable. As Mary Douglas put it:

> Institutions systematically direct individual memory and channel our perceptions into forms compatible with the relations they authorize.

They fix processes that are essentially dynamic, they hide their influence, and they rouse our emotions to a standardized pitch on standardized issues. Add to all this that they endow themselves with rightness and send their mutual corroboration cascading through all the levels of our information system ... Any problems we try to think about are automatically transformed into their own organizational problems. The solutions they proffer only come from the limited range of their experience.

(Douglas, 1986, p. 92)

A particularly interesting variant of neo-institutionalism is what is called "the logic of confidence" argument (Meyer and Rowan, 1977). The argument is that institutions do not necessarily have to be successful to survive; they only have to appear to be doing the things that people expect such an institution to do. In other words, it is often their appearance that engenders trust rather than their results. Or, as James Herndon put it more colloquially, "An institution is a place to do things where those things won't be done" (Herndon, 1972, p. 99). The logic of confidence argument seems especially applicable to schools, since everyone has gone to school and so has a sense of what a school "should" be like, and indeed was originally developed in regard to schools.

Wilson (1989) shows clearly the degree to which government action is affected by the institutional nature of government and bureaucracy as well as by political factors. Far from chastising public sector managers for their weaknesses – though he recognizes that such weaknesses exist – Wilson concludes that "Given the constraints on the managers of public agencies, it is a wonder that there is any management at all ... often, goals are hopelessly vague, activities sadly ineffectual, and powers sharply limited" (1989, p. 154). This is itself a result of the very public way in which governments must operate, and the scrutiny they are constantly under from people whose interest lies in discrediting what is being done.

Neo-institutionalism gives a theoretical expression to the common empirical finding that policies are transformed by those who have to turn them into action. Issues of implementation are discussed more fully in Chapter 6. However, it is clear that policies do not move neatly into practice, and that some of these alterations are inherent in the nature of large organizations.

Organizational learning

A more optimistic vein of work concerns the ways in which organizations come to change their practice through learning. A number of writers (e.g. Senge, 1990) have argued that in the face of increasingly complex environments, organizations must be oriented to learning as a way of coping with change. Majone concludes his discussion of ideas and arguments in policy-making with the importance of learning:

learning is the dominant form in which rationality exhibits itself in situations of great cognitive complexity. This suggests that the rationality of public policy-making depends more on improving the learning capacity of the various organs of public deliberation than on maximizing achievement of particular goals.

(1989, p. 183)

Although organizational learning is an appealing concept, it has some serious conceptual difficulties. For example, it is not clear whether an organization can learn, as distinct from the people who make it up. What does organizational learning actually look like? The idea of organizational learning also inevitably has a normative character in that it assumes that some kinds of learning are desirable while others are not. Presumably learning that leads to outcomes valued by the writer is the right kind of learning, while learning leading in other directions is wrong! Yet without a normative element, one could only conclude that all organizations are learning something or other – even if only to keep on as they are – all the time.

James March (1991) has developed the distinction between the *exploration* and *exploitation* of knowledge in organizations. He argues that organizations will tend to do what they already know: to exploit accumulated skill and knowledge. This is sensible in that it is through exploiting knowledge that efficiencies can be produced. Looking for new approaches and methods is expensive and often wasteful. At the same time, organizations that do not seek new knowledge and new ways of doing things will eventually face problems as the situation around them changes and their ways of doing things become less and less functional. The problem is to find the appropriate balance between these two elements. It might well be argued that school systems have focused very heavily on exploitation, and that relatively few resources have been devoted to finding new ways to educate people. Certainly the formal investment by governments in research and development in education remains very small almost everywhere in the world (Guthrie, 1996). On the other hand, it may be that the exploration of alternative approaches to learning is being carried on – perhaps appropriately – outside the formal education system by profit-making organizations, information technology companies and community groups.

Another approach to the question of learning can be found in Charles Lindblom's work on problem-solving. As Lindblom puts it,

One can say ... that there exist countless social problems for which no adequate solutions come into sight unless and until people reconsider the positions they have taken and consequently alter them ... It follows that ... the only prospect of solution lies in further inquiry. The path to a solution is through inquiry and knowledge that will make a politically imposed solution not now possible eventually possible.

(1990, p. 6)

Like Dror, Lindblom sees clearly the many obstacles to effective problem-solving. He writes eloquently about what he calls "impairments" to effective problem-solving (one of which is inadequate and closed-minded education), but also believes that improvements can be made. He argues for many approaches, including but not limited to the contribution of social science. Lindblom also contends that partisanship in policy can be valuable, helping over time to move towards better understandings of issues and possibilities: "There would seem to be more hope for good policy in the contestation of partisan participants, each aided by social science, than in policy-making by an inevitably partisan single decision-maker falsely perceived as or postulated as above partisanship" (1990, p. 265).

History and culture

The most important determinant of present arrangements is usually past practice. What has gone before and how people think about their present situation shape what is either desirable or possible at any given point in a jurisdiction. Each nation, or each region within a nation, thinks and acts within its history and its sense, often taken for granted, of what is right. All of the overarching elements discussed earlier in this chapter will themselves have different manifestations in each concrete setting. Elements of social structuring, such as issues of social class, language, religion and ethnicity, are especially significant in influencing education policy. The structure of political institutions and the nature of political culture also affect the way in which education policy issues are played out. Each of these elements is in turn shaped by unique historical events.

Consider first issues of social structure. Family background continues to be the single most important predictor of educational and life outcomes, but its role in education policy debates varies a great deal across the settings. In England, with a long history of social class divisions, class and elitism are defining elements in all debates about education policy. Edwards and Whitty (1995) have argued that in Britain the entire structure of education policy and provision can only be understood within a framework in which rankings are what matter, and most people's objective is to have their children as high on the academic ladder as possible. Certainly, questions of class were a key part of the debate over reform in Britain. In New Zealand and Canada, on the other hand, social class has historically been less prominent than in Britain, and class issues figured much less prominently in debates over education. In the United States a strong history of individualism means that social class tends to be largely absent from mainstream political debates.

To take another example, ethnic diversity is an important feature in each country, but the legacy of slavery in the United States carries completely different implications for ethnic relations than does Britain's relatively recent Commonwealth immigrant population. In the US every policy question is looked at through the lens of its racial impact so that, as one example, debates about school choice are often also debates about racial segregation. In Canada and New Zealand relations with Aboriginal peoples have been vital policy issues, though for a variety of reasons Canada has been less accepting of special status for its Aboriginal people than New Zealand has been in regard to the Maori. In the United States, although the situation of Aboriginal people displays many of the same problems, their numbers are, except for a few states, too small to have much impact on overall policy.

Religion also plays an important but quite different role in each country. In the United States, the constitutional separation of church and state coupled with a revival of evangelical Protestantism have exacerbated the suspicion of state schooling and fueled conflict around how schools might accommodate differing religious beliefs. Canada, Britain and New Zealand, on the other hand, have all had state religion at one time, and all have a history of at least some sectarian schools being supported by state funds.

Differences in history and culture are also affected by the differing geographic and demographic situation in each country. Thus Scotland, though nominally part of the British system, continues to have quite different education policies for various historical reasons (Raab *et al.*, 1997). In Canada, because of the state's origins in struggle between French and English, every educational issue also has to be considered from the standpoint of regional interests, language and religion. The country's history of immigration and its current demographic diversity mean that equity issues are always on the political agenda but in complex ways because of different views about the appropriate place of ethnic identity (Riffel *et al.*, 1996).

Geography matters, too, even in our digital age. It is far easier to get key people together in a small country such as Britain or New Zealand than in a large and dispersed country such as those in North America. Where people meet less often, certain kinds of political and organizational relationships are less likely to develop. On the other hand, Canada has a small population despite its size, meaning that elites in all sectors are small, certainly compared with the United States, or even Britain.

Both Canada and the United States are federal states, while Britain is largely unitary and New Zealand entirely so. Canada's history and geography have led to a highly decentralized system of education in which the national government has a very limited role. However, Canadian decentralization is quite different in spirit from that in the United States. In Canada, governments have historically been seen as positive and important instruments for achieving social purposes, unlike the United States, where local control is fuelled by a strong orientation towards individual rights and concomitant suspicion of all things done by governments. Canadian provincial governments have always been important actors in education.

The structure of political institutions is also a vital factor. Unitary states such as Britain and New Zealand can take actions that are impossible in federal states such as Canada and the United States. Parliamentary systems provide a quite different set of political opportunities and constraints than does an American-style system with its separation of the legislative and executive functions. The separation of executive and legislative control in the United States creates dramatic differences in political practice – for example, in the ability of an executive to implement its program. One can only conjecture about the fate of, say, Thatcherite reforms had the Conservative Party in England not had a parliamentary majority. In the US system there is almost inevitably more compromising and making of deals in any legislative program than a majority parliamentary government would face.

Political culture also influences the way in which reforms occur. Jurisdictions vary in how polarized their main political parties are, which in turn affects the nature of political debate and the sharpness of the policy options that may be put forward. Where parties are trying to claim the political center, policy differences may be blurred. Where a party is trying to appeal to true believers, differences may be sharpened.

All of these factors shape the range of options that policy-makers will even contemplate, as well as the strategies they might use to pursue an issue. No country is the result of a process of rational planning, so the net effect of context is to increase the complexities and contingencies that surround education policy.

Conclusion

These strands of analysis provide useful ways of thinking about policy creation and implementation. They direct our attention both to the promise and to the limits of public policy. Governments are inevitably involved with shaping public policy and activity. This is an important task. At the same time, governments, especially in open political systems, have only limited ability to create the world as they might wish it. Although the analysis in this chapter gives considerable emphasis to the limits of government action, it does also suggest that we can learn from our efforts and improve our capacity to analyze and act on important matters. Public policy remains, whatever its limits, a central way for societies to shape themselves.

This is precisely why empirical evidence about reform is so important. As Howlett and Ramesh point out,

> Researchers [may] forget the contingent nature of the hypotheses gener-
> ated by the various approaches and the need to test them. Instead of
> using the study of public policy to test the hypotheses and assess the
> explanatory capacity of their theories, analysts simply read public policy

making in terms of the theoretical framework, models, or metaphors they are using.

(1995, p. 40)

The discussion in later chapters attempts to balance a theoretical understanding with empirical evidence, neither underestimating nor overestimating the importance of government policy to the lives of people involved with schools.

3   The Five Settings and the Reform Programs

A Brief Description

The following pages provide a brief description of the context and the main reform events in each of the five jurisdictions. An overview is necessary to provide the background for the analysis in the following chapters. Putting a description of each setting and the complex events around education reform into a single chapter is an impossible task. What follows is much condensed and leaves out more than it includes. All that can be accomplished is to give some sense of the context and main events in a way that is not terribly misleading. Additional details on each setting are included in later chapters as well. Those wanting a fuller picture should also consult the chronology for each jurisdiction in Appendix 2, and the additional readings described in Appendix 1.

England

Context

Although Britain remains as of this writing primarily a unitary state, the school systems differ considerably between England and Wales (generally spoken of as one unit for purposes of education), Scotland, and Northern Ireland, with recent constitutional developments likely to magnify these differences over time. This discussion focuses on England, which was most strongly affected by the reforms in question.

England has a population of about forty-seven million people. Most are Caucasian, but the country had large numbers of immigrants after World War II from its former colonial possessions, especially the West Indies, India, Pakistan and Bangladesh, and now has a visible minority population of about 5 per cent, much of which is second or third generation. The population is mainly urban, and the minority population even more so.

Britain's recent political history is as a two-party state, with the Labour Party historically associated with the unions and the industrial and working-class northern part of the country, and the Conservatives associated with business, the middle and upper classes, and much more entrenched in the south. Although other parties have had a national presence, none has had any serious chance of forming a government in recent years. Each of the major parties has had substantial periods in governments since the end of World War II.

Although British politics have been highly polarized for some time, the center of gravity in national politics shifted beginning with the selection by the Conservatives of Margaret Thatcher as their leader in 1976. Three years later Thatcher's Conservatives won the general election, defeating Labour, and were re-elected in 1984, 1987 and 1992. Although the entire period of Conservative rule bears strongly Margaret Thatcher's imprint, she was overthrown as party leader and prime minister in 1991, and replaced by John Major. Major won the 1992 election, but was then decisively defeated by Labour in 1997. The long period of single-party rule in Britain is a significant difference from some of the other settings under study (though both Canadian provinces have also had relatively long-term Conservative governments).

Thatcher introduced fundamental changes in almost every aspect of the public sector during her term as prime minister. She was very strongly committed to neo-liberal ideas about privatization and the value of market forces, as well as to neo-conservative ideas about returning to old standards of quality and exclusivity. She was determined to move away from what she saw as excessively collectivist ideas of government towards a much smaller state and much more emphasis on market provision of services. Immediately after she took over the Conservative leadership, Thatcher and her supporters created a number of think tanks and other organizational vehicles designed to promulgate these ideas so that they became fundamental to Conservative Party thinking and policy (Lawton, 1994).

Social class has long been the dominant organizer of the English social system. The English school system has historically been elitist at all levels, with a very small number of schools, many of them private (although called "public schools" by the British), seen to be at the top of the heap, educating the children of the well-to-do and the upwardly mobile.

Until 1988, the general approach to education in Britain had been shaped by legislation at the end of World War II when the school-leaving age was raised and a genuine commitment was made to provide secondary education for all. During the 1960s and 1970s a serious attempt was made to move to a less elitist system by turning secondary grammar (academic) schools into comprehensive schools that would serve children of all ability levels. However, there has been a persistent belief in some influential sectors that quality of education declined as schools became more open and less selective. The secondary school system of final exams and of two levels – GCSE and A level – of academic qualification, with relatively few students obtaining the latter, was a further reinforcement of a system that was predicated on low participation rates at the higher levels. Indeed, until very recently

Britain had one of the lowest participation rates in advanced education of any of the industrialized countries.

The English school system in 1988 consisted of about 22,000 schools. The majority were operated directly by about 120 local authorities. The local authorities were (and still are) elected and are responsible for all municipal services as well as education. During much of the Thatcher period, local authorities, especially in the large urban areas (including central London), were dominated by Labour. The dispute between the Conservative central government and the Labour local governments was doubtless one of the reasons that the powers of local authorities, not only in education but in many other areas, were so drastically reduced by the Thatcher government.

For various historical reasons the British system also included a number of other arrangements. Voluntary-aided schools were mostly religious in orientation, and operated under the local authority but with more control over some aspects of their operations, such as admissions. A small number of voluntary-controlled schools, chiefly operated by long-standing foundations, had an even greater degree of autonomy from local authorities. "Public" schools – actually private – continued to educate a significant portion of the children of the well-to-do. In London, the Inner London Education Authority, with its own separately elected Council, had responsibility for schools across eleven local authorities until 1988. All schools also were supposed to have governing bodies made up of teachers, parents and local citizens, mostly appointed by the local authority, though these played, in general, a fairly minor role until 1986.

Although some local authorities operated their schools in a bureaucratic and hierarchical way, there were prior to 1988 relatively few hierarchical controls on academic practices in schools other than the high school examinations. Britain had no national curriculum so schools were free to adjust both content and modes of teaching to suit themselves or their local community. Large-scale testing occurred only in secondary schools at the end of year 11 (the GCSE).

Before 1988, the national Department of Education (though it operated under a changing series of names) played a relatively small role in England in comparison to the other jurisdictions in our study. The Secretary of State for Education had few statutory powers. The absence of a state curriculum eliminated one major function of a state agency. The high school examinations were done by independent organizations. Money for schools went from the national government as part of local authority grants, but not from the Department of Education. To simplify the description of a very complex process, local authorities are funded by the national government at prescribed levels for the entire range of services they provide. Local authorities then make decisions about how much will be allocated to schools as opposed to other services. The Department of Education is not involved in the central decisions about funding of local authorities. Although the

Thatcher government took a number of steps to reduce and control spending by local authorities, these initiatives did not come from or through the Department of Education. One very important function of the department was to operate an inspection system through Her Majesty's Inspectors (HMI), experienced educators who visited schools and also did special studies on particular issues of interest.

Britain in 1988 had five teacher unions or associations, but collective bargaining occurred at a national single table for all. Salaries and some working conditions, such as extra-curricular obligations, were part of collective agreements. Until 1986, unions played a very powerful role in education policy-making. In its earlier years the Thatcher government challenged and greatly weakened unions in many areas of the British economy. Teachers were one of the later targets. However, in the period from 1985 to 1987, the Thatcher government directly confronted the teacher unions, in the end passing legislation that substantially reduced union powers and effectively ended their ability to provide strong organized opposition to changes in policy (Ironside and Siefert, 1995). The Teachers' Pay and Conditions Act in 1987 ended collective bargaining of teachers' wages and working conditions; salary scales since then have been set unilaterally by the government after recommendation by a commission. The teacher unions differ in their approach to issues, with some being more militant and more like trade unions while others try to define themselves as being more like professional associations. The existence of multiple unions has very probably lessened teachers' political influence.

The reforms

Reforms in education need to be seen in the context of the overall Thatcherite project of reducing the role of the state and relying primarily on market forces for all forms of service provision, while also strengthening some traditional aspects of British society such as its emphasis on elitism. Education was not one of the first major targets of the Thatcher government. Some policy changes were made in the early Conservative years, notably to end the requirement for comprehensive secondary schools and to increase the role of parents in both choosing and governing schools. The Conservatives also introduced in 1981 the Assisted Places Scheme, which provided financial support for high-achieving students to attend selective private schools. Keith Joseph, a confirmed advocate of markets over state provision, was Secretary of State for Education from 1981 to 1986, but despite several discussion papers and much behind-the-scenes policy work (Lawton, 1994), the main reform legislation came after Joseph retired.

In the 1987 election, education was a major focus of the Conservative program partly because of the long and bitter labor dispute with teachers over the prior years. The Conservatives promised "to compel schools to respond to the views of parents" as a way of bringing the benefits of the market to education (Gewirtz *et al.* 1995). Action on their program began immediately thereafter. In a series of bills between 1986 and 1993, many important changes were made, with the 1988 Education Reform Act being the most important single piece of legislation. In retrospect the Conservative program can be described as having had nine main elements:

- City Technology Colleges were created as an attempt to have industry support model inner-city education programs with a strong technical and vocational focus.
- School governing bodies, consisting primarily of elected parents and co-opted community representatives, were given most of the formal authority over schooling. Governing bodies were also required to report regularly to parents on the school's plans and achievements.
- Many of the management responsibilities for schools, such as determining staffing and budget allocation, were moved from local authorities to schools (local management of schools, or LMS). Local authorities were required to pass on the vast majority of funding to schools on a formula basis.
- Schools were given the right to opt out of the control of their local authority, and be directly funded by government and controlled by their governing body of parents, teachers and community members (grant-maintained or GM schools).
- Parents were given the right to choose the school their children would attend. Schools were given the right to make academic ability a part of their admissions policy – a partial return to "selection," which Labour governments had attempted to eliminate during the 1960s and 1970s.
- A National Curriculum was introduced to cover all subjects and all grades.
- A program of national testing was created to test student achievement in the main subject areas at four age levels, with public reporting of the results on a school-by-school basis.
- The Office for Standards in Education (Ofsted) was created to conduct regular inspections of schools with the results to be made public.
- Much of the responsibility for teacher education was moved to schools and local authorities in an effort to reduce the influence of the universities in this field.

The City Technology College initiative was announced in 1986, before the other main provisions of the 1988 Reform Act, but was included in that bill. Some of the 1988 provisions were extended in 1992 and 1993, and Ofsted was created in 1992. However, the bulk of this program was contained in the 1988 Education Reform Act, an enormous document. The original version of the bill was 200 pages in length with 255 clauses, and by the time it was passed, 290 pages and 308 clauses. The bill also abolished the Inner London Education Authority (ILEA), which had been responsible for education through most of London and was dominated by Labour. The responsibility for education in London was given to the individual boroughs.

It could be argued that the Conservative approach to education, while consistent in some important ways across their entire eighteen years in power, also evolved and arguably became steadily more radical over time. For example, the required delegation of funding from local authorities to schools increased, grant-maintained schools were given more powers, and the capacity of schools to select students based on ability was increased.

City Technology Colleges (CTCs) were intended to demonstrate that schools located in inner-city areas of England could produce very high levels of achievement using a strong emphasis on high technology. They were to be partnerships between the public and private sector, with the latter contributing large amounts of money to the schools' development and operations. In the event, this initiative fell far short of plans in the number of CTCs created, in the degree of private sponsorship and in the actual nature of the schools.

School governing bodies were to consist of parents elected by other parents, teachers elected by the school staff, and co-opted governors – people from the community recruited on to the governing body to provide a particular perspective or expertise. Parents and co-opted members were required to form a majority of the board. Within the requirements of the National Curriculum and its enforcement through testing and inspection, governing bodies were given substantial authority over the school. They received the great bulk of the budget as a lump sum from the local authority. The governing body hired all staff, was responsible for school premises, set all policies on such matters as admissions, program and discipline, and had obligations to report to parents formally on an annual basis.

Local management greatly diminished the power of local authorities, who were now required to pass on 85 per cent (later increased to more than 90 per cent) of the funding they received for education directly to schools. Their ability to adjust school funding to recognize differing needs was largely eliminated. Although they remained the official employers of staff, all hiring decisions were to be made by school governing bodies. Schools were also given control over external services such as program consultants and transportation, so local authorities would have to bid for contracts from individual schools in order to sustain these services at a district level.

The grant-maintained schools initiative allowed individual schools to choose through a ballot of parents to become completely independent of their local authority, in which case they would be funded directly by the national government. The governing bodies of GM schools were given complete managerial authority over all operational aspects of the school, including hiring, pay levels, program, discipline, facilities, and community relations. A separate funding agency was set up to channel funds to these schools. In later legislation, all school governing bodies were required to make a formal decision each year as to whether they wished to pursue grant-maintained status.

School choice was to operate at two points – the beginning of primary schooling and again at the beginning of secondary schooling. Parents would be free to apply to any school in the country. Schools were required to have a plan for deciding which students would be selected if there were more applications than places. These enrolment schemes could not use academic ability as the selection criterion for more than a small portion of the total student body (though this portion was increased in 1992).

The National Curriculum prescribed for all students in England a course of studies in every subject, including proposed time allocations, through all the years of schooling. The national testing program was intended to be tied closely to the National Curriculum. Tests were to be given at ages 7, 11 and 14, described as Key Stages 1, 2 and 3 respectively. The existing GCSE exams at the end of Year 11 were left in place, but with much more public reporting of school-by-school results. As described in Chapter 6, the assessment initiative became a major source of difficulty in the implementation of the Conservative program.

The creation of Ofsted replaced the inspection function that had previously been done by HMI (Her Majesty's Inspectors, a group of civil servants under the Secretary of State for Education). Ofsted was created as a separate agency, reporting to the prime minister rather than the Education Secretary and so could operate with considerable autonomy from the Department of Education. Moreover, the inspection program was privatized; school inspections were put out for bids by groups who conducted them under contract to Ofsted. A considerable number of retired teachers and inspectors, as well as consultants, took the training to qualify as Ofsted inspectors.

One important area that did not change under the Conservatives should also be mentioned. English secondary schools have as their high point the "sixth form," a two-year period during which students study a small number of subjects in great depth in preparation for A-level exams, which are the entry points to universities. The A-level system has had the effect of reducing secondary school completion rates and has also been criticized as encouraging students to specialize too early. Nonetheless, despite several efforts to change it, the sixth form and A-level system remained intact throughout the Conservative period.

Despite this exception, the total impact of the changes made by the Conservatives was very great indeed. As Ranson (no supporter of the Tory policies) puts it,

> The Conservatives have since 1979 placed before Parliament a historically unique torrent of legislation to rewrite the governance of education. Its

driving obsession is to wipe out any lingering infection of social democracy as much as to create a new polity that expresses and organizes an alternative vision of education and society.

(1994, p. 69)

New Zealand

Context

New Zealand is a unitary state of about three million people, most of whom live on the country's North Island. The population is quite dispersed, however, so that the country has many small schools – in 1989, more than 60 per cent of primary schools had fewer than ten teachers. The population is primarily of European ancestry (called *pakeha* in New Zealand) with important and growing minorities of Maori (Aboriginal inhabitants before the European arrival) and more recent immigrants from other parts of the South Pacific. New Zealand has particular obligations to the Maori population under the Treaty of Waitangi, made in 1840. The education system and New Zealand society generally have many elements borrowed in the colonial period from the British system. However, as a country settled primarily by immigrants, the social class divisions of Britain were more muted in New Zealand.

New Zealand has no formal written constitution, so the elected parliament has almost unrestricted powers. For example, the country's upper house was abolished in 1950 by a simple act of the lower house – something unimaginable in the other settings in this study, all of which have two houses with constitutional status. In effect, a majority government in New Zealand can push through almost any program if it is willing to accept the political consequences. At the same time, New Zealand has a relatively weak executive. For example, the members of the Labour cabinet were elected by the caucus rather than appointed by the prime minister, whose authority was limited to assigning ministerial roles for those so chosen.

New Zealand national elections take place every three years. The country's politics were traditionally dominated by two main parties – Labour on the left and the National Party on the right – although this configuration changed substantially when, for the 1996 election, the country moved to a system of proportional representation with the consequent creation of more political parties and coalition governments. In the 1970s and 1980s, however, governments alternated between Labour and the National Party. The small population and more muted class influence tended to make politics less polarized than in Britain; many politicians inevitably had connections with each other across party lines. However, debate in parliament can be very acrimonious and quite personal.

Until 1989, New Zealand operated a national system of education in which the national Department of Education was by far the most important player. The country had 2,700 schools, about 700,000 students, and about 40,000 teachers. More than 85 per cent of students attended state schools, but New Zealand did have a number of private schools (enrolling about 3 per cent) and integrated schools (enrolling about 9 per cent) – the latter with state funding but private management, and often organized on religious lines.

Primary schools were organized into eleven regional boards, but neither these nor the school governing bodies for secondary schools had very much authority. Curriculum, staffing, financing and organization were controlled from the capital of Wellington. The department managed many aspects of schooling, including capital facilities, teacher training and curriculum support, in great detail. The country had a set of national curriculum syllabi that were in the process of major revision at the time of the reforms. Some of these syllabi had been in place for quite a long time by 1988. Student assessment was the responsibility of each school, with the exception of the national school-leaving exams at the end of secondary school. The Department of Education had a staff of inspectors who did regular inspections of schools, evaluated teachers and provided a considerable amount of consultative assistance on matters such as curriculum implementation.

There are two teacher unions in New Zealand – the New Zealand Educational Institute (NZEI) represents teachers in the early childhood and primary system, and the Post Primary Teachers' Association (PPTA) represents secondary teachers. The teacher unions have historically played a powerful role in education policy, with extensive involvement before 1989 in almost every area of education policy. Collective agreements are national for each union, but include few working condition issues.

The reforms

The New Zealand education reforms can be seen as having several phases. The first phase was a commission on the administration of education that recommended sweeping changes in the way schools were organized and governed. Many but not all of these recommendations were then put into law by the Labour government in 1989. When the National Party replaced Labour in office in 1990, the reforms were altered in some significant ways, and were later expanded by the National government to deal with issues of curriculum, assessment and qualifications. However, the reforms in education in New Zealand must be understood in the context of a massive set of changes in economic and social policy during the 1980s.

In 1984 a newly elected Labour government began a series of major changes in New Zealand's very extensive public and regulated sectors. The government, led by Finance Minister Roger Douglas, adopted policies that led to deregulation of many economic sectors, privatization of many state agencies and services, reduction of public spending in many areas, and a general move towards a much smaller state sector with fewer benefits, services and regulations. Crown corporations were sold off, many sectors were entirely deregulated, collective bargaining was largely abolished and unions disestablished, and government expenditure drastically reduced. The civil service shrank from 66,000 in 1984 to 35,000 in 1994 (Boston *et al.*, 1996, p. 55). Union membership fell from more than 40 per cent of the labor force to less than 20 per cent (cited in Jesson, 1999).

The main lines of these reforms were strongly in accord with neo-liberal economic theories of privatization and market mechanisms, and were especially influenced by agency theory and contract theory as understood and promoted by two key agencies – the Treasury (or Finance Department) and the State Services Commission (SSC), which was a central agency that controlled government organization and staffing.

During the government's first term, its focus was on economic policy. In 1987 the Labour government was re-elected. Prime Minister David Lange also took on the Education portfolio. Shortly after the election the government created a whole series of working groups to look at various aspects of social service provision. Three such groups were established to look at education – one for early childhood (the Meade Commission), one for post-secondary (the Hawke Committee) and one for the schools sector (the Picot Taskforce). The latter, under the leadership of businessman Brian Picot, was set up to suggest reforms to the management of education.

The Picot Taskforce included five people. In addition to the chair these were a professor of education, a teacher educator, a Maori professional and another businessman. Their report specifically mentioned that they were chosen to represent these various interests. In addition, staff from the Treasury and the SSC were attached to the Taskforce. The Taskforce's terms of reference were specifically around management structures and cost-effectiveness, and did not include issues of curriculum, teaching or assessment. However, Brian Picot apparently insisted that the Taskforce should not be a cost-reduction exercise (Butterworth and Butterworth, 1998).

All the New Zealand commissions held public hearings and received briefs. Picot's group met with or heard from more than 700 individuals and organizations during its nine months of work. The report of the Picot Commission, entitled *Administering for Excellence: Effective Administration in Education*, was released in May 1988.

The Picot Report concluded that the education system in New Zealand was overly centralized, unresponsive and inefficient. It recommended a radically devolved system of education in which individual schools would be largely independent and governed by boards made up mostly of parents. Most operating authority would be removed from the Department of Education to individual school councils. The regional boards would be abolished. Schools would operate on the basis of a charter – a kind of contract with the government as to what the school would do – combined with inspection and review by government agencies. A number of vehicles would be created to foster public input and dialogue about education beyond the individual school. The Picot Report also suggested substantial change in the role and structure of the Department of Education, making it a smaller organization that would focus on policy rather than service delivery. The latter functions were to be devolved to schools or to special purpose agencies.

In August 1988, after a brief but intense further period of consultation and internal staff review, the government released its response to the Picot Report. This document, entitled *Tomorrow's Schools*, provided the basis for the subsequent reforms in school governance and administration in New Zealand beginning in 1989. The government adopted many but not all of Picot's proposals. The main components of *Tomorrow's Schools* were:

- creating governing councils in each school with a majority of elected parents and giving these boards control over budget, staffing and school policy;
- having each school develop a charter – an agreement on the school's nature and purpose – that would be approved by the minister of education and would be evaluated from time to time;
- giving parents a degree of choice in the school that their child would attend;
- eliminating most of the functions and staff of the Department of Education (which would be renamed as the Ministry of Education), moving these tasks either to schools or to autonomous quasi-governmental agencies;
- creating an Educational Review Office (ERO) which would monitor and report publicly on the quality of schools.

Tomorrow's Schools also included a significant emphasis on equity issues and especially on obligation to Maori people. These provisions were implemented in legislation in 1989, somewhat prior to but linked with extensive reforms in the early childhood and tertiary sectors. The government launched a large-scale advertising campaign to support *Tomorrow's Schools* and to encourage people to be candidates for the new governing boards.

The key feature of the reforms was the establishment of individual schools as the central structure of the education system. Each school would have a governing body that included the principal, one elected teacher, five elected parents and, in secondary schools, an elected student. The governing body would be responsible for all aspects of the operation of the school including staffing, school policies and program, and facilities. Picot's intention had been to delegate all funding to schools, but the government decided that teachers would continue to be paid by the national government, with schools getting a formula allocation for staffing rather than the actual funds to pay staff.

The school charters were intended as a contractual relationship between each school and the national government. Each charter would outline the nature of the school's goals and program, and would be the basis on which the school's success would be evaluated. School charters would be required, however, to give attention to a number of national policy issues including equity policy and Maori education, as well as to such administrative issues as personnel, financial management and property management. (Some typical elements of school charters are in the text box on page 49.)

In the proposed new system parents would be able to apply for their children to attend any school. Schools would, however, have to give attention to a number of equity issues in making admission decisions if there were more applications than places, and students who lived nearby would have first right to attend a school. Government would also set an official enrolment limit for each school, which could not be unilaterally altered by the school.

The role of the Department of Education, which had run almost all aspects of education in New Zealand, was changed quite drastically. The new ministry was to be a relatively small policy unit, giving advice to the minister and government. Many of its previous functions were now to be taken over by schools. A new and independent body, initially called the Review and Audit Agency, later changed to the Education Review Office, was to be created to be responsible for the auditing and inspection of schools to ensure they were complying with their charter and national policies.

In addition to these proposals, the government made other important changes across the public sector that reduced the influence of unions, collective bargaining and pay systems for all public sector workers, including teachers. Collective bargaining for most workers was effectively abolished, with teacher unions being one of the few large remaining labor organizations.

The Labour education program did not contain any major provisions around curriculum or assessment, or indeed other aspects of school program. The National government, however, did begin to address these issues, giving more attention to curriculum, assessment and the rationalization of qualifications. In 1993 New Zealand began to develop an extensive national curriculum, but the country never adopted a system of national achievement testing beyond its secondary-school leaving exams, despite several attempts to do so.

Within a few months of the coming into effect of *Tomorrow's Schools*, the Labour government commissioned an additional review of the status of the reforms (the Lough Report), resulting in recommendations for still further change. The Lough recommendations took the reforms further in the contractualist direction preferred by the Treasury. It also changed the nature of the school charters to make them one-way commitments from the schools to abide by government direction rather than the two-way relationship envisaged by the Picot Report (Ramsay, 1993).

In the fall of 1990, Labour was defeated in a general election and replaced by the National Party. The National Party's Education Amendment Act in 1991 left intact most of the Labour reforms, but extended them by placing greater emphasis on parental choice, standards and inspection. The requirement for schools to have equity provisions in their charters was dropped, and schools were also given much more latitude to select students.

Gradually during the first few years of the 1990s, the National government became more interested in substantive educational issues, including more attention to curriculum and assessment. Work began on a national curriculum for the country. The government moved, through the New Zealand Qualifications Authority (NZQA), to create a single framework of qualifications that would govern all levels of education and provide integrated movement from one level or kind of education to another. A proposal for national achievement testing in primary schools was made, but never put into place. Changes were made in teacher training, special education and a number of other areas. Also, National made ongoing efforts to move to bulk funding of teachers' salaries, and about 30 per cent of schools had taken this step by the time Labour was re-elected in 1999 and announced an end to bulk funding.

Table 3.1 outlines the main modifications made to the recommendations of the Picot Taskforce.

Table 3.1   *Main changes to reforms in New Zealand*

Issue	Picot proposal	*Tomorrow's Schools*	Later Labour changes	National changes
Schools as central units	Each school to have responsibility for most operating matters	Payment of teachers' salaries left at national level		Ongoing efforts to give each school control over teachers' salaries and property management.
Charters	A two-way contract between the school and the government on objectives and activities	No change	Accountability only from the school to the government	Charters focused increasingly on compliance with government guidelines
Inter-school co-operation	Establishment of regional units and forums	Not fully implemented and very limited effectiveness		Some efforts to promote consolidation or closing of small schools

Parent governance	National parent advocacy council to help parents govern	Established	Disbanded	No change
Choice provisions	Local students given first right to attend; enrolment schemes with strong equity provisions	Established	No change	Equity provisions weakened; schools given right to set own admissions criteria
National guidelines	Outlined key national policies for inclusion in school charter	Adopted; many guidelines, especially on equity issues	No change	Guidelines reduced in number; equity provisions weakened significantly
Education Policy Council	Intended to provide additional source of public policy advice	Not accepted or established	No change	No change
Role of Ministry	Limited to policy advice and property management; many functions delegated to schools or to other statutory bodies	Many ministerial policy directives left intact; not all services removed		Still many ministerial policy directives to schools and still some services provided directly
Review and audit	To be set up in an independent agency	Adopted; focus on compliance with charter requirements	Size and scope of ERO scaled back considerably	Move to include audit of school quality as well as compliance with charter and national guidelines

New Zealand school charters

School charters in New Zealand were intended originally to outline the unique character of each school, against which its actual accomplishments would be gauged. The first charters were often the result of a great deal of work and debate by governing bodies (Ward interview; Thrupp interview). However, as the government changed the nature of the charters towards compliance with central directives, they began to look more similar to each other. The following analysis of a dozen randomly chosen charters gives some of their flavor.

Many charters employ very similar initial language on school purpose, such as this excerpt:

The needs of children and their learning shall be the focus of this charter.

By following the guiding principles of the charter, the board of trustees will ensure that all students are given an education which enhances their dignity. This education shall challenge them to achieve personal standards of excellence and to reach their full potential. All school activities will be designed to advance these purposes.

Although there is much common language around students' achieving their full potential, lifelong learning or stimulating learning environments, schools also vary in the apparent emphasis they place on these ideas, with some seeming to stress a more child-centered conception of education and others giving more emphasis to ideas of excellence and high standards. Some but not all charters provide a description of the local community.

Each charter must include some common elements, in particular a plan for meeting the ten National Educational Goals and statements as to how the school will comply with National Administration Guidelines on curriculum, personnel, finance and property. Some charters do this in two or three pages by making broad statements about school objectives, for example:

Programme delivery and content: – to meet the New Zealand curriculum goals and objectives; to develop programmes that meet local needs; to ensure the curriculum is balanced to cater for needs of all students integrating the essential skills as embodied in the Curriculum Framework.

Or

Finance: to manage the college's finances to enhance the education of all students, in a manner that supports the intentions of this charter and allows the college to meet its immediate and longer term needs, goals and objectives.

Other charters run to fifteen or twenty pages and provide much more detail on how the various education goals will be met. For example:

Goal 2: Equality of educational opportunity for all New Zealanders, by identifying and removing barriers to achievement. This school will endeavour to provide equality of educational opportunity by:

1   identifying barriers which operate to the educational disadvantage of students in the school; e.g. physical and medical handicap, intellectual ability or disability, social dysfunction, emotional difficulties, behavioural problems, socio-economic circumstance, racial, ethnic or cultural differences, gender, financial hardship, family structure, religion, age, parental expectation/values, inappropriate teaching methods, or obstructive administrative structures.
2   identifying individuals and groups of children affected by such barriers;
3   adapting environmental factors within the Board's control;
4   lobbying other agencies (e.g. Ministry of Education, Special Educa-tion Service) to meet their responsibilities to help provide the resources required to counter identified achievement barriers;
5   providing training for staff to ensure available resources are utilised in the most appropriate manner to help remove or overcome barriers, or to in some way compensate for the effects of barriers;
6   enhancing learning by providing role models, such as girls, women, and people from different ethnic groups in positions of leadership and authority and boys and men as caregivers, so

that children can understand the meaning of equity in the behaviour they observe from day to day;

7 developing teachers' awareness of the need for, and the ability to use, teaching strategies which ensure all groups and individuals in the classroom have equitable learning opportunities and outcomes.

Originally, charters were required to include statements about Maori issues, and although the National government ended the requirement to do so, most charters continue to give attention to Maori equity issues.

The Canadian Context

Canada is a country of thirty million people. It is constitutionally a federal state, comprised of ten provinces and three territories. Canada is officially a bilingual country (English and French) with a multicultural population. The distinct status of approximately one million Aboriginal people is slowly being given increasing recognition. About one quarter of the population, largely though by no means entirely in the province of Quebec, has French as a mother tongue. There is a sizeable Anglophone minority in Quebec, just as there are Francophone minorities in other parts of the country. At the same time, Canada has a large population, living in all parts of the country, with other mother tongues and cultural backgrounds.

The original Confederation in 1867 of four provinces – Nova Scotia, New Brunswick, Ontario and Quebec – that led to the creation of Canada involved delicate compromises around the place of Quebec in a majority Anglophone country, and guarantees of religious freedom in schooling for Christian but not other religious minorities. These have taken on different forms in various parts of the country. All provinces have a public school system, but several provinces also maintain a publicly funded system of minority religious schools, called "separate schools." Many provinces also provide some level of public financial support for private or independent schools, which may have a religious, ethnic or other focus. French and English minority groups, where they exist, also have guaranteed educational rights. In addition, Canada's hundreds of Aboriginal First Nations are each responsible for education on their own lands (formerly reservations). So in many Canadian provinces there are effectively four or five school systems receiving significant public funds, making the boundaries between state or public schools and private or independent schools complex and often blurred.

Canada's constitution assigns the responsibility for education to provincial governments. However, responsibility for Aboriginal education in First

Nations is currently jointly held between the federal government and Aboriginal groups themselves, while provinces are also involved because many Aboriginal children attend public schools. The federal government is also involved in one way or another in many aspects of education including labor force preparation, language education, cultural education and support for education research. The Council of Ministers of Education (CMEC) is a creation of the provincial governments that does play a co-ordinating role but has no powers over any of the provinces. Because the country is so large with such a small population, because six of the ten provinces have populations of a million or less, and because of the pervasive influence of the United States on almost every aspect of Canadian life, Canadian educators and policy-makers may be more knowledgeable about developments in the US than about developments in neighboring provinces. Curriculum, assessment and other key policy controls have been provincial, though in recent years there have been some steps to develop regional or pan-Canadian curricula and testing programs.

Canadian education politics can only be understood if one realizes that the most heated issues in Canadian education historically have been around language and religion. In the last few years Canada has had enormous public debate over proposed changes in these arrangements in several provinces. Many of these proposals have led to constitutional court cases as well as to heated political argument. Furthermore, Canadians are still trying to sort out the impact of schools that for many years denied Aboriginal people any opportunity to control their own education or to learn about or practice their languages, cultures and religions.

In 1982 Canada adopted a Charter of Rights and Freedoms somewhat similar to the United States Bill of Rights. As in the US, one result of this move has been a much greater role for courts in ruling on various aspects of education policy.

Education reform has been present in all provinces in Canada in recent years. While there are common elements in what provinces have done, there are also important differences among provinces, so that generalizations are always risky (Young and Levin, 2000).

Manitoba

Context

Manitoba is a province of about one million people in the center of Canada. About 70 per cent of the population lives in or near the capital city of Winnipeg, but the remainder is dispersed over a very large rural and northern area including some quite isolated communities, resulting in many small schools. The population includes large numbers of people whose origins two or three generations ago were European (from almost all parts of

Europe), a new immigrant community that is increasingly composed of visible minorities, and a significant and rapidly growing Aboriginal population (now more than 10 per cent of the total). There is also a small but politically important Francophone minority. The economy is diversified among agriculture, manufacturing and services, but the province is in the bottom half in Canada in wealth, and the provincial government is quite reliant on fiscal transfers from the federal government to support its programs and operations.

For the last thirty years, Manitoba has alternated governments between the Progressive Conservatives and the New Democrats (a social democratic party), with the Liberals as a third party. On the whole, Manitoba politics could be characterized as ranging from "small c" conservative to populist. There is little tradition of political radicalism on the part of any of the main parties; Manitoba is usually a follower of political trends rather than a leader. The rural and wealthier urban parts of the province have tended to vote Conservative, while the poorer urban areas and the north have tended to vote NDP. Most Manitoba elections are decided by small shifts in vote, so while politics are often partisan and acrimonious, the major parties tend to stay quite close to the political center. During the period of this study, a Conservative administration was in office, having been elected in 1988, and re-elected in 1990 and 1995.

About 95 per cent of the province's 200,000 students attend Manitoba's 700 plus public schools, but there are also private schools that receive substantial public financial support. Public schools are organized into about sixty school districts or divisions with locally elected boards of trustees who are then responsible, under provincial legislation, for the operations of the schools. The districts range in size from fewer than 500 students to more than 30,000, with a majority of districts covering large rural areas with small populations. About 200 schools are officially classified as small schools. Financing is shared between provincial support and local property taxation through a complicated series of arrangements; Manitoba is one of only two provinces to still have a significant component of local property taxation as part of the financing of schools. Most schools have parent committees, but these have a purely advisory function. Aboriginal students are found both in First Nation schools and in public schools, especially in urban Winnipeg and in northern Manitoba.

The province has always laid down school curricula in some detail, and the provincial Department of Education, in addition to being responsible for the provincial share of school finance, also regulates many aspects of school operations, including the amount of time to be devoted to each subject, the qualifications of teachers, the school calendar, and so on. Achievement testing has a changing history, with provincial examinations abolished in the early 1970s but with other forms of provincial testing beginning in the 1980s. The 13,000 teachers are unionized through a single organization, the

Manitoba Teachers' Society, but collective bargaining occurs at the school district level. Collective agreements are largely focused on salary and benefit issues, though there are some working condition clauses in some contracts. Manitoba does not allow teachers to strike, requiring settlement of contract disputes through binding arbitration.

The reforms

The Conservative government which took office in May 1988, replacing the New Democratic government which had been in power from 1981, was committed to reducing the province's deficit, to limiting tax increases (and later to tax reductions), and to reducing the size of the public sector. During their eleven years in office they reduced many programs, cut the size of the civil service, eliminated some public services, increased user fees and eventually balanced the provincial budget. Funding for public services including education was limited, with several years of no increase or actual decreases. The Conservatives also took a number of steps to limit collective bargaining in the public sector. They passed legislation to reduce salaries of public sector workers, including teachers, through compulsory days off without pay. However, the Manitoba Conservatives were less committed to severe budget cuts and extensive privatization than were Conservative governments in a number of other provinces.

The Conservatives made few significant moves in education in their first several years in office. A commission was created to consider reform to the Public Schools Act. This commission held extensive public hearings and reported in 1993, but none of its recommendations were officially accepted or implemented.

As part of a cross-Canada trend to look at reducing the number of school districts, Manitoba also created in 1993 a commission to review school district boundaries. That commission reported in 1994 with a recommendation to reduce the number of school districts from sixty to twenty-one. However, after a period of study, the government announced in 1996 that it would not act on those recommendations and that school district boundaries would remain largely unchanged. This decision differs from action in almost all other provinces to reduce the number of school districts, with the most drastic example in New Brunswick, where local school districts were entirely eliminated in the early 1990s but are to be reintroduced in 2001.

The main package of education reforms in Manitoba relevant to this study was announced in July 1994 by Education Minister Clayton Manness, and was called *New Directions*. The *New Directions* document included these major planks:

- a definition of essential learning embodied in a prescribed curriculum with a reduced number of options for students;
- an increased program of student testing with public results;
- a requirement for each school to have a development plan;
- creation of advisory councils in all schools to provide more parent and community input;
- some parental choice of the school children would attend;
- greater use of distance education and technology in schools;
- changes in teacher education.

Some of these, such as the curriculum and testing proposals, were relatively well defined in the document. Others, such as the changes in teacher education, were expressed in quite general terms. The discussion of essential learnings took ten pages of the thirty-four page document; the discussion of parental and community involvement occupied four pages, and teacher education took a single page.

The provincial curriculum requirements were tightened by giving more time to the major subject areas, especially language, mathematics and science. The high school program was re-oriented to provide a greater degree of specialization in the last two years. Some subjects, such as physical education and history, were made optional at an earlier age.

Parent advisory committees were required in each school. These committees were to be elected annually by parents. Parents who were themselves teachers were prohibited from holding more than one place on a council. The councils were given a set of tasks, such as reviewing school development plans, but were to operate as advisory only to the principal. Schools were also required to create development plans on an annual basis.

Parents were given the right to apply to have their child attend any public school. However, students in the local area were to be given first preference, and schools were given a number of criteria they could use to determine if they would accept any external application, including their view of their capacity and any special needs that an external student might have. The legislation gave school principals final authority over admissions questions.

Provincial testing was to be extended to include the major subject areas of language (English or French), mathematics, science and social studies in Grades 3, 6, 9 and 12. The provincial tests would constitute an increasing portion of students' final marks as the students got older. In addition, the province required schools to give percentage marks on student report cards in all grades in addition to whatever other letter grade or anecdotal reporting they did. Exam results would be made public on a school-by-school basis.

A number of other provisions were also contained in the reforms. One that proved controversial was a proposal (never actually enacted) to allow teachers to suspend students from their classes without requiring permission from the school administration.

At the same time as *New Directions* was being implemented, education was also greatly affected by the government's efforts to eliminate the provincial deficit without increasing income taxes. Funding to schools was cut in several years and held to zero in other years. The salaries of teachers and other education workers (as in other sectors under provincial control) were unilaterally reduced by 2 per cent per year by the government, through legislation that overturned established collective agreements. When these reductions were allowed to lapse, in 1996 and 1997, the government passed further legislation that changed collective bargaining provisions for teachers so as to reduce the scope of bargaining and favor the wage offers of school boards. Although not officially part of the *New Directions* effort, these measures were a key part of the context in which the reforms took place.

A number of aspects of the *New Directions* proposals did change during the implementation process. Some of the changes in high school requirements were altered (notably keeping Canadian history as a compulsory subject). Parents who were teachers were allowed to be elected to advisory committees. Schools were able to retain existing parent councils rather than having to re-establish them under the new legislation. A proposal to allow teachers to suspend students from their classes was dropped. A number of elements of the curriculum and assessment timetable were deferred or changed altogether. However, the basic directions remained intact. The Conservative government was re-elected to a third term in 1995, but Clayton Manness retired from active politics and a new education minister was appointed. In the 1999 general election the Conservatives were defeated by the New Democratic Party.

Alberta

Context

Alberta is a province of three million people on the eastern side of the Rocky Mountains in western Canada. Its population, which is growing rapidly, is concentrated in two large cities (Edmonton, the capital, and Calgary) and several smaller cities, but it also includes rural and northern areas and isolated communities with small schools. The population is very mixed in background, includes a relatively large immigrant community that is increasingly made up of visible minorities, and the province has a significant and rapidly growing Aboriginal population.

Alberta is also one of Canada's youngest provinces, created only in 1905, and still sometimes regarded as retaining elements of a frontier mentality. Its economy has been heavily dependent on the oil and natural gas industry, with consequent cycles of boom and bust. However, overall Alberta has been growing fairly rapidly and has had net in-migration from other parts of the country.

Politically, Alberta has been one of Canada's most conservative regions, regularly electing conservative representatives both provincially and nationally. It tends to keep political parties in office for very long periods of time, and then make a dramatic change. The Social Credit Party formed the government for more than thirty years until it was defeated by the Conservatives in 1971, and the Conservatives have been in office continuously since then. Alberta's conservatism is drawn both from traditionalist and neo-liberal strands. On the side of the former, the province has a large strongly religious population in the south that tends to be very traditional on matters of morality and social policy. The boom-and-bust oil economy that dominates the province has also brought an element of American-style market-oriented thinking to Alberta. The consequence has been low tax rates (Alberta is the only province in the country without a sales tax) and a strong tendency towards individual self-reliance. At the same time, Alberta's oil revenues did allow the province for many years to spend at quite high levels compared to other provinces, even while maintaining low tax rates. However, in the 1980s Alberta began to reduce public spending so that by the time of these reforms it was no longer a high-spending province in regard to education.

Most of Alberta's 525,000 students attend one of the 1,800 plus public or separate schools, but private schools do receive state financial support (about half the public school level) and enroll about 4 per cent of students. The province also has a substantial number of small schools in its rural areas. Alberta has Canada's largest proportion of children being home-schooled, although the numbers remain small. As of 1993, the public schools were organized in about 140 school districts with locally elected boards of trustees that were then responsible, under provincial legislation, for the operations of the schools. Schools often had parent associations, but these were purely advisory in nature. Prior to 1994, financing was shared through a complicated series of arrangements between provincial support and local property taxation.

As in most provinces of Canada, the Alberta Department of Education provides provincial funding for schools, sets detailed school curricula and regulates many other aspects of school operations. Indeed, Alberta has had one of the most active and interventionist Departments of Education in the country. Achievement testing has occurred continuously but has expanded steadily in the last fifteen years or so. Teachers are unionized through the Alberta Teachers' Association, but collective bargaining occurs at the school district level.

The reforms

In Alberta the reforms of interest in this study were those introduced by the Conservative government of Premier Ralph Klein in 1994. Late in 1992, Klein, a populist former mayor of Calgary, became leader of a Conservative government that had been in office for twenty years but had run into serious political difficulties. One main issue was the province's large annual deficit. In the spring of 1993, Klein called an election, running on a program of eliminating the deficit through reduced spending and greater efficiency in public services. He was rewarded by the electorate with a very convincing renewed majority mandate in the June election. The 1993 Conservative election program had relatively little to say about education, however.

Beginning at the end of 1993, the Klein government undertook a sharper cut in spending and a greater amount of privatization than in Manitoba, in keeping with a generally more conservative political culture in Alberta. The largest single item in the government's approach was to eliminate debt by reducing spending. Budgets of all services were cut significantly. The reduction in education funding, at 12 per cent over three years, was one of the smallest reductions. To reach their spending target, the Alberta government used a variety of devices, including privatization of a number of services such as telephone and liquor sales. Government departments, including education, were reduced in size quite substantially. Staffing in the Department of Education fell by more than half (Peters, 1999). In some other cases cuts in spending were linked to specific service reductions. For example, many hospitals were closed. The government also made legislative reductions in the pay of many public sector workers, including teachers. A large share of the reductions, however, was simply given to intermediate agencies such as school boards and hospitals to handle as best they could.

A package of education reforms was announced in January 1994 by Education Minister Halvar Jonson. The proposals included:

- a 12 per cent cut in education spending over three years, including legislated roll-backs of teachers' salaries;
- the elimination of provincial funding for kindergarten;
- a substantial reduction in staffing in the Department of Education;
- elimination of local property taxation to support education, with all funds being provided by the province;
- a reduction in the number of school districts from 141 to 60, and a reduction in the number of members on each board;
- the authorization of a limited number of charter schools;
- an increase in provincial testing to include all students in Grades 3, 6 and 9;
- increased capacity for parents to choose the school their child attended;
- a requirement for provincial approval for the appointment of all district superintendents (formerly solely the responsibility of elected school boards);
- a requirement for the Department of Education and all school districts to develop and publicize an annual business plan.

Some of these provisions were subsequently withdrawn or changed in the face of very strong opposition from school boards. The province changed its provisions on the appointment of school superintendents, though it retained a greater role in that process than it had previously. Several lawsuits by school boards also resulted in the province restoring some local taxing ability to the separate (primarily Catholic) school boards. However, legislation to implement the rest of the reform program was introduced in February and passed in May of 1994.

The United States Context

The United States is a country of nearly 300 million people organized in fifty states, ranging from not quite half a million in Alaska or Vermont to more than thirty million people in California. The US has always been a country of immigrants, but its demography has shifted rapidly in recent years with increasing numbers of Hispanics as well as about 10 per cent of the population that is African-American. Current estimates are that the US population will be about one-third African-American, Asian and Hispanic within another twenty years (as cited in a presentation by Dr Gary Orfield to the University Council for Educational Administration, Minneapolis, 31 October 1999).

The US political system operates on the basis of a constitutional separation of powers between the executive and legislative branches of government and generates very different political processes than are found in parliamentary systems such as those in Canada, New Zealand and Britain. Heads of state – the president nationally and governors in each state – are elected directly. Cabinets are appointed directly by executive heads and cabinet members do not have to be elected. The separation of the executive function from the legislative means that the president or governor does not necessarily command a majority in the legislature. Even if his or her party has a majority, the structure of party discipline is much weaker than in parliamentary systems, since the government cannot fall on a confidence vote. This means that political initiative can come from almost anywhere. Any legislator can introduce a bill and, if she or he can garner the necessary support, have it passed into law. Legislators often use this ability to put issues on the agenda or to pressure the executive to take particular actions. At the same time, the governor must put together a majority for each legislative proposal. The result is a much more decentralized process of political initiative and a much greater need to compromise on proposals in order to generate enough votes to have them passed. In a close vote, individual legislators may be able to have their pet ideas built into a bill as a quid pro quo for their support.

The US both nationally and in almost all states has effectively been a two-party system. Both Republicans and Democrats have normally needed to seek middle ground to be elected. Perhaps for this reason, American politics can be extremely bitter and personal, with the growth during the last twenty years of so-called "attack advertising," in which candidates impugn each other's characters on television and radio.

Education in the United States is highly decentralized and diffusely governed. Education is a responsibility of each of the fifty states, with the federal government playing a limited but important role in setting overall policy direction, in providing financial support for a wide variety of initiatives, and in promoting research. Though there are many significant national organizations in education, they tend to have an advisory or influence role rather than a direct share in governance.

At the same time, most states are less controlling of education in the US than are Canadian provinces or Australian states. Most states (Hawaii is the exception) have delegated a great deal of authority to individual school districts, of which there are about 15,000 in the country, ranging in size from a few hundred students to New York City's one million plus students. Compared with Canada, school districts in the United States generally have more autonomy and more financial responsibility. Whereas school finance is largely – and increasingly – provincial in Canada, it remains substantially local in many parts of the US. Variations in spending between states and across districts within many states can be enormous, with some districts spending twenty times as much per pupil as others, depending primarily on their wealth. The result can be huge inequalities in school facilities, staffing, class sizes and other resources. A further result of this decentralization, of course, is that centrally mandated changes are extraordinarily difficult to make. The diversity of arrangements in the United States means that there are counter-examples to almost any generalization about education.

Although the fifty states are independent in matters of education policy, they do tend to watch each other fairly closely, and policy proposals often spread quite rapidly from state to state. Indeed, the policy-making apparatus in the United States is often described as being subject to fads that take hold and sweep across states for a time, only to be replaced by the next popular policy proposal. At the same time, each state has its own political culture and history. For example, governors tend to be stronger actors in some states than in others, and interest groups such as teachers may have much more power in some states than in others (Mazzoni, 1994).

The courts play a larger role in policy-making in the United States than in any of the other countries. Many important educational issues, including financing, race relations, the role of religion and issues of individual rights, are subject to far-reaching decisions made by courts. Legal challenges to state policies are therefore quite frequent.

Another important feature of state policy-making is the constitutional requirement in many states for a balanced budget. State revenues tend to fluctuate more than do those of the federal government, so states may move in a short time from substantial surpluses to large budget cuts. Since education is the largest single budget item for most states, these swings in financial fortunes can have drastic and sudden implications for schools.

In 1983 the United States government issued the report of a national commission on education. The report, entitled *A Nation at Risk*, argued that education in the United States was in serious difficulty and that large-scale changes were needed to improve quality if the country were to be able to continue to compete economically. The report set off a massive wave of education reforms across the country over the next several years as governors and legislatures tried to respond to the political demand for reform. However, as Mazzoni points out,

> Interpretations that narrowly single out national influences give too little recognition to state activities that preceded *A Nation at Risk* and too much recognition to similarities – rather than to differences – in how state education policy systems sought in the 1980s to improve their public schools.
>
> (1994, p. 55)

Mazzoni locates the increased state activism of the 1980s not only in specific political events, but also in the growing policy capacity in state governments and a buoyant economy that gave states some extra money to spend on new initiatives. He also notes the number of state governors and individual state legislators who were active in promoting education reforms (1994).

Minnesota

Context

Minnesota is a state of about four and a half million people located in the north center of the United States. Its main population center and capital is the twin cities of Minneapolis–St Paul, which have well over half the state population. Much of the rest of the state is rural or small towns. Minnesota became a state in 1858. The population is about 90 per cent Caucasian, much of it descended from the Scandinavian settlers of 150 years ago. The economy is quite diversified, although like most other parts of the United States it was undergoing quite rapid change during the first half of the 1980s. As a relatively prosperous and homogeneous state, Minnesota had less of the social upheaval that has characterized many parts of the United States over the last thirty years.

Minnesota has a reputation as a politically liberal state and has had strong ties to the Democratic Party, which in the state is called the Democratic Farmer Labor party (DFL). Although the state tends to vote Democratic in national elections, it has elected Republican governors and senators reasonably often. The state government has two elected houses – a House of Representatives and a State Senate. The DFL has dominated the legislature for many years. Minnesota has been considered a "weak governor" state, in which more of the legislative initiative tends to rest with the legislature (Roberts and King, 1996). As has been the case throughout the US, Minnesota legislators have become increasingly sophisticated, with growing support staffs. In the 1980s the governor did, in addition to other powers, appoint the nine-member State Board of Education and the Commissioner of Education.

The State Board of Education and State Commissioner of Education are uniquely American structures, designed originally to provide an independent and presumably less partisan locus for education policy. State boards, including that in Minnesota, have varied in importance over time. Sometimes powerful boards or commissioners have challenged governors for the key role in initiating policy. The powers of the Minnesota Board had been reduced during the 1970s – for example by giving the governor control of the appointment of the State Commissioner of Education. In the mid 1980s the Board had been re-energized as a player in education policy and a countervailing influence to the governor and legislature, but in an increasingly politicized environment with more and more active participants, the State Board is one player along with many others.

Minnesota's 840,000 students attend primarily the 1,750 public schools and learning centers, which are organized into about 350 school districts. About 9 per cent of students attend private schools, which receive some funding for transportation, materials and support services but no direct public funding. The State Department of Education provides financial and regulatory as well as support functions to districts, and provides policy advice to the governor and the State Board of Education. However, Minnesota had no state curriculum.

The state was considered a national leader in education in many ways. It was a liberal spender on education; in 1982 it spent 122 per cent of the US average per capita (Roberts and King, 1996). It also has relatively good outcomes, including high rates of high school completion and good scores on the Scholastic Aptitude Test (SAT). The state government provided a large proportion of total school revenues, although this depends each year on the overall state budget. As a result of its constitutional provision prohibiting a budget deficit, Minnesota's state share of school funding dropped from 71 per cent to 45 per cent during the recession of 1981–2 (Roberts and King, 1996, p. 33). At the same time, the Reagan administration was reducing federal support to education.

Like other US states, but unlike many parliamentary systems, Minnesota has an extensive system of non-governmental organizations that may work actively on education issues. These include, in addition to the usual insider groups (teacher, superintendents, school board members), several university centers focused on policy research and several foundations that supported research or policy analysis in education. In addition, the largest corporations in Minnesota had set up the Minnesota Business Partnership to mobilize public opinion and to lobby on important public policy issues. Minnesota also housed an organization called the Minnesota Citizens' League, a non-partisan and non-profit organization that was active on a wide range of public policy issues. As a more liberal state with higher levels of education, Minnesota is less prone to "insider" politics than are some other states. The fact that the state's capital is also its largest city, which is not the case in most states, also has political implications, as it makes legislators more accessible to a range of interest groups.

Teachers in the US are organized through two different unions – the National Education Association (NEA) and the American Federation of Teachers (AFT), with the former generally considered to be somewhat more like a professional union and the latter seen as being more like a traditional trade union. (In Minnesota the two unions have merged since the events described below.) Collective bargaining is at the local level, with one of the two umbrella organizations representing teachers in any given jurisdiction. Agreements do frequently include some working condition issues, such as preparation time.

The reforms

In Minnesota, rather than a program of reform this study looked at two specific reforms that occurred several years apart. Neither the development of school choice nor, later, of charter schools in Minnesota was part of a larger program of government reform as was the case in each of the other settings.

In the early 1980s several important organizations in Minnesota had issued reports calling for reforms in education. In January of 1985, Democratic Governor Rudy Perpich outlined a series of proposals for education reform which he called *Access to Excellence*. His proposals included a greater share of state funding, more state evaluation of achievement, more scope for local districts to define programs, and parent choice of school, which proved to be the most controversial proposal. Perpich's initial attempt to pass the necessary legislation failed, as he was unable to create the required coalition in the legislature, especially given strong combined opposition from all the major education interest groups. The only feature to be passed in 1985 was a post-secondary options program that allowed students in the last two years of high school to move directly to a college or university if they were admitted, and to take their state grant monies to the post-secondary institution. Minnesota was the first state in the United States to adopt a law of this sort, one that has still not been widely adopted in other states.

Following the defeat of his main proposals, Perpich began a consultation process aimed at building enough support to pass a more significant reform program. He created a "Governor's Discussion Group" of sixty-one people with a mandate to develop a plan for education in Minnesota. This group eventually did agree to a revised and limited plan for school choice, the most contentious element of Perpich's program. In 1987 the Minnesota legislature adopted the K-12 Enrollment Options Act, which allowed school districts to opt in to choice plans. Other elements of Perpich's earlier proposals, however, such as state competency testing, were not adopted.

In 1988, the legislature made the choice provisions compulsory for all districts by the start of the 1990–91 school year. Although Governor Perpich had not publicly sought such an extension of the plan, he did support efforts by several key legislators who championed the new measure. "On May 6, 1988, at his hometown high school in Hibbing, Minnesota, an ebullient Perpich signed the $38 million Omnibus Education Bill that established the nation's first mandatory K-12 school choice program" (Roberts and King, 1996, p. 65). The plan as adopted in 1988 was very similar to what Perpich had initially proposed in 1985.

A few years later, in 1991, now under Republican Governor Arne Carlson, Minnesota went through a similar process in regard to charter schools: that is, schools specially created for a particular defined purpose and operating outside the normal state and district system. Governor Carlson was not a prime mover of this initiative, which came largely from other legislators, the Citizens' League and some of the same policy entrepreneurs who had been involved in the earlier debates (Mazzoni, 1993). Once again there was heated debate and strong opposition from mainstream education groups to the proposal. However, the supporters of the policy were able, through effective lobbying and use of political influence, to get legislative support for the measure. Carlson did eventually endorse the measure and eventually promoted it strongly at the national level. It passed the legislature on the first try, and in 1991 Minnesota became the first state to adopt a law authorizing the creation of charter schools. The law authorized the creation of up to eight such schools under a relatively restricted set of conditions.

The open enrolment and charter school proposals were by no means the only reforms being proposed or adopted during these years. By 1986 the state was quite involved in looking at outcome-based education (OBE) for its high schools. The legislature approved efforts to develop OBE curricula, testing and demonstration programs. OBE turned out to be very difficult both technically and politically, not only in Minnesota but in other states as well (Boyd *et al.*, 1996), and became a major source of controversy that continued for a decade. It has never been widely adopted in the United States, and has been abandoned or sharply curtailed by several states that had invested heavily in it. Both school choice and charter schools, however, were subsequently widely imitated by other states, hence the interest in those issues and in Minnesota as a case study of reform.

4   Origins

Theoretical Framework

Where does a particular program of educational reform come from? How does it come to be on the political agenda? These deceptively simple questions turn out to be very difficult to answer. Once an issue has been adopted by a government, it is difficult not to see it as having been inevitable. Much of the commentary on reform treats it as arising primarily from ideological commitments. Yet the evidence suggests that the process is complex, and that there is nothing automatic about any issue assuming a place of importance in political agendas that are inevitably too crowded and full of controversy.

This discussion of the origins of reform begins with John Kingdon's excellent study of agenda setting in US politics (1994), though some of Kingdon's analysis needs to be modified because of the important differences in political processes between the US system and that of the parliamentary governments in the other jurisdictions in this study. Kingdon sees political agendas as being created from the intersection of three processes – political events, problem recognition, and policy proposals. Each of these "streams," as Kingdon calls them, can serve either as an impetus to action or as a constraint on it. An issue takes an important place in the political agenda only when the three streams come together such that there is a political recognition of something as a problem, a political opportunity to take action, and an acceptable proposal as to what action will be taken. These processes are in practice very closely interconnected, but it is analytically useful to think of them separately.

Political events

Consider first the most straightforward of the three elements – political events. A government comes into office with commitments to do some things and not to do others – a program. As public trust in politics has waned, one response of politicians has been to place more emphasis on making and fulfilling a specific set of commitments. A political program sets limits to what will be done, but the extent to which and ways in which any political program actually comes into effect is not predetermined.

Kingdon refers to "policy windows" – a political situation that allows some action to be taken. At any given moment there are many political issues swirling around any government. The decision as to which of these will be acted on is dependent at least in part on the ebb and flow of political events. Governments face competing pressures, including pleasing key supporters, meeting election commitments, dealing with emerging issues, meeting fiscal goals and living within available revenues. Choices among these are further affected by the positioning of various individuals and interest groups. The range of elements that can affect any given policy choice is very large indeed. Is there an election looming? Are ministers positioning themselves for a future leadership campaign? Is a cabinet shuffle anticipated? Does an opposition party have to be mollified? Is there an emerging problem that requires attention or from which it is desirable to divert attention? Do key constituencies or important individuals want or oppose a particular policy? Has a particular issue suddenly grown large in the public consciousness? Will the budget allow something substantial to be done? In any of these situations political leaders and their advisers may see the need for bold action or great caution. I was involved in one major reform in education that was triggered because the minister wanted to launch an initiative that would make it harder to change his portfolio in a rumored-to-be-imminent cabinet shuffle. Ideas that had been rejected for months were suddenly rushed forward for action.

Governments do attempt to plan an agenda over a term in office, often with more difficult choices made earlier and good news saved for closer to an election. However, the best efforts of governments to plan an agenda are often rendered null by unexpected events. A sudden crisis in one or another sector may divert everyone's attention from even the most important and long-term project. A colleague and I a few years ago studied a Canadian government department that had spent two years carefully developing a strategic plan with extensive staff and stakeholder involvement, only to have much of it tossed aside because of the need to address an unexpected crisis. Crises may also be fomented or created by governments as a basis for radical action. The Ontario minister of education in 1995 became infamous over a remark he made about the need to create a crisis in order to justify changes in education, and similar accusations have been leveled against US policy-makers by Berliner and Biddle (1995). The crisis strategy is commonly used either by governments themselves or by external pressure groups to press for action on many issues. Examples include the alleged crisis of government debt in Canada in the early 1990s or the alleged crisis of crime rates in the United States.

For all these reasons, decisions about political agenda items are highly contingent on the particular circumstances. The realities of government are well-captured by New Zealand academic and politician Liz Gordon:

> One of the things I have found in moving from the academic to the political sphere is how little policy planning actually takes place, and how ephemeral such plans are, exposed to the whims of ministers. There is no blueprint being carried out and no automatic unfolding ... Policies are being reinvented constantly. Often politicians appear to be confused about the implications of their policy actions – Not blueprint, then, but mantra.
>
> (1999, p. 249)

Problem recognition

Kingdon's category of problem recognition has to do with the perception that a particular policy issue is actually a problem that requires government attention. It is possible to think of many issues that emerged as recognized problems rather suddenly – and often faded away almost as quickly. The environment became a prime focus of public concern in the 1980s, for example, and although environmental issues remain important they have in recent years been far lower in priority than they were a decade or two ago. The relative degree of attention to issues such as inner cities, or tax cuts, or unemployment, or welfare has also shifted considerably over time. These shifts are not always related to objective conditions, either. For example, welfare reform in the United States captured attention at the same time as unemployment rates and welfare uptake rates were dropping.

If political events are difficult to categorize, the factors related to problem recognition are even more so. Although many potential sources of issues and problems are identified in the literature, there does not appear to be anything like a commonly accepted typology. The model in Figure 4.1 is an attempt to represent the various influences on policy emerging in this study. This model suggests that there are both more and less proximal sources of problem recognition, with many of the less proximal influences acting through other channels.

Obviously nothing becomes a political issue unless important politicians accept it as such. They make the decisions as to which items will be acted upon. The immediate pressures on politicians come from both political and institutional sources. The former include political parties, other collective political organizations such as cabinet or party caucuses, and individual politicians. The latter include those problems bubbling up from the operation of institutions, both within and outside the government. These agendas are themselves constructed in the context of pressures from political and institutional sources within and outside government, and may be strongly influenced by the broader context of ideas at a national and international

Figure 4.1   *A general model of influences on the policy process*

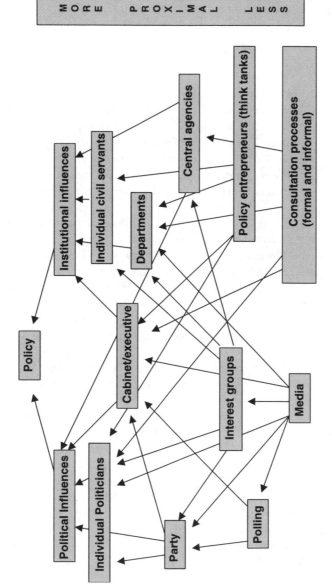

MORE PROXIMAL LESS

Policy

Institutional influences

Individual civil servants

Central agencies

Departments

Policy entrepreneurs (think tanks)

Consultation processes (formal and informal)

Cabinet/executive

Political Influences

Individual Politicians

Interest groups

Media

Party

Polling

The general climate of ideas – 'what everybody knows'

level. Relationships among these various levels can be interactive as well, such that perceptions of political interests may affect the kinds of issues that other actors bring forward.

Within-government pressures

Kingdon, looking at US political systems, sees individual politicians as especially important in shaping political agendas – much more so than are civil servants (1994, p. 30). The situation is different in parliamentary systems, where political proposals must be vetted through cabinets and sometimes through party caucuses, giving a stronger role to the collective. Nonetheless, individual politicians can shape agendas in fundamental ways in all systems. A powerful cabinet member can obtain resources and support for a program which a weaker politician might never be able to mount even if it is part of the government's agenda. As former Manitoba Education Minister Clayton Manness said, "In our democratic system, ministries were meant to be held by strong ministers. That's the way it is supposed to be. And you can tell in every government who is in control of their ministry and who isn't" (Manness interview). Even in cabinet systems, government leaders sometimes have to give way to key cabinet ministers to maintain order and solidarity in the government. The political views of individual ministers can also have enormous effects on the nature and content of a reform program. In some cases the key politician may be the elected official responsible for education (such as a minister), while in others the head of the government (prime minister, premier, governor) may be setting the agenda. In American states, individual legislators may be the key people in developing and moving forward an agenda.

The importance of legislative bodies depends almost entirely on the specific setting. Where a parliamentary government has a comfortable majority, legislatures are of little consequence; the executive determines policy. However, in minority government settings, or in the US system, in which the executive can never presume a majority on a given issue, the legislature can be a decisive influence on policy.

The official political party apparatus is clearly another source of pressures and ideas, though again less so in the United States. Issues may come from election commitments or from official party policies. Party commitments may, of course, be different than those of ministers responsible for education or from those of the cabinet or executive as a whole. Typically, a political party contains a wide range of views that are competing for primacy; one cannot completely predict from the party's official name what its policies will be. As events described in this book show, similar kinds of reforms may be introduced by parties describing themselves as conservative, liberal, or socialist. This means that within any government there will usually be very active debate about which policies should be pursued, and the outcome of this debate depends very much on personalities and internal power relationships as well as on external pressures. In some cases parties are dominated by activists who are seeking to push a government further in a particular direction than the elected politicians may feel able to move. In other cases, however, those holding office may lead opinion in the party, pushing the government further than the political apparatus may have anticipated or wanted. For example, Margaret Thatcher and Keith Joseph were well ahead of majority opinion in the Conservative Party on many issues when Thatcher became leader.

At the next level are structures that are in direct contact with the political apparatus. One of these is the bureaucracy, whose views and routines often have substantial impact on political agendas, either by way of modifying the ideas of politicians or in terms of bringing forward requirements for new legislation or political action that grow out of the routines of government. As departments and other government agencies do their work, they frequently determine a need for political action or intervention. Circumstances change such that old policies are no longer workable and require new political attention. Sometimes these routines are of small political importance, but in other cases issues emerging from the bureaucracy can assume considerable political salience – for example, a proposal to change environmental assessment procedures or a proposal to alter the way in which schools are financed. In countries that have written constitutions, the courts can also play an important role in putting issues on the political agenda.

Individual civil servants can be important on occasion in advancing specific ideas, if they can find the right political moment. In some US states, the chief school officer is elected, and functions part-way between a politician and a civil servant. In some cases education agency heads in the United States have publicly challenged their governors (Mazzoni, 1994), something unthinkable between a minister and deputy minister in a parliamentary system. The civil service is also important in shaping the ways policies move into practice, as discussed in the next chapter.

Relations between politicians and civil servants embody some inherent tensions rooted in the different role each group plays. Politicians are necessarily concerned about the broad political agenda, about the hot issues of the moment, and about how policies will be perceived. Their time horizons tend to be short. Civil servants, on the other hand, are usually mainly interested in the long-term welfare of their policy area. Civil servants may not only lack understanding of the vicissitudes of politics, but may actively dislike many aspects of politics. Nonetheless, political direction usually ends up operating through the civil service, so the structures and culture of bureaucracy will almost always end up having an impact on the substance as well as the process of policy.

The impact of the bureaucracy will also depend on the way in which the civil service is structured in any given setting. The department responsible for education may be a very powerful institution or it may have quite a limited role. In Britain, for example, funding of schools was not part of the responsibility of the Department of Education, which greatly limited the department's scope for affecting policy. Even where education departments are given a key role, policy agendas are rarely entirely controlled by the politician or department responsible for education. They are often shaped by other parts of the government apparatus, both bureaucratic and political. The balance of influence in any policy field between the cabinet official and department responsible, on the one hand, and central agencies of government, on the other, is always a point of contention. Some observers of politics have also noted a trend towards more centralized management by government leaders of political agendas within parliamentary systems. When education is high on the political agenda, as it usually is during periods of reform, it gets more attention from leaders of governments (premiers, prime ministers, governors) and from central agencies and central policy units, thus reducing the ability of the responsible cabinet official or department to shape policy. Other departments of government may influence aspects of education policy. For example, education policies may be affected by efforts to reduce crime or to improve health outcomes.

Most importantly in many cases, including several of those in this study, education may be seen not so much as a policy field in itself, but as another exemplar of more general political concerns, such as an overall wish to reduce state provision or to privatize services. In this case the political agenda for education may be set elsewhere in government, either at the political or bureaucratic level. For example, Whitty *et al.* argue that education policy in England under the Conservatives was

> positioned within several policy sets that were becoming central to the Thatcher government's overall strategy ... explicit commitment to common policies across different policy areas has served to reduce the relative autonomy of education policy and made it easier to demonstrate a relationship between education initiatives and other favoured projects ... Thus, in seeking to make sense of the origins and the contradictions of ... policy, it is important to recognise its relationship to the broader economic, political and cultural projects being pursued by the Thatcher government.
>
> (1993, p. 5)

A particularly interesting example of this wider view concerns the role that money played in the reform process. During the 1980s and 1990s, reduction in deficits became a central concern of governments everywhere, almost regardless of political stripe. Few governments were willing to increase taxes, so reductions in spending on public services were widespread. Many education reforms were at least partly about efforts to control costs or to improve productivity. These financial pressures and controls were generally imposed on education departments by finance or treasury departments or by central government policy direction.

External influences

Another powerful set of influences on political agendas comes from the great variety of lobbying to which governments are subject. Many different groups attempt to influence and shape government agendas. In education the list would include professional groups, parent groups, business groups, and a wide range of others with interests in particular aspects of education. Because education is seen to have such broad social consequences, almost any interest group is likely to have at least some interest in the policy agenda for schools. When education becomes a political priority, a wider range of lobby groups is often involved. For example, a move to privatize elements of provision may bring to bear the interests of those, such as consultants or potential private providers, who now see themselves as having a potential stake in events.

While interest in education policy may be broadly distributed, the ability to influence government actions varies considerably from one group to another. Quite a bit of work in political science analyzes the ways in which interests work to have their views come to be generally seen as desirable (e.g. Lindblom, 1980). Chapter 5 has a fuller discussion of the range of vehicles that are used by the various parties to influence the policy debate.

The role of business, and especially big business, is particularly important. Lindblom (1980) pointed out years ago that business exercises an enormous influence on the policy process because of its status as a main generator of wealth. As education has become more and more tightly connected to an economic agenda, business interests have come to play a more and more important role in education policy formation. Mazzoni describes the emergence of big business interest in education in the United States as "The most dramatic political change associated with the 1980s reform movement" (1994, p. 62). The last two decades have also been a period in which business has had an exalted status, with models of business management often being held up as examples for the public sector, and business views and interests given a great deal of play in public policy discussions (Borman *et al.*, 1993; Manzer, 1994). Organizations representing large businesses – the New Zealand Business Roundtable, the Minnesota Business Partnership, the Canadian Business Council on National Issues – are increasingly seen as having an important and legitimate point of view on almost every public policy issue. Ross Perot, for example, personally had a large impact on education reforms in Texas in 1984 (Mazzoni, 1994).

At the same time, business does not always speak with one voice and is not always able to get its own way, even in the United States. Public policy-making has been undergoing a general shift towards more active lobbying and greater emphasis on consultative processes. The number of organized groups trying to influence policy and their willingness and ability to pursue their policy objectives has increased. Policy challenges through overtly political as well as judicial processes are more common than ever. Governments have responded to this trend by placing more emphasis on consultation in policy formation; such devices as commissions, public hearings or white papers are now frequently used before policy changes are actually announced, even if they are perceived sometimes as cynical ploys rather than real dialogues.

Although it is widely accepted that government actions are very heavily influenced, if not determined, by perceptions of public opinion, latterly augmented by large amounts of polling, analysis of political opinion is surprisingly muted in the education policy literature. Many analysts of education seem to give primacy to ideology over politics, arguing that programs are shaped by core beliefs much more than by political vicissitudes. Such a view may sometimes be correct. Some governments are committed to certain courses of action almost regardless of voter opinion. One thinks of Margaret Thatcher and the poll tax. But these situations are likely to be in the minority, with governments generally much more attuned to what will be found acceptable than either the critics or proponents of particular policies might like. As Kingdon put it, whatever politicians' inclinations may be, their sense of the public mood and what people are likely to find acceptable has a powerful effect on their choices in almost every case. After all, the poll tax ended up playing a considerable role in Mrs Thatcher's fall as Conservative leader.

Kingdon does not see the media as particularly powerful in shaping political agendas. However, the media do play an important role in giving attention to some kinds of ideas while ignoring or undermining others. An individual case, such as a crime, a proposed deportation, a bankrupt farmer, or a plant closure can become the rallying point for a demand for government action that politicians ignore at their peril.

The nature and impact of media coverage of political events is a hotly debated issue. Media coverage does tend to be a primary source of information about policy issues for most people, but the extent to which it creates perceptions as opposed to reflecting them is an open question. Some claim that the privately held nature of much of the mass media and its dependence on advertising as a main revenue source will lead inevitably to its reflecting the views of the corporate world. Others take the view that the prime interest of the media is readers (or viewers or listeners, as the case may be) and that coverage other than editorials will focus on what draws attention. In that case the emphasis would tend to be on conflict.

> The amount and depth of media coverage vary not so much by policy substance as by policy-making drama ... Media writers and producers seem attracted most to issue conflicts that can be personalized as disputes between attractive, repellent, or provocative antagonists. Hence basic school funding bills may receive only perfunctory coverage, while a policy fight involving a colorful governor and combative adversaries will be seized upon to provide one captivating – if not always enlightening – account after another.
>
> (Mazzoni, 1993, p. 371)

Other oft-cited concerns about the media role in public policy include tendencies to superficial reporting of events that does not lead to a truly informed public, and to rapid shifts of attention from one story to another such that the first disappears from the news. Unfortunately, the empirical evidence on the role of the media in education reform is very limited (although Wallace, 1995, 1998, are helpful starting points).

The relationship between the identification of problems and proposals for their solution can be a complex one. Sometimes problem identification leads to proposals, but in many other cases people already have proposed solutions and are looking for problems to which to attach them, as described many years ago in the "garbage can" model of decision-making (Cohen *et al.*, 1972). Kingdon suggests, in fact, that the availability of a policy response is one of the factors that determines whether an issue is actively adopted by a government (1994, p. 142). We turn our attention, then, to the nature and sources of policy proposals.

Policy proposals

By "policy proposals," Kingdon means what might be called ideas about what should be done. Where ideas come from "in the first place" turns out to be a vexing question, and perhaps an unanswerable one. At any given time a huge number of ideas about political issues are floating around in one way or another, so the relevant question is why some are actively taken up, or how some ideas come to be dominant at a given historical moment. Here Kingdon is pessimistic, suggesting that we simply cannot know this. Ideas can come from anywhere, and there is "an infinite regress of tracing" such that "Even a brief examination of public policy case studies would lead a researcher to despair of ever finding a given source of initiative that seems to be important across several cases" (p. 71). He goes on to talk about the "extraordinary looseness of the information system. Ideas, rumors, bits of information, studies, lobbyists' pleadings – all of these float around the system without any hard-and-fast communication channels" (p. 77).

Despite Kingdon's pessimism, it is possible to talk about more immediate and more remote sources of policy proposals in a parallel fashion to the discussion of influences on political agendas. The sources in Figure 4.1 are relevant both to problem identification and to policy proposals.

Wherever policy proposals originate, they must eventually be taken up by political actors. Just as politicians decide what issues will be given priority in the political process, so they are the final arbiters of policy ideas.

Mazzoni (1991) describes this as "arena politics" and notes that

> Outside forces press demands for policy innovation; these demands – even when backed by powerful social groupings, promoted by policy entrepreneurs, and accompanied by anticipated budget surpluses – meet with little responsiveness in the subsystem area; elected officials (if a political constituency can be envisioned and new revenues are available) seize upon the proposed innovation, publicize it through popularizing symbols, and thus create the macro arena.
>
> (1991, p. 119)

An important part of the policy proposal process is the deliberate generation of suggestions by various contending parties. All the organizations described earlier – bureaucracies, central agencies of government, political parties, and so on – are sources of policy proposals just as they are sources of problem identification. Every organization involved in political lobbying is likely also to be generating, or at least advocating, particular policy proposals. Labor unions, parent groups, business organizations, professional associations, community groups, ethnic associations – all may be involved in proposing and supporting a policy agenda.

Efforts to influence public policy have become more extensive and more sophisticated in recent years. Of particular interest is the increasing role of idea-generating organizations in shaping education policy. Think tanks and policy institutes have multiplied, with the explicit purpose of affecting policy. These organizations are often created and funded by groups with particular agendas that they want to promote; think tanks may be seen as a way to dissociate the ideas from the immediate interests of the sponsors. Policy organizations are also becoming increasingly sophisticated in their approach to influencing public policy, including the way they disseminate ideas and the nature of their relationships with the media, with other interest groups and with politicians. Conservative groups in the United States, for example, have developed a number of organizations and techniques to develop and propagate conservative political ideas, with substantial funding and often with considerable success (National Committee for Responsive Philanthropy, 1997). Think tanks have gained prominence in Britain and Canada also, with most of them funded by business or conservative interests.

Think tanks are homes for the people Kingdon calls "policy entrepreneurs." These are individuals who make it their calling to promote particular policies. Policy entrepreneurs come from quite varied backgrounds. Some are academics, but many other kinds of people also get involved, for a wide range of reasons, in the business of policy promotion. Policy entrepreneurs may be tied to a particular political organization, or they may be individuals who have strongly held beliefs that they want to see adopted. Other policy entrepreneurs are found in the bureaucracy – people with a strong interest in particular ideas or approaches looking for opportunities to advance these. Policy entrepreneurs may play a critical role in keeping ideas alive, waiting for the right combination of circumstances in the other two streams (see Mintrom, 2000, for a full discussion). Roberts and King further subdivide policy entrepreneurs by their degree of activism, distinguishing between policy intellectuals, who generate ideas but do not engage in policy design work, and policy advocates, who "not only contribute to invention or develop innovative ideas, but ... mold an idea into a proposal, and press for its acceptance" (1996, p. 13). They see policy entrepreneurs as absolutely vital to major policy changes, in terms of formulating ideas, pressing for their adoption and supporting their implementation. However, this view is likely more appropriate to the US context in which the capacity to develop and initiate ideas is more diffuse than in parliamentary systems.

On the whole, research appears to play a small role in the development of political agendas for education. While research is rarely decisive in any policy field, it has been especially absent in education policy. It is quite common for education policy proposals to be advanced and adopted without anyone thinking that empirical evidence ought to be asked for. The reasons for the limited impact of education research are much debated. Some attribute the problem to poor-quality research, far removed from the problems of policy and practice. Others argue that research could make a much more significant contribution if the culture of education were more receptive to it. Still others believe that the problem is that far too little research is being done in education. The level of investment in research in education remains very small compared with other public policy sectors, especially health.

Research is, however, often used as a tool to promote particular policy approaches in education and elsewhere. Various parties may commission their own studies or seize on work that supports their position as part of the public argument. Part of the work of think tanks is to do or commission research that will give credence to particular policy proposals. Research funding generally may be tied to whatever happens to be of current interest, so that the general climate of opinion influences what gets studied.

Just as the media help to shape conceptions of problems, they may also play a role in advancing particular policy ideas or solutions. For example, extensive coverage of school-by-school test results may either openly or implicitly advance an agenda of parental choice. In some cases the media, especially some print media, can be much more blatant in crusading for particular policy approaches, such as the drive by newspapers in many countries in recent years to support reduced taxation rates.

The broader context

The discussion of the influence of the media is a reminder that the debate over policy ideas at any given moment occurs in a larger context. Three aspects of that context are discussed here: the overall climate of ideas, the role of ideology in reform programs, and the impact of globalization.

The climate of ideas

At any given moment there tends to be a conventional wisdom about what is true in any policy area. Donald Schon (1971) refers to these as "ideas in good currency." These fashions in thinking occur in all areas of social life, including such diverse areas as child-rearing, nutrition, crime, tax rates or international relations. Although we know that ideas held to be true a few years or decades ago turned out to be wrong, we continue to behave as if today's ideas will turn out to be immutable.

Historical studies illustrate how conceptions of what is important, true or worthwhile shift over time. Silver and Silver (1991), for example, trace changing views in the 1960s and subsequently about the importance of poverty in education, and about the strategies that should be used to address it. Manzer (1994) traces changing ideas about the appropriate organization of education in Canada, showing how different conceptions of the purposes of education came to be dominant at different times. Livingstone and Hart (1998) have used years of polling data in Ontario to show how certain ideas about education policy, such as the merits of testing, have gradually become conventional wisdom. Many other works could be cited in the same vein.

How and why these shifts occur may be impossible to know. In part, the prominence of particular ideas is shaped by changing material conditions, such as the optimism about education that followed massive economic growth in western countries after World War II. Krahn (1996) shows how ideas in Canada about links between schools and work followed the pattern of economic cycles. When employment conditions worsened, more attention was given to the need for schools to tie more closely to work, but when conditions improved, concern shifted to other aspects of education policy. The influential US report *A Nation at Risk* was written at the end of the recession of the early 1980s, at a time when economic uncertainties were very high. Triggering events may also play a role, such as the way in which the Russian launch of Sputnik in 1957, in the context of enormous US–USSR rivalry, resulted in important efforts to change education in the United States and, in the usual echo effect, also in Canada.

Another factor affecting the general climate of ideas may be a dialectical process in which the disappointments of the past lead to different ideas about what to do next. A considerable element of the debate about education has revolved around levels of public confidence. Action by government is much more likely if there is a perception of public dissatisfaction and political reforms are generally sold on the basis of promises of improvement, but political promises tend to be large, and the nature of human action is such that it is almost impossible to deliver everything that has been promised. The result is almost inevitably a disenchantment with policy outcomes. Thus the neo-conservative move in education policy in the 1980s was at least partly fueled by the failure of earlier reforms to deliver as much benefit as had been promised. Manzer (1994) shows how in Canada both the development of ideas about progressive education and opposition to these ideas were in large measure reactions to previous ideas and policies. One can trace the same pattern in Britain around the promise of comprehensive schools. We may yet see a similar reaction to the reforms of the 1980s and 1990s as people discover that they do not yield the promised benefits either.

It is also the case, as already pointed out, that various actors work to alter the climate of ideas to advance their own interests or convictions. This is, after all, a main part of what politics is about. A particularly important question in looking at education policy, then, is the degree to which policies arise from and reflect ideological convictions.

The role of ideology

Recent education reforms have often been criticized – and defended – as representing a particular intellectual perspective. Confusingly, this perspective may be referred to by both supporters and critics as either neo-conservative or neo-liberal, both of which appear to be encompassed in the more general term "New Right."

Like most terminology around ideas, the word "ideology" has a variety of definitions and is used in many different ways. Donald and Hall provide a definition that has been widely used.

> The term ideology is used to indicate the frameworks of thought which are used to explain, figure out, make sense of or give meaning to the social and political world ... They define a discursive space of meaning which provides us with perspectives on the world, with particular orientations or frameworks within which we do our thinking. Without these frameworks we could not make sense of the world at all. But with them, our perceptions are inevitably structured in a particular direction by the very concepts we are using.
>
> (1986, pp. ix–x)

This definition shares with most others the notion that ideology is a framework for thinking about social and political matters – one that simultaneously allows us to see or understand certain things and, as the obverse of the same coin, prevents us from seeing other things.

An important feature of the discussion of ideology is that it is at one and the same time described as a relatively coherent set of ideas that drive thought and action, and also as being full of contradictions and inconsistencies. So, in contrast to the definition cited earlier, Apple (1990, p. 15) notes that

> Ideologies [are] filled with contradictions. They are not coherent sets of beliefs. It is probably wrong to think of them as beliefs at all. They are instead sets of lived meanings, practices, and social relations that are often internally incoherent.

And Billig *et al.* (1990, p. 2) take a similar position: "In contrast to the cognitive psychologists, we stress the ideological nature of thought; in contrast to theorists of ideology, we stress the thoughtful nature of ideology." Ideology and thinking generally are full of dilemmas; ideology is never complete and unified, so individuals still have to think through what to do in any given situation. However, this raises the question of how ideological thinking is different from any other kind. Many contemporary social theorists regard every position as in some sense ideological (Stone, 1988). However, if every position is regarded a priori as ideological, the term may cease to be very useful as an analytic device; to paraphrase Wildavsky (1973), if ideology is everything, then maybe it is nothing.

Some analysts describe ideology as one of the central drivers of education policy. Edelman's (1988) views have already been mentioned. As another example, Manzer has produced a historical review of education policy in Canada that is framed by ideological concepts of liberalism and conservatism.

> Political ideas constitute meanings of politics and policies because they form the language through which people understand their place in the political world, and thence articulate their interests, conceive modes of associations with others in their political community, and devise courses of collective action … In judging public policies there are no criteria without ideological contexts.
>
> (1994, pp. 6, 9)

The term "ideology" is often used normatively. For adherents of a particular view, ideology is the script of belief – thus the fierce battles within ideological communities over what may seem to outsiders very minor points of doctrine. Critics, on the other hand, may use the term as a pejorative, implying that those who are ideological are not thoughtful, or are blind to important realities. Here ideology is seen as the opposite of pragmatism. For example, Lawton describes Conservative education policy in England by linking ideology with prejudice: "Unfortunately, the legislation has been a mixture of attempts to enforce ideological prejudices, out-of-date traditions and then more legislation to patch up earlier over-hasty drafting" (1994, p. 104).

Not all analysts identify ideology as a main determinant of policy, for several different reasons. Some commentators note the important differences of opinion within groups that are sometimes seen by opponents as homogeneous. Political parties almost always contain quite wide spectrums of opinion within themselves. Another set of analyses focus on the extent to which policy-making is dominated by immediate political practicalities.

> Interpreting policy via a reading of a correspondence between ideological preferences and concrete proposals is a hazardous procedure, and one which may overlook the complexities, contingencies and competing interests which we believe are so much a part of the policy-making process.
>
> (Fitz and Halpin, 1991, p. 135)

Further, the same policies may be supported by people from quite different political persuasions. School choice is supported in the US by some liberals and inner-city activists as well as advocates of markets and Christian conservatives. Cibulka describes US policy as, at least in some cases, arising from odd coalitions of groups. He concludes that, given typical political constraints in the US, "policy will seldom meet any stringent test of substantive or instrumental rationality; its *raison d'être* is the maintenance of social and political consensus" (1995, p. 25).

Manzer summarizes the problem analysts of ideology face.

> The interpretation of policy principles as elements of rival political ideologies is admittedly problematic. Where policy designs are the result of political compromise or historical evolution, participants in policy-making are unlikely to have articulated explicitly ideological justifications and explanations for the outcomes. Where policies have been explicitly chosen, the ideological assumptions of policy design may remain unstated and unexamined, perhaps for the good reason that everyone involved at the time simply took them for granted and got on with the practical details.
>
> (1994, p. 50)

Manzer's analysis leads one to distinguish between ideology as a public justification or rationale for reform, and ideology as an actual constituting element of reform, whether so stated publicly or not. Any combination of these possibilities could exist – that is, reforms could be ideological in their justification, in their actual constitution, in both respects, or in neither.

The debate about ideology and policy is akin to the debate about theory and practice in education. Some take the view that all practice emerges from some kind of theory, even if the latter is unarticulated. From this perspective efforts to clarify theoretical assumptions are a vital step in understanding and changing practice, just as efforts to understand ideology are vital in understanding and changing policy. Others see the worlds of theory and practice as being fundamentally different in important ways, so that while there is a connection it is rarely tight or complete. Practice is always distinct from theory to at least some degree, and can be entirely unrelated to a theoretical position. Influential work in organization theory (Argyris and Schon, 1978) suggests that there are important gaps between what people say they believe and how they actually behave, and that people may in fact be incapable of acting in accord with their espoused values. The same may be true at times of ideological positions.

One of the best statements on the mixed influences on education reform comes from researchers who interviewed British minister Kenneth Baker.

> Any vision of policy-making as a rational process was undermined in this interview with a skilled, ambitious and relatively senior member of the Cabinet. It was a reminder that reforms happen for quite pragmatic, party political reasons. The importance of the political agendas of the government and the personal ambitions of ministers as aspects of the policy process came through strongly ... Educational reforms proceeded, not necessarily because they were needed or because they were right, but because the private opinion polls suggested educational reform was a vote winner.
>
> (Fitz and Halpin, 1994, p. 46)

All of this suggests that discussion of the role of ideology in education reform needs to be well grounded empirically, and that analysts need to be clear what they mean when they make claims about connections between ideology and policy.

Policy as international

An important question in any comparative study of education reform is the degree to which reform in various countries is an international phenomenon. A comparative literature (outlined in Appendix 1) has developed, looking at reforms such as school choice and decentralization. This work provides a variety of views about the importance of the international element in education reform.

Some commentators argue that actions in various countries embody a common set of ideas about needed improvements. For example, Lawton (1992) presents rationales for reform that are held to apply across countries and Guthrie (1996) describes common reform elements across many countries. Gewirtz *et al.* (1995) note the extent to which policies advocating greater use of markets have been adopted, albeit in varying forms, in many countries. Whitty *et al.* (1998), looking at the US, England, New Zealand, Australia and Sweden, see policy convergence towards "a marketized model in an evaluative state" (p. 11).

How the movement of policies across boundaries – a concept described in the literature as "policy borrowing" – takes place is still a largely unexplored question. However, a growing literature in this field (Finegold *et al.*, 1993; Rose, 1993; and Halpin and Troyna, 1995) identifies a number of factors that promote policy borrowing.

Some see these policy movements as deliberately orchestrated by particular social and economic interests – what is usually referred to as "the New Right." Conservative governments and big business are seen to be working together to reverse some of the changes of the 1960s that redistributed wealth and attempted to reduce inequality. These commonalities are often linked to the larger economic and social phenomenon termed "globalization." Globalization is itself a disputed concept, used to refer to such disparate phenomena as the increasing impact of international organizations, the increasing movement of ideas across political jurisdictions, or, most frequently, changing economic production and finance structures that are seen to have diminished the power of the nation state (Davies and Guppy, 1997). Governments have certainly invoked globalization as a rationale for particular policies, sometimes arguing that they have no choice in the face of international developments but to follow particular policies such as reduced public spending. In any given situation, concerns about globalization, whether valid or not, may be a real motivation for policy, or they may act as an excuse for policies that are desired on other grounds, such as ideological conviction.

Other explanations have also been advanced for policy movement across settings. Howlett and Ramesh (1995) propose what they call a "convergence thesis" – that as countries move towards similar levels of industrialization they also tend to face similar issues and consider similar policy responses, but that this similarity is a matter of convenience rather than inevitability. Such an hypothesis would explain why developing countries tend to imitate the practices of more industrialized countries rather than the opposite.

Another approach can be found in dissemination theory (Rogers, 1983), which looks at the ways in which ideas of various kinds move across settings. This work has tended to focus on the spread of technologies. Rogers argues that technologies move in a characteristic pattern in which adoption rates are autocatalytic, increasing rapidly over time but not necessarily ever achieving complete dissemination. In a historical application of the same general concept, Diamond (1997) looks at the ways in which practices such as writing and agriculture spread across civilizations, and argues that ideas were adopted over time where they were seen as holding advantages for influentials. An extension of both these approaches (Levin, 1998a) has compared the spread of education reform ideas to the movement of diseases as described in the epidemiological literature. The diffusion of disease is held to be dependent on the three elements of agent (the carrier of the disease), host and context. Diseases only spread where all three factors line up appropriately, and the same might be said of the movement of policies in education. The value of the epidemic metaphor is to draw attention to the combination of factors that may be necessary for a policy to have impact in other settings.

These comparisons are a reminder that political ideas have always traveled, since ancient times (Fowler, 1994). Universities around the world still retain many of the qualities of their medieval origins. When mass education was developed in the nineteenth century many of its features were also borrowed by countries from one another. Whether there is now more such borrowing or whether the movement of policies is more powerful than in times past are empirical questions that have not been carefully examined, at least in education.

Ideas can move through personal contact as well as through electronic and print transmission. All of these have become increasingly international in recent years. The people involved in generating policy alternatives — academics, staff of think tanks, civil servants and politicians — travel more and see more of what others are doing through, for example, trade missions, conferences, involvement in international organizations, and such events as the World Economic Summit in Davos, Switzerland. International organizations such as the OECD also play a role in this regard (see box on page 84), disseminating ideas and research across the world. The World Bank and the International Monetary Fund have certainly had a powerful impact on social policy in many developing countries (Boyd, 1999).

Print vehicles, too, are more and more international as newspapers are distributed world-wide, academic journals become international, and publishing houses are increasingly part of multinational companies. The electronic media move easily across boundaries and borrow stories from each other. The rise of all-news TV networks has resulted in more exchange of information across countries.

The rapidly expanding use of the Internet and the World Wide Web has also made international contact much more feasible. Personal links at an international level have expanded dramatically because of e-mail, and academic work has become much more internationalized. Instant access is available to media sources around the world from everywhere in the world. The World Wide Web also offers vastly better access to policies and documents from around the world; much of the documentary background to this book was pulled from the Web, and many educational organizations are now linked to counterparts in other countries in this way.

People do use these international sources, too – witness the extent to which a piece in the *Economist* or the *New York Times* is likely to be read and cited in many countries and several continents. Use of international media is also likely to be greater among policy influentials.

Despite these elements pushing towards commonality in policy, there are also grounds for being cautious about claims that policy developments move easily or readily from one country to another. It is easy to pull out statements by politicians or examples of similar policies and claim a greater degree of commonality than actually exists. For the most part, those who have looked more carefully across jurisdictions have generally concluded that differences among countries are at least as important as the similarities (e.g. Halpin and Troyna, 1995; Whitty, 1997). Policy by definition tends to have a broad sweep, but practice occurs in concrete and particular settings.

Looking beyond the English-speaking industrialized countries also changes the picture considerably. An OECD report on education reform and evaluation, for example, stressed the degree to which continental European countries were far less drawn to reforms based on stricter assessment and accountability regimes (Kallen, 1996). At the same time as the United States, Canada, Britain and New Zealand were experiencing policies of retrenchment and privatization, other countries, such as Japan and much of continental Europe, were moving in quite different directions.

Federal states provide another interesting instance of the variability in reform across settings. A large and dispersed country such as the US faces quite different prospects in implementing reforms than does a small national state such as New Zealand. In the United States few reforms, no matter how popular, are actually adopted across all or even almost all of the states. Mintrom (2000) has tracked the diffusion of open enrolment and charter schools across states. Open enrolment (cross-district choice) began in Minnesota in 1988, and by 1994 had been adopted by nineteen states, with no further adoptions as of 1999. Charter schools began in Minnesota in 1991, and by 1999 had been enacted into law in thirty-six states, though in a number of these in a very weak form. The likelihood of adoption was influenced by a number of contextual factors, and states varied considerably in their interest in borrowing ideas from other states. Much depends, Mintrom concludes, on the presence of effective policy entrepreneurs.

An International Agency – the OECD and Education Policy

The OECD is a policy and research organization made up of most of the world's industrialized countries. It has been seen as one of the vehicles through which ideas about public policy move around the globe because of the way it brings together politicians, civil servants and academics and other promoters of ideas. In education there has been some suggestion that the OECD has advanced an agenda of privatization, market forces, reduced spending and tightened accountability requirements. For example, Taylor *et al.* (1997) make this argument in some detail, especially in regard to higher education policy in Australia.

However, the OECD view, at least as expressed in its public documents, is more ambiguous. Various OECD reports could just as easily be read as being very cautious about the value of reforms such as privatization and stricter accountability. Here are excerpts from some recent OECD documents on these issues.

From a report for the 1996 meeting of OECD ministers:

> When weight is given to the full range of education outcomes, a case can be made for *public* rather than *market* provision.
>
> (OECD, 1996, ch. 5, p. 6)

And

> Criticizing the standards achieved by students, teachers and schools may prove counter-productive in the long run. To the extent that high esteem and expectations are extended to schools and teachers, this can be passed on to the many students, parents and communities who themselves have only modest expectations. An outstanding policy challenge is thus to raise expectations as well as the general attractiveness of the system, and especially to ensure that this is felt in those hard-pressed schools.
>
> (ch. 7, p. 8)

A 1995 OECD report on school evaluation concluded that:

- external assessment and friendly advice to schools are both important;
- performance indicators can be valuable, but are hard to define and can be costly;
- accountability itself won't lead to improvement, but may be desirable for other reasons;
- it is important to build on teacher skill and to use staff development to create a climate of self-review.

This report was also cautious about the role of parents in school improvement.

> The idea of the "parent" in some countries is an ideological construct just like any other – embodying various assumptions concerning what

parents want, which happily coincide with what the government desires. But several countries are finding that parents are reluctant to play their new consumerist role to the full.

(OECD, 1995, p. 22)

These snippets of evidence do not necessarily contradict the claim by the Australian researchers. It would also be fair to say that many OECD documents are organized around currently popular themes in policy such as the potential value of choice or decentralization. Moreover, the OECD does provide a venue for people from various governments to exchange ideas on agendas and how they can be advanced. However, the role of the OECD is, like other elements of the political process, complex and ambiguous rather than simple and straightforward.

Evidence From Our Cases

How do the five cases in this study inform the theoretical framework that has just been developed? What do these cases tell us about the ways in which education reform programs originate? The next few pages provide a review of the evidence on these influences more closely, first by looking at the dynamics in each of the settings and then by considering some overall issues across the cases.

England

Of the five settings in this study, it is England in which education reform was most clearly linked to an ideological program (though one that had its contradictions and inconsistencies), most consistently identified with a few key ideas, and in which short-term political calculations played the smallest role. Within this overall frame, individual politicians were quite important, but interest groups appear to have played a relatively small role.

In Britain, the education reform agenda came mainly from the Conservative Party, was part of the party's electoral commitment, and was integrally connected to the overall agenda of the Thatcher and Major governments. The intellectual origins of education reform, however, came from two different and in some respects contradictory elements. One key element of policy thinking in England was traditionally conservative. Much of the Conservative critique of education was an attack on changes that had supposedly lowered standards, and a call for a return to traditional methods of teaching and forms of organization. A myriad of specifics fit under this general heading, such as more emphasis on British content, stricter discipline, the return to grammar and other selective schools, and an attack on so-called "progressive teaching." The analysis had a particularly British character, relying on beliefs about the importance of hierarchy and differences in ability. Many of the original promoters of this critique of progressive teaching and comprehensive schools were themselves intellectuals with backgrounds in schools and in universities, a particularly ironic situation given the tendency of the Conservatives to dismiss academics and their work as foolish and irrelevant at best, communist at worst.

The second main aspect of Conservative policy was the desire to reduce the role of the state through privatization and the use of market-based provision of services. Even before she became leader of the Conservative Party, Margaret Thatcher and colleagues set out to make this the dominant element in the party's program. Lawton (1994) and Ranson (1994) both provide extensive (and not very sympathetic) discussions of the way in which Conservative thinking evolved during the 1970s and 1980s. Thatcher, with others such as Keith Joseph, set up new conservative think tanks to promote the virtues of free enterprise and market policies and to counteract what they saw as the ascendancy of liberal and collectivist ideas, even within the Conservative Party. These policy institutes or centers began to generate ideas about what a Conservative government could and should do, in education as well as other fields, to change the direction of public policy and the role of the state. Many of the individuals who were prominent in these organizations, such as Stuart Sexton, Rhodes Boyson, Cyril Taylor and Brian Griffiths, occupied important positions in the Conservative government after 1979, so were in a position to help turn their views into reality. Various forms of privatization, including selling of Crown assets (such as British Rail), privatization of many services (such as water and bus services), and introduction of market-like elements into other services (such as health) were all part of the Conservative program.

These various elements of Conservative ideology had an uneasy coexistence. The critique of progressive, multicultural and comprehensive education was explicitly an argument about education itself, and the remedies it suggested involved extensive use of the state's power to shape education provision. The argument for privatization, on the other hand, was part of a larger interest in neo-liberalism, was developed primarily outside the education sector, and always advocated reducing the role of the state.

Lawton concluded, after studying Tory education policy throughout the Thatcher and Major years:

> The dominant feature of the Tory Mind that has emerged from this study is, unsurprisingly, an exaggerated concern for tradition and past models of education and society. But what did surprise me when reading so many speeches and autobiographies was the Tory *fear* of the future and of the non-traditional ... the kind of fear which took the form of an almost paranoid belief in conspiracies among the "educational establishment" ...

The Thatcherite "market solution" is a dramatic change in direction for Toryism. Almost as surprising as the Tory conspiracy theory is conversion to the belief that market forces can be relied upon to produce the kind of social system needed for the twenty-first century, including education.

(1994, pp. 144, 146)

In practice, Conservative policy included elements of both approaches. The 1988 Education Reform Act, which gave schools much more authority over their own management, also dramatically increased the legal powers of the Secretary of State, adding, by one count (Ribbins and Sherratt, 1997), more than 200 new powers. The National Curriculum and national testing both tended to increase uniformity of provision by judging all schools against the same standard. The advent of Ofsted inspections a few years later intensified this effect. At the same time, provisions for parent choice, local management of schools, opting-out and competing for students were all efforts to make education more like a market.

Despite these contradictions, the Conservatives themselves described their program throughout their time in office with a few key ideas drawn from both traditions. These are well exemplified by Kenneth Baker's speech introducing the Education Reform Act in the House of Commons for its second reading in late 1987. Baker's very first words were: "Raising the quality of education in our schools is the most important task for this parliament." To do so,

> We need to inject a new vitality into that system. It has become producer-dominated. It has not proved sensitive to the demands for change ... This Bill will create a new framework, which will raise standards, extend choice and produce a better-educated Britain.

Baker concluded his speech: "I would sum up the Bill's 169 pages in three words – standards, freedom and choice ... one cannot improve standards without at the same time increasing choice and freedom" (1 December 1987).

The same themes of improving standards through parent choice are found in every important Conservative policy document. In 1992 the government issued a paper entitled *Choice and Diversity: A New Framework for Schools*. This paper had an introduction from Prime Minister John Major which said:

> Our reforms rest on common sense principles – more parental choice; rigorous testing and external inspection of standards ... transfer of responsibility to individual schools and their governors; and, above all, an insistence that every pupil everywhere has the same opportunities through a good common grounding in key subjects.

(1992, iii)

In 1996, near the end of the Conservative reign, another minister, Gillian Shephard, had this to say in parliament:

> This Education Bill is the latest in a succession of education Bills that have, over the past seventeen years, transformed our education system. The Bill will continue the drive for reform by carrying forward the basic principles in which we believe – principles that we have applied consistently in our efforts to raise standards in schools.
>
> First and foremost of those principles is the right of parents to choose the education that they want for their children, and to be able to choose, wherever possible, from a wide range of different types of good schools. That choice and the diversity of schools that we have promoted have been the strength of Conservative policies since 1979.
>
> (11 November 1996)

The main lines of the Conservative project in education thus remained intact over seventeen years and seven ministers. At the same time, accounts show the influence that particular ministers had in shaping specific pieces of policy or legislation (Lawton, 1994). Mark Carlisle, Thatcher's first education minister, moderated early calls for vouchers in education and was replaced, it appears, because Thatcher found him ineffective. His successor, Sir Keith Joseph, was very close to Thatcher and a key figure in developing the whole Thatcherite agenda. However, it was Joseph who put a final end to the vouchers idea, thus scuttling one of the most desired reforms of staunch neo-liberals. Kenneth Baker, who replaced Joseph, is a particularly important figure. By all accounts Baker had an important role in shaping the 1988 Education Reform Act and especially the nature of the National Curriculum, despite Prime Minister Thatcher's rather different view on a number of the issues (Lawton, 1994). Wilcox and Gray (1996, p. 34) suggest that John Major's strong support in the face of stiff opposition, soon after becoming prime minister, for the bill to establish Ofsted inspections, was at least partly motivated by his desire to "set his own distinctive stamp on the Thatcherite legacy he had recently inherited." Still, reading the interviews with all the Conservative education secretaries reported by Ribbins and Sherratt (1997) gives one an impression of a strong degree of uniformity of view, even if there were differences in emphasis.

The policy organizations set up by the Conservative Party, and a number of other bodies such as the Hillgate Group, did play an important role in helping to shape the government's approach to education. The documents they produced and the proposals they tabled helped set the frame within which the government developed its approach. This role was indirect, however; few of the policies proposed by these groups were adopted wholesale, in part because of the need to try to marry the market-liberal and traditionalist wings of the party.

Interestingly enough, there is little evidence in the British case that business interests were particularly important in shaping the government's agenda. In the one case where policy did envisage a substantial private sector commitment – the City Technology College initiative – the result was quite unsatisfactory to the government, as the desired support did not emerge. Perhaps business was not particularly involved because it was clear that the Conservatives were already so sympathetic to private sector perspectives.

For similar reasons, the Conservatives distrusted the civil service, especially in the education ministry. As Kenneth Baker put it in his memoirs:

> Of all Whitehall Departments, the DES [Department of Education and Science] was among those with the strongest in-house ideology ... The DES represented perfectly the theory of "producer capture," whereby the interests of the producer prevail over the interests of the consumer. Not only was the Department in league with the teacher unions, University Departments of Education, teacher training theories, and local authorities, it also acted as their protector against any threats which Ministers might pose.
>
> (1993, p. 168)

Similar comments were made by Keith Joseph (Ribbins and Sherratt, 1997) and by Margaret Thatcher (cited in Lawton, 1994). It was clear in the British case that policy was very much made at the political level, with the bureaucracy's responsibility mainly limited to implementation issues. This tendency may have been exacerbated by the relatively weak nature of the Department of Education, which had throughout the 1970s an "inadequate array of powers and instruments in order to secure its policy objectives" (Ranson, 1994, p. 56). The Education Reform Act and subsequent Conservative legislation changed this situation considerably by dramatically expanding the powers of the Secretary of State and hence of the department she or he headed. This expansion had been, Ranson (1994) suggests, a long-standing policy objective of the department, so at least to this extent Conservative reforms did move in tandem with civil service objectives.

Almost none of the public discussion of reform in Britain focused on money. The lack of attention to money may be in part because of the complicated way in which education is funded in Britain. Still, the small amount of attention paid to funding issues in Britain is remarkable given the apparent reductions that took place in a system that was not all that well financed to begin with.

The Thatcher government did, of course, set out to reduce public spending generally, and their efforts in this direction certainly included limiting the funding of education. Keith Joseph was one of the strongest advocates of reduced public expenditure, even during his time as education minister (Jenkins, 1988). The Conservatives also disliked the local authorities (municipal governments), many of which were dominated by Labour, and introduced a variety of controls on how much the latter could spend as well as how they could spend it. Labour critic Jack Straw made the point in parliament during the ERA debate that the national government had reduced spending on education by some 20 per cent, an amount that had to be made up by local authorities from other sources (1 December 1987). However, the issue of funding was not particularly central to Labour's critique of the Act, and complaints about lack of funding hardly appear in the literature on reform in Britain, even in news sources such as the *Times Educational Supplement*. Discussion focused on the policy issues of opting out, national curriculum, assessment, inspections, and local management, with levels of funding hardly mentioned. The exception is the frequent mention of the additional resources that were provided to favored Conservative projects such as grant-maintained schools and City Technology Colleges.

New Zealand

The New Zealand reforms in education have to be seen in the context of the country's massive public sector restructuring, although the process in education was different in some important ways from that in other sectors. By 1987, when the education reform process began, there had already been three years of very substantial change in many aspects of economic and social policy. Some discussion of this larger process is necessary before turning to the origins of the program of education reform.

The overall reform program in New Zealand after 1984 is an extraordinary historical event. A government ostensibly of the left undertook one of the most extensive programs of market-oriented change in the world. The New Zealand case is also unique in the degree to which large-scale public sector reform was carried out largely in accord with a relatively unified set of theoretical precepts. This vision is generally described as having arisen primarily in the New Zealand Treasury Department, where a small group of senior policy analysts had become convinced that New Zealand's economic difficulties were largely a result of excessive state intervention and could only be solved through much greater use of free markets. The general Treasury analysis is made clear in their *Brief to the Incoming Government* in 1984, and its application to education is in a similar brief prepared for the new government in 1987. The latter document suggested in regard to education that:

> In sum, government intervention is liable to reduce freedom of choice and thereby curtail the sphere of responsibility of its citizens and weaken the self-steering ability inherent in society to reach optimal

solutions through the mass of individual actions pursuing free choice without any formal consensus.

(New Zealand Treasury, 1987, p. 41)

The New Zealand strategy applied some well-developed theoretical concepts. In addition to a belief in the efficacy of markets, Treasury (and later the State Services Commission) applied ideas from public choice theory, agency theory, and transaction-cost analysis to the full range of public services in New Zealand (Boston *et al.*, 1996). All of these form what has come to be known as the "New Managerialism" or "New Public Management" (NPM). These ideas are rooted in a limited concept of the state and a belief that self-interest is a paramount factor best controlled through specified contractual and managerial relationships between service funders and service providers. Contractualism was at least as strong an element in New Zealand reforms as was the desire to expand market mechanisms.

The question of how the Labour government came to embrace and implement these ideas is a fascinating one. One view is that these changes were a recognition that previous social and economic policy in the country was unsustainable – that New Zealand's economic performance was deteriorating because the country was trying to operate in isolation from global economic and social trends which required changes in many areas of policy. Within this general orientation some people are very enthusiastic about what was done while others see many negative consequences but do not feel that there was any available alternative. Moreover, this perspective maintains that the reforms were always subject to political direction (M. Wilson interview).

A second view is that the New Zealand government was captured after the 1984 election by a small group of politicians, economists and business people who set out to implement a neo-liberal agenda. Advocates of this view (e.g. Jesson, 1989) argue that a climate was systematically created in the country to lead to public acceptance that there would have to be radical change in many New Zealand policies and institutions if the country was to survive. They cite the degree to which many sectors of the New Zealand economy and society were subject to the same set of policy approaches under NPM, and point out that Labour had not made these changes part of its 1984 election platform.

The evidence gathered in this study suggests that a number of elements came together in a quite unusual manner to produce the Labour reform program. There were economic performance problems in New Zealand by the early 1980s; the country had serious problems with its balance of payments and its relative economic performance seems to have been declining for some time. A short-term concern about currency devaluation at the time of the 1984 election also fueled a sense of economic crisis.

The particular individuals who occupied some key roles are also very important to what took place. Roger Douglas, the finance minister, was probably the most important – so much so that the entire New Zealand reform process became known as Rogernomics. Jesson (1989) notes that Douglas, an increasingly strong advocate of free market policies, had almost single-handedly produced the Labour economic program before 1984. Once Douglas became finance minister, he was being advised by a group of economists who were all very strongly committed to NPM solutions to all economic issues. One source noted that this group were all men, without children, and included several very conservative evangelical Christians.

Douglas as finance minister had enough support in cabinet, including from Prime Minister Lange, to push his program through. Institutional structures were also important. The New Zealand government had a relatively weak Prime Minister's Office and a very strong Treasury, which allowed that arm of government to take initiative that would not have been possible in many other settings. The country has no written constitution, so no system of formal checks and balances. The legislature is unicameral, and Labour had in 1984 just been elected with a comfortable majority, partly because of a sense that the previous National government had been unwilling to make changes.

All these factors made it easier to take bold action. Douglas was not only a strong promoter of the ideas of the Treasury, but also a proponent of political strategy that called for changes to be made very rapidly so that there was no time for opposition to organize. All of these elements came together to create the New Zealand events of 1984–9.

As Boston *et al.* note,

> Exactly why the various theories and approaches ... were embraced with such enthusiasm in NZ is a fascinating question. Clearly, part of the answer lies in the gathering together of a group of reform-minded policy analysts in the Treasury, their familiarity with the new institutional economics and public choice, and their sustained efforts to apply this literature to the problems of governance in the public sector. Of course, these efforts might well have been in vain had it not been for the openness of senior ministers to the Treasury's proposals and their willingness to implement them, notwithstanding the political risks involved.
>
> (1996, p. 28)

Although the New Public Management was widely adopted by Labour in New Zealand in the 1980s, the New Zealand Labour Party certainly had no official inclination towards it. There was a great deal of debate in the Labour Party about the government's actions, so much so that in 1989 a number of important people left the government to set up a new party that they felt was truer to Labour principles. After Labour was defeated in 1990, Lange himself made several highly critical references in parliament to the influence of the Treasury under his own administration – such as this comment on 31 October 1991, during debate on National government legislation on education:

> The problem with what has happened since that time [1987] is that Treasury papers have hung like an awful spectre over the way in which education has developed. The Minister, wittingly or unwittingly – I want to acknowledge how one can unwittingly advance Treasury's agenda – has taken the thrust forward in a kind of biscuit-factory approach to education.

This seems a remarkable admission that his own administration had been wrongly captured by Treasury views.

By 1987, the government's attention was shifting from economic reforms – where most of the focus had been over the previous three years – to social policy issues. Shortly after the 1987 election, the government began a whole series of reviews of almost every aspect of social policy, including the three reviews related to education. The focus on social policy sharpened the political conflicts within the government. In its first term, the government had spoken of economic reform as necessary to protect social programs, so there was increasing resistance to extending NPM. The reviews of social policy, including education, became battlegrounds between those in the government who sought to extend NPM ideas and those who wanted to protect education and health from what had happened in other sectors. The Picot group itself had some serious conflicts among its members over the extent to which it would support the Treasury/ State Services view (Ramsay, 1993). Lange told me in an interview that he took on the Education portfolio himself after 1987 partly because he hoped to protect education from some of the worst aspects of the reforms in other fields. During Labour's second term, as Douglas sought to introduce a flat tax system and to extend NPM principles to all areas of social policy, Lange and Douglas moved farther and farther apart. In late 1988 Lange fired Douglas as finance minister, but when, in the summer of 1989, Douglas was voted back into cabinet by the Labour caucus, Lange himself resigned as prime minister.

Tomorrow's Schools, the report on which the main New Zealand education reforms were based, certainly had elements of NPM philosophy in it. The basic idea of individual schools with charters that were like contracts with the government is quite consistent with contractualist ideas within NPM. So is the decision to have a separate agency for audit and accountability purposes, and the decision to restructure the Department of Education into a much smaller policy unit, with all its services devolved to other organizations. The acceptance of parental choice of schools fits within a market model of education, in which consumers create quality and accountability by their decisions about what services to take up.

At the same time, *Tomorrow's Schools* departed from NPM and free market ideas in some important respects. Most importantly, it turned governance of schools over to locally chosen bodies made up mostly of parents – clearly an attempt to extend local control over schools. Both the Picot Report and *Tomorrow's Schools* contained quite strong commitments to equity issues, especially for Maori but also for women and other groups, which were to be a compulsory part of every school charter. Lange put considerable stress on equity issues in all his public comments on the reforms. The commitments to Maori education were to be maintained, and the rules around school choice were framed to make it difficult for schools to become selective. As Willis put it, the Labour government

> was itself internally divided between new right, centrist and left-wing factions. In general, the major education reforms in New Zealand initiated by the fourth Labour Government have been driven by the ideology of the new right. However, the market-led tendencies in its education policies are held in check by an insistence that the policies of equality of opportunity should play an important role in a restructured education system.
>
> (1992, p. 206)

Labour was also committed to maintaining or increasing the funding of education. Lange made this commitment an important part of his comments in introducing the legislation, although there is some controversy as to whether these additional funds were ever actually given to schools.

Tomorrow's Schools was certainly not presented publicly as a way of carrying forward the ideas of New Public Management, but as a long-needed adjustment to the organization of schooling in the country. In introducing the bill in parliament on 27 July 1989, Lange said:

> This is a historic occasion. A long-overdue reform is being introduced. Since the passage of the Education Boards Act in 1876 and the Education Act in 1877, the structure of education administration has remained basically the same. During the century four working-parties ... all called for radical reform, but, down the years successive Governments did not respond to the challenge ...
>
> Charters guarantee standards and fairness. In relation to standards, basic skills must be taught and existing syllabuses followed. In relation to fairness, the Government's policies on equal opportunity and its advocacy of the principles of the Treaty of Waitangi [with the Maori] are advanced.

The link between these policies and improved education was never made very explicit. Lange wrote in the introduction to *Tomorrow's Schools*:

> The government is certain that the reform it proposes will result in more immediate delivery of resources to schools, more parental and community involvement, and greater teacher responsibility. It will lead to improved learning opportunities for the children of this country.
>
> (New Zealand 1988, p. iv)

However, the link from administrative change to learning was not so neat. As Lange put it, speaking in parliament on the second reading of the bill,

> It [the government] never thought for a moment that such a change in administration inevitably would result in some benefit to the quality of learning ... In tandem with those administrative changes the Government started to work on the whole question of standards in education.
>
> (19 September 1989)

The election of the National government in 1990 brought a change in emphasis to the Labour provisions. The National minister, Dr Lockwood Smith, played an important role in giving new direction to the reforms, and especially in giving more attention to educational issues such as curriculum and assessment. Among the first National actions was to reduce the emphasis on equity in favor of one on competition. Smith gave his rationale for these amendments in 1991:

> It is important to address the reason that the legislation is important for education. There are at least five reasons, the first of which is freedom of choice. Freedom of choice in education is important to enhance educational standards ... The legislation will breed healthy competition among our schools.
>
> (11 June 1991)

Smith then went on to mention the Porter Report on competitiveness in New Zealand, and its indication that the country lacked a competitive culture in education.

> The legislation will allow the development of healthy competition – exactly what the Porter project called for – to enable the economy to get going and to allow the spirit of enterprise and competition to start to pervade the culture of our education system so that it can become relevant to this modern competitive international economic environment

... The government wants the highest standards in our schools and one way to breed higher standards is healthy competition.

(11 June 1991)

The other three reasons had to do with the impact of the previous enrolment limits and provisions in particular situations, which Smith described as "freedom from stupidity."

The National amendments weakened the equity provisions around reform in several respects. The National government was also much less interested in maintaining or increasing funding levels. The government itself estimated that schools' purchasing power had declined by 10 per cent between 1989 and 1995, and despite improvements in 1996 and 1997, funding to schools declined almost 7 per cent in real terms between 1990 and 1997 (Wylie, 1997, p. 23).

One possible reason that the New Zealand reforms had so little educational substance is that there was in New Zealand no equivalent to the British argument about standards, selectivity and progressive teaching methods. New Zealand did not have a strong traditionalist conservative element. The country had had several previous inquiries into education that had called for greater devolution of responsibility from the Department of Education to schools, but opinion among commentators is divided as to the degree of public dissatisfaction with the system in 1987. Hirsh, discussing New Zealand in the context of an international report for the OECD, concluded that:

> Until the late 1980s, New Zealanders regarded their schools as of fairly even quality, and the scope for choice as limited; a neo-liberal government borrowing and exaggerating recent British policies has not merely caused much political rancour, but also helped change the way many New Zealanders view their schooling, opening up "rich" seams of competitiveness and envy.
>
> (Hirsch, 1995, p. 159)

On the other hand, a number of sources suggest that there were many complaints about the education system (Macpherson, 1989, 1999). Left-wing critics had attacked the old system as being inequitable and unresponsive (Ramsay, 1993). Lange's opening comments, cited earlier, drew attention to this ongoing demand for change. He described the education system as "a cumbersome, hopelessly overstaffed, underworked, complex, crazy, multitiered, administrative, monolithic octopoid which would carry along over time by momentum" (Lange interview). Gordon, a strong opponent of the reforms, nonetheless described the pre-1987 situation as one in which "policy became whatever was agreed at long and tedious sessions at Lopdell House [the Department of Education's training center] with input from every conceivable education group. Education was corporatist heaven" (Gordon, 1999, p. 248).

Big business did play a role in education reform in New Zealand, though less so than in other areas of policy change. Brian Picot, the head of the commission on reforming educational administration, was a supermarket magnate, though one with a long affiliation to the Labour Party, picked by Lange because "He had good ideas. He was a man of goodwill, and he also was a practical man" (Lange interview). The New Zealand Business Roundtable took a public and generally supportive position on the Picot reforms. After the initial reforms had been passed into law, the Roundtable hired Stuart Sexton, one of the leading British Conservative theorists, to write a report that suggested the reforms had not gone far enough and needed to move towards a voucher model (Sexton, 1990). None of the commentators on New Zealand, however, seem to regard Sexton's report as having been very influential, and neither Labour nor the National Party moved towards a voucher system in any significant way after the initial *Tomorrow's Schools* implementation, despite the Treasury's continued advocacy.

Manitoba

In Manitoba more than in any of the other settings, education reforms were shaped by a single person. There is general agreement among observers that the 1994 reform program would not have occurred without the efforts and powerful political support of the education minister of the day, Clayton Manness (see box on p. 100). The Conservative government of Premier Gary Filmon had already been in office for six years, with no large-scale action in education, when the 1994 reforms were introduced. Manness agreed that he had been appointed minister because Premier Filmon "wanted something to be done."

Manness had previously been finance minister, had considerable clout in the cabinet, and was seen as an organized, decisive person who, once embarked on a course of action, would stick to it and make it happen. He was also influential in the more traditionally conservative, rural element of the Conservative Party, and had been Gary Filmon's opponent for the Conservative Party leadership in 1983.

Although Manness played a key role, the Manitoba reforms also had other antecedents. In interviews, senior civil servants talked about the reforms as a logical progression from initiatives that were already happening. They felt that the reforms would have occurred in any case – though perhaps in a different fashion – and were well under development before Manness became minister (Carlyle/Loeppky interview).

Manness said that the reforms came out of his commitment to change and his work with both the civil service and other education groups. It was not, in his mind, particularly a matter of partisan politics. He had some strong ideas about what ailed the school system. He felt that standards of achievement had declined and that too many students were simply not learning what they needed. At the same time, he did not begin with a clear idea of how to bring about the changes he wanted. The reform program of 1994, called *New Directions*, was articulated by Manness and others in the government as being a way of improving and modernizing schools in light of changing economic demands and within the context of fiscal exigencies. Neither the *New Directions* document nor the statements made by the minister in introducing it in the legislature articulated clearly just how the reforms would lead to improvement. There was no equivalent to the British Conservatives' belief in markets and choice, or the New Zealand Treasury commitment to contract theory as levers for improvement.

The Manitoba government also did not argue publicly in relation to education reform that reduction of the public sector was a good thing for its own sake, or that changes in finance or governance would themselves produce improvements in service. To be sure, the Conservatives did privatize or attempt to privatize a number of other public services, the most important of which was the sale of the Manitoba Telephone System in 1995. However, even here the public rationale had more to do with the requirements of changing market conditions and the need for a level of investment beyond what the public sector could afford, than it did with any presumed automatic superiority of the private sector. No doubt many within the Manitoba Conservative Party did hold the view that private enterprise was better in principle than public, but this was not a strong element in the official rhetoric, and the actions of the Manitoba Conservatives were less dramatic than those of Conservative governments in other provinces such as Nova Scotia or Ontario.

The reforms were broadly consistent with what might be seen as conservative approaches to education, in that they included stricter controls on curriculum and increased testing as well as some rather modest steps towards parental choice. However, in some other ways the reform program, at least on paper, was not wedded to conservative values. For example, the *New Directions* document did have many references to equity issues, including gender equity and, especially, the need for more effective education for Aboriginal students. The support documents that were prepared as part of the implementation of *New Directions* embodied many elements of accepted progressive education practice, such as a strong emphasis on differentiated instruction and curricula that emphasized higher-order thinking skills. These inconsistencies seem to have been a result of the very different agendas of key actors, both politicians and bureaucrats, in the process.

Interest groups did not appear to play an important role in education reform in Manitoba. There is no evidence of any active business lobby on education, though in a small province such as Manitoba the informal links between politicians and other community leaders are often quite important. The Conservative government had close ongoing ties with many business leaders, so it may be that a formal lobbying effort was not needed. The government did organize a series of public consultations around reform, but these occurred after *New Directions* had been tabled and were limited to people invited by the government.

More central to the Manitoba reform program was the government's strong political commitment to eliminate the provincial deficit without increasing income taxes. Beginning about 1992, deficit reduction became the main focus of almost everything the Manitoba government did. Grants to schools, as well as to hospitals and universities, were frozen or reduced for several years. Cuts were made to many other government programs. A large number of staff positions were cut in all departments, including Education. More importantly for purposes of reform, the government made unilateral reductions to the pay of teachers (as well as civil servants and others paid from public sources). The number of days allocated for teachers' professional development was also reduced.

When the unilateral salary reductions came to an end, about a year after the introduction of *New Directions*, the government passed new legislation to change collective bargaining for teachers. These changes removed most working conditions issues from the scope of bargaining, and also instructed arbitrators to consider school boards' ability to pay – which is largely a function of the amount of money the province gives them – in determining salary awards to teachers. All of these measures, of course, generated a great deal of opposition from teachers that inevitably carried over into their view of the entire reform program.

A Minister's View

Following are extended pieces of an interview with former Manitoba Education Minister Clayton Manness on 8 September 1998, in which Mr Manness was asked to reflect on the education reforms he introduced and sponsored. It deals, briefly, with three of the four elements of this study – origins, adoption and implementation. Some elements of the interview have been reorganized for this presentation, and grammar and syntax have been altered where necessary to conform to standard conventions of written English.

Origins

I was the education critic in opposition from 1983 to 1988. The various groups, and those who embraced education as if it were their own, made representation to us, of course, because they sensed that someday we might be in a position to affect policy. I listened to everybody. I listened to the Teachers' Society and the School Trustees and parents' groups. I did some reading. I did not do so much reading that I was a disciple of the reform movement outside. I didn't with passion believe that because a certain model was being practiced in certain jurisdictions we therefore had to practice it here. I wasn't struck at all by so-called outside success stories. First, I was not that deep a thinker, and second, I just didn't have time to read all of the available material. As a matter of fact I was criticized very harshly throughout my stay in the ministry as someone who really had not done a lot of research. The department had not done a lot of research with respect to the policies that we brought forward in *New Directions*. I just did not have the time.

I gave many public presentations on my views on education. I would often read from a primary reader and then ask the audience, "What vintage do you think this is?" It was a pretty advanced elementary reader. The audience would almost always say that it had to be in a range from Grade 4 to Grade 6. And I said, "No, you are not right. It is actually a Grade 1 reader." Then I asked, "What year do you think this was the prescribed reader?" The answers I received were that it must be from the 1950s. But actually it was a 1902 reader. People were overwhelmed – just shocked. I would always complete my comments by saying, "Now I understand why my grandfather, for instance, who only had Grade 3 education, wrote letters that were very well composed. In his own way he was a very learned person because whatever formal education he had obviously was solid and he was able to build upon it." And my father, who only had Grade 8 education, he wasn't quite as learned as my grandfather but still he was able to read and write. And so I said that I did not know if there was a message here or not, but nobody has to tell me that we have not been there and have not done a lot of this level of training before.

Apart from that, who has the most impact on me isn't my great-aunt, who was a teacher in a one-room school, or the Teachers' Society, or the Trustees. It was mothers – you don't see many fathers – who came into my office after I became minister. They usually had children in Grade 9 and 10. Generally they just broke down as they told me that they recently realized their children can't read and write. They generally come from a lower economic standing. They bought the dream that education would be the great equalizer. They were now desperate people looking for immediate solutions to their children not being able to read and write. This happened many times, and if it happened many times in my office, then it is real. Those who come at me and say it is an argument about money, I say I will fight you and I will beat you. This issue alone became a passion for me.

I could tell you I went to one international education meeting (I did not go to many as I was the former finance minister and I didn't believe in throwing money around). I attended an international education conference of Pan American states in Buenos Aires. I'll never forget the minister of education from one of the Caribbean states. She said, "We are going to catch you, and we are going to beat you economically because education is still number one, two and three in priorities in our families." I realized that is the way it used to be here. There was a time when nothing was more important in our society than education. This is no longer the case – certainly not at the home setting.

So then, this is the totally unsteeped and traditional educational background and foundation that guided my thinking in the development of *New Directions*. Certainly I had people talking to me about charter schools, urging me to try those, or the voucher system.

At the same time I had an experience with my youngest son. I have four children. Three of them went to the public school system. The youngest one came to live with me in Winnipeg when I had just come into Education and he went to [a private school]. I'll never forget after three or four months I finally had the courage to ask him what was different from the public school. He said, "It's not much different other than here it is cool to do well. That's the only difference." He didn't even know what he was saying.

When I was a young parent I did everything to keep alive our small school – a two-room school. I was involved in a community where there were many people who volunteered because resources were short and the history of the community was that you don't complain, you just go out and do it yourself. We received the necessary personal resources when husbands and wives who were not working away from the home came to the school and helped under the direction of the principal.

Adoption

Coming in to be the minister of education I had a mandate from the premier to be pretty aggressive. He gave me license to be forward-thinking and that, of course, is the most important thing a premier can give any minister if action is wanted. I really do not care who the minister of education or the minister of finance is; when there are large initiatives to be taken, a minister better know that he is in step with the premier. No doubt one of the reasons the premier brought me in was because he wanted something to be done. He maybe didn't know for sure what, but he wanted something done.

So I then said, "What are we going to do?" I went to the deputy minister, who I knew was ready to do something, and I asked for the best people in the department. I said I didn't care what their past political affiliations were, I don't care where they were ranked in the department. Include some of our best younger people. If we are going to build a team I don't want more than four or five or six people, and we are going to try and accomplish something.

So we had an inside department team. I then went to the main stake-holder groups and invited them to be part of a larger group. Of course, they were very skeptical right from the beginning. That would make sense. I had been the same minister who had hammered them hard in funding and I knew there was not a lot of trust. And so it was a large table. There were six from outside and then all of us inside. I stated we were going to embark upon meaningful reform. Government wanted reform in education and would accomplish it in some fashion. "I just think it is important that you be aboard and that you have a chance to input what you think is crucial and I will react to it," I said. "I know we are not going to be able to go the whole distance together. Let's hope we can, but the reality is that we probably can't. But let's go together as far as we can. I'll promise that I'm not going to abuse your input. I hope you will give me the same cour-tesy. I'll take seriously everything that you say." And believe it or not, that was not a bad exercise. There was more commonality than people would have ever thought possible, but through it all there was also an under-standing that I was serious, that it was not just a political exercise, that we were going to go forward and that I would try and be as honest as I could.

Eventually it became clear to me that one group was trying to delay the process waiting for the next election. I made the decision that this was as far as we could go together and that there were political motives for trying to draw it out another six months. And then, of course, I needed time to move the reform package through my government. It had to be given legislative support. I had to wage many battles internally.

It was my sense that the best way to introduce reform was to allow greater competition. I am not a competition freak; I don't really sense that everything is wonderful in and around competition, but it has a place on the social policy side. I certainly believe today that it has a place in educa-tion, because there are groups that have entrenched positions that will never move and government is powerless to make them; I say this of trustees as much as I do of superintendents or of teachers.

Although teachers wanted to portray me as someone who was always running them down, not on one occasion in print or in private did I ever, ever criticize the profession or indeed the Teachers' Society. I once said to them, "You can do anything you want to besmirch me or the government. I'm reaching beyond you. If you want to be an active, positive part of reform, wonderful." But ultimately, what their continuing opposition convinced me was that the only way to do anything meaningful was through competition, and so to that end I pushed very hard for a number of things.

One was that parents have a greater say through school councils. I didn't see, for instance, that as the panacea. I knew that they could go off the track very quickly, so we had some remedial action built in. Some political friends of mine were people I wouldn't trust to run a school council. But in communities where well-meaning people want to come together and have greater influence, genuine influence, whether they were parents or non-parents, the public school system belongs to all of us and they had a right to be part of that council. That was the competition put in place for trustees.

There are good schools and there are many tremendous classrooms out there. There are many remarkable teachers. I wanted to make sure that good teachers that couldn't care less about the "small p" politics swirling around were given every instrument possible to do their job. So I pushed for the right of teachers to be able to remove very difficult students from the school, just to make the point that nothing was more important than supporting teachers in the classroom. Ultimately the government backed down on this issue immediately after I left.

But now let's move to the programming area. First, I didn't want any more of these parents to come in when their children are in Grade 10 and the kids can't read. And when I ask, "How come you didn't know?" they say, "The report card was saying my child was doing relatively well." So I wanted to have more standards testing. The parent has every right to know along the way how their child was doing, in a very honest fashion. The parent had the right to know in Grade 3 how that child was doing compared to some standard. Not in the school, not in the school division but by some standard, in this case across Manitoba, and I hope some day across Canada. To that end we put into place standards tests in Grades 3, 6, 9 and 12.

The guts of the reform package was the restructuring of the curriculum. I thought that a lot of our students were not being at all challenged through age 14. I wanted to see a compression of skills for the formative years of Grade 1 to Grade 6 or 7. I really thought our students could learn more, could achieve more, because they had in past generations. I thought that in Grade 9 or 10, where so many students are not being fully challenged, they should be given an opportunity in a much more challenging way to be introduced into skill areas. And indeed, in Grade 10 or 11, if they are not doing anything but wasting time and yet they've achieved the basic skills of the ability to read and write, that they be allowed to leave the system without any stigma. Similarly, those who wish should be given an opportunity to take advanced courses, whether in mathematics or language, history or a more rigorous introduction to science. And I think all of it could work toward better use of resources.

My family was not particularly happy that I was taking on this challenge, but deep down I wanted to do something meaningful. So I came in with a mission. But I also knew we only had a year and a half. I also knew that I most likely would not be running again for office, so time was short. In our democratic system, ministries were meant to be held by strong ministers. That's the way it is supposed to be. And you can tell in every government who is in control of their ministry and who isn't. I was a senior minister. I had the support of the premier for reform, but there still were many battles inside. We had former educators in the caucus who thought that this reform was too new, it was happening too quickly. But because I had come out of Finance, and we had gone through this terrible agonizing period of downsizing and I had challenged ministers through that period of time, I just simply refused to moderate the reform package. I would hear the arguments and the counter-arguments, I wouldn't stand for them because time was too crucial. Action had to be taken.

Int: One of the interesting things in your account is that you've said almost nothing about political factors in the whole process.
CM: No. This was not a political process, at least it was not to me.
Int: This didn't come out of the party?
CM: Yes and no. The party wanted it, yes. The party wanted a political benefit. But their polling told them there would be a political benefit. To me, the mission was more important than the politics.

Implementation

In retrospect we were missing something in our planning group. We did not have individuals who were really in tune with the administration of education to make sure how credits flow, timetabling, etc. So we really weren't terribly prepared to answer all the questions on the details of implementation. I turned over to the department the responsibility to develop an implementation strategy. I was pushing for a two to three year timeline and put a lot of trust in other people. This is where some of the implementation difficulties arose, because the bureaucrats, bless their souls, wanted to please, and I believe they took some chances and, of course, I always was a chance-taker so we moved into some risky implementation approaches, or options.

Int: If you look at the present, to what extent is the plan that you developed in place now?
CM: People say it is. I think it has been moderated. I think it has been moderated too much. But I understand why that happens. There are different people there now.

Alberta

Education reform in Alberta seems to have been shaped more by the government's desire to reduce spending than by any other consideration. The Alberta government under Ralph Klein articulated a strong Conservative program around eliminating the province's debt, reducing taxation, and privatization. Education was actually cut less than most other areas, but Alberta, despite its wealth, remained a low spender among provinces on public education.

The Alberta reforms need to be seen in the context of a very powerful Department of Education that had always played a lead role in education policy. Unlike many other provinces, Alberta had never eliminated provincial exams, and in the 1980s had developed a series of other policy responses in areas such as teacher evaluation that could be considered part of an overall effort to manage education in a corporate manner. Alberta had begun a process of "business planning" in government, including the Department of Education, well before the Klein reforms.

As in Manitoba, the Alberta education reforms of 1994 were announced without reference to a broader education program. There was no mention in the press releases or in the statements in the legislature of the virtues of privatization, choice, decentralization or markets. Instead, the government justified the reforms in terms of efficiency, with a strong orientation towards preparing students to meet the needs of the economy. The Department of Education business plan, *Meeting the Challenge*, justified the reforms:

> We can provide the quality education our students need despite reduced resources by restructuring the education system. This means setting a strong provincial direction ... reducing layers of administration and allowing schools and their communities to make decisions that directly benefit their students.
>
> (Alberta, 1994, p. 3)

In commenting in the legislature on the introduction of the reforms, Premier Klein provided a similar rationale:

> quite simply the Minister of Education has said on a number of occasions quite clearly that the frontline attack relative to education is on the fundamental administration of the system, and basically we want the dollars to follow the students into the classroom so they can get good quality education.
>
> (14 February 1994)

Later in the debate, the education minister, Halvar Jonson, a former president of the Alberta Teachers' Association, had similar comments, noting that the reforms were "designed to focus resources on students in the classroom, to ensure more decision-making at the school level, to lower administrative costs, and to put into place a fair system of funding education" (12 April 1994).

An interesting feature of the parliamentary debate on the reforms in Alberta is that words such as "choice" and "competition" were almost never mentioned. Charter schools were discussed only very briefly, with the Liberal opposition describing them as "one of the few things in that Bill that we could live with" (19 May 1994). The discussion in the legislature was mainly around the degree to which the government was centralizing authority at the provincial level.

David King had been education minister under an earlier Conservative government and now headed the Public School Boards Association of Alberta. King felt that the entire reform program had been driven by financial concerns and by the government's desire to increase its control over the system.

> I think that the government is driven entirely by a fiscal agenda and by a concern that it should be able to centralize management control of the system. Certainly they are centralizing in the Department of Education but there is no evidence that they are centralizing management control because they have a vision or because they have a plan for the reform of the educational system.
>
> (Interview, March 1999)

As in Manitoba, however, the civil service saw the reforms as reflecting largely their proposals and ideas. The former deputy minister, Reno Bosetti, suggested that the government's desire to control spending provided an opportunity to move forward other proposals that the department had long wanted. For example, efforts to change the provincial financing system for schools had been attempted for years without success but were now adopted. Certainly the Alberta reforms are consistent with the strong "statist" orientation of the Department of Education. The 1994 proposals as tabled would have shifted a substantial amount of power from school boards to the province, including 100 per cent provincial financing as well as control over the hiring of the school boards' CEOs. The measures to strengthen parent voice or to introduce choice were, by comparison, quite muted.

Individual political actors did play important roles in some respects. Premier Klein's commitment to spending reductions was vital. Charter schools appeared in the Alberta reforms, according to Deputy Minister Bosetti, because Minister Jonson had read something about them and liked the idea (Bosetti interview).

Business interests also occupy an important place in Alberta, which has generally been the Canadian province with the strongest orientation to private sector interests (Taylor, 1996). However, there has been consistent conflict in Alberta on education policy between the government and some of its other supporters. For example, although Alberta has relatively liberal provisions around home schooling, fundamentalist religious groups have consistently regarded these as too restrictive, and have argued for greater parental control. Alberta has also had a strong lobby for a much more market-like system. Joe Freedman, a physician from southern Alberta, has led this campaign with funding from the conservative Donner Foundation. However, the weak charter schools provision in the 1994 legislation was far less than Freedman had sought.

Minnesota

The origins and development of the Minnesota choice and charter school initiatives reflect a number of the elements of the US political system. Much of the policy initiative came from outside the education system. External groups and individuals played a critical role in putting the ideas on the agenda and keeping them there until they were adopted by the powerful political sponsors such as the governor or a key legislator. Whatever the sponsorship, eventual passage by the legislature depended on support from legislators and other political insiders. A coalition of people with rather different interests and a series of compromises around various aspects of the proposals were necessary elements for success.

Because political action in the US develops through a process of cross-party compromise, one rarely finds the same kind of explicit rationale that a party with a parliamentary majority can lay out for its proposals. In Minnesota, both choice in 1985–7 and charter schools in 1991 were ideas that were developed and promoted by people outside the traditional education power structure. Choice was taken over and promoted by some key legislators and the governor of the day, a common feature of the American system in which politicians are constantly looking for new proposals that might boost their stock among voters. Charter schools were promoted primarily through a non-legislative coalition. Neither initiative had been part of a party program during the previous election.

The adoption of open boundaries, choice and charter schools in Minnesota was very largely the result of the efforts of individuals committed to an idea that did not have any particular political salience or constituency. A half-dozen policy entrepreneurs who came primarily from the university sector worked together and strongly promoted the need for reform, and their own proposals for reform, for several years. They used personal contacts with politicians and other leaders, work with groups such as the Citizens' League, university teaching, media work, position papers, and other means to keep both their issues and their solutions alive. They carefully cultivated senior officials in the state government as well as politicians. They lobbied continually and looked for the right opportunity to move their proposals into law.

An important feature of these efforts was the unusual coalition of supporters. While in many settings both school choice and charter schools are seen as reforms of political conservatives, in Minnesota the group supporting these measures was actually dominated by political liberals. Joe Nathan, for example, one of the main promoters of both initiatives, supported them because of his concern about inequality in schooling and his belief that they would help minorities and the dispossessed get a better deal from schools (Nathan, 1996).

Demand for changes in education policy in Minnesota in the 1980s came initially from outside the education and political systems. Two groups – the Minnesota Citizens' League and the Minnesota Business Partnership – both began in the early 1980s to lobby for changes in education. The League, a non-profit policy analysis organization, issued a report to the legislature in 1982 (*Rebuilding Education to Make It Work*) that called for some form of parental choice and more authority at the level of each school through making the system less hierarchical and bureaucratic. However, these proposals were controversial enough that no legislator would sponsor them (Roberts and King, 1996, p. 75). Nor did the proposals have very much support within the education system, especially because the report argued that more funding was not a critical factor in reform. As Roberts and King note:

> by the mid 1980s in Minnesota, we see the emergence of two currents in the river of educational reform. One attempted to shift the course of the river, while the other sought to improve the existing riverbed with an increased flow of monetary support.
>
> (1996, p. 43)

The following year the Minnesota Business Partnership commissioned its own study of the public school system, which concluded that the state's school system was good but could be better, and needed significant change for that to happen. Among their specific recommendations were the suggestions that high school students be able to move to post-secondary education before completing high school, that schools be given more decision-making powers, and that state-wide tests be developed to assess student progress on key objectives – ideas that were characterized as deregulation, decentralization and accountability. Minnesota was ahead of most other jurisdictions in developing these as central policy themes.

Despite opposition and earlier failures to get support in the legislature, Minnesota Governor Rudy Perpich came out in favor of school choice, to considerable public surprise, in a speech to the Citizens' League in January 1985. Public polling in 1985 did not indicate very much interest in school choice, for example (Mazzoni, 1993). The group of policy entrepreneurs was able to meet with the governor late in 1984, when he was casting about for a set of education proposals that would be workable and politically attractive. Apparently Perpich had not been happy with the proposals put forward by the State Department of Education. Perpich's 1985 program, called *Access to Excellence*, included a greater share of state funding, more state evaluation of achievement, more scope for local districts to define programs, and parent choice of school. "The package was virtually identical to the basic ideas on education redesign that had been recommended by the Minnesota Business Partnership and the policy entrepreneurs" (Roberts and King, 1996, p. 80). Perpich's announcement of his support for these policies was made with no prior consultation either with educational groups or with legislators. He also promoted his proposals at the national level as part of the ongoing discussion of education reform. Although these proposals were not adopted by the legislature in 1985, they did garner support from some important politicians from both parties. Several lobby groups were created to move them forward, such as People for Better Schools and the Brainpower Compact. These groups and the 6M coalition of education stakeholder groups engaged in a very open public battle over the proposals. After a two-year process of debate and modification, some of the key elements, including school choice, were adopted into law.

Six years later a very similar group of policy promoters took on a similar crusade in favor of charter schools in the state. The governor, Republican Arne Carlson, did not support this initiative until it was well advanced. The promoters were able to put together a team of legislators and others to sponsor the measure, with support again from the Citizens' League. This time, though substantially watered down from the original proposal, the measure passed into law on its first attempt with quite broad bi-partisan legislative support. The perception that school choice had been reasonably successful and had not disrupted schools as its opponents had claimed was one of the reasons that the charter schools proposal was acceptable. Once charters were adopted in Minnesota, Carlson also promoted them nationally.

In neither of these cases could Minnesota be said to have been copying ideas from elsewhere, since it was not only the first state to adopt the proposals but also did so ahead of countries such as England and New Zealand.

Although big business was active in the Minnesota debate, it was not able to have its proposals adopted in their entirety or even very substantially. The Business Partnership proposals were at first rejected entirely by the legislature, and some of them were never adopted. The Citizens' League, however, did turn out, over the long term, to be influential. "No other [external] organization matches its staying power or sustained influence as an agenda-setter on educational reform issues" (Mazzoni, 1993, p. 365). Educational organizations including teacher unions and school trustees were influential, but also unable to get their own way on many important issues.

The climate of ideas, ideology and globalization

At the broadest level, reform in all five settings drew on some common themes that are linked to broader international economic and social developments. There is little doubt that some kinds of ideas about education and public policy were in vogue in the late 1980s and early 1990s, especially in the English-speaking industrialized countries, while others ideas were largely absent. The policy papers of governments, the concerns of international agencies such as the OECD, and the topics that were often taken up in both academic and popular publications did tend to focus on a set of similar issues. These included the need for more efficient use of limited resources, the presumed link between schools and economic competitiveness, the need for greater accountability, and the importance of parental choice and involvement. All of this discussion itself took place in the shadow of overall government efforts to reduce both the role of the state and the public's expectations of it by eliminating deficits and debt, by curtailing public spending, and by trying to use private sector operations and models.

Public confidence

All of these reform programs postulated significant public unhappiness with the schools as a key rationale for reform. However, the evidence does not support this allegation. In each of the countries in this study, there is evidence of substantial public satisfaction with schools, especially among parents of school-age children (Barlow and Robertson, 1994; Berliner and Biddle, 1995). One of the most comprehensive reviews of public opinion on schooling is by Livingstone and Hart (1998), who review evidence from Canada and elsewhere and conclude that public confidence in schools has remained more substantial than in most other institutions. Data on parents' reasons for choosing schools in England and Scotland also suggests that most parents are reasonably satisfied with local educational provision (Woods *et al.*, 1998; Levin, 1997). Polls conducted by various groups during the reform process in New Zealand, Minnesota, Manitoba and Alberta also indicated positive public attitudes to schools (e.g. Wylie, 1999; McEwen, 1995). In no setting was there much evidence of a high degree of dissatisfaction. Yet the reforms proceeded despite this absence.

Hart and Livingstone (1998) also note that corporate executives have a much more critical view of schools than do other groups, and support policies like those adopted in the cases in this study to a much greater extent than do other groups in the population. In fact, it has been suggested (Dehli, 1996) that the degree of ongoing support for schools and teachers has been a disappointment to governments that have been hoping to find in public opinion additional justification for their proposed reforms.

Polling data can be read in various ways, of course. Davies and Guppy (1997) review twenty years of Canadian data and come to the conclusion that public confidence in schools has been declining over time, albeit slowly. Loveless (1997), looking at US polling data, concludes that support for schools remains quite strong, and that public actions even more than polls show such support. For example, Loveless notes relatively low levels of enrolment in private schools. In Canada, even with much increased public funding, private school enrolments have grown only modestly.

A reasonable conclusion would be that public schools, while certainly not free from criticism, enjoy as high a level of public support as do other public institutions, if not higher. This conclusion does not suggest that schools need no changes, but does suggest that there is no crisis of public confidence. However, the strong support for particular reforms by business leaders also illustrates the extent to which policy can be driven by a specific set of interests rather than a broad public agenda.

International impacts

There is plenty of evidence about the movement of education reform ideas across the world. Links existed between political parties – for example between the Thatcher and Reagan/Bush administrations (Whitty and Edwards, 1992). New Zealand's Roger Douglas, architect of many neoconservative changes there, was often in Canada as a consultant to or guest of Conservative provincial governments interested in similar policies, while British Conservative policy consultant Stuart Sexton wrote an influential report on education for the New Zealand Business Council (Sexton, 1990) and then turned around and held up New Zealand's reforms as an example for Britain to emulate. British Conservative ministers traveled to several countries promoting their brand of education reform, and Kenneth Baker was apparently influenced by a visit to the US in 1987 to look at magnet schools. The London *Sunday Times* sponsored a book by two Americans (Chubb and Moe, 1992) about the implications of British reform for the US. Many other examples could be cited.

All of this supports the view of education reform as being in large measure an orchestrated international phenomenon. Certainly some observers have made this argument, as suggested earlier in the chapter. The commonalities in some of the central ideas and approaches that have been described earlier in this book lend credence to this view of reform.

At the same time, while there clearly are international connections, when one looks more closely at national experiences the differences across jurisdictions are also compelling. In England the reforms were extensive and in many ways transformative of schooling. In New Zealand they were primarily about governance issues and had little impact on many aspects of school practice. In Alberta and Minnesota issues of spending reductions, greater provincial control, increased – though still quite limited – parent involvement, and more assessment were central. In Minnesota reforms centered around the introduction of market-like mechanisms.

In interviews the participants themselves played down the role of external influences. In Manitoba both Minister Manness and the key civil servants said that they did not directly borrow policies to any considerable extent, and Prime Minister Lange in New Zealand made the same comment. However, they did acknowledge that developments elsewhere helped shape the context in which they operated.

> The international community ... now shares information, picks it up on the Internet. We are all reading the same authors. There is quite a community of interest that influences us ... I would simply say policy-making now ... is seldom if ever us trying to invent the wheel. Having said this, we can still come up with some approaches that may be different.
>
> (Carlyle interview)

Not only did the content of the reforms differ considerably, but an adequate understanding of what happened also requires careful attention to the specifics of context and culture, as the elements already mentioned take shape and interact in unique ways in each setting. The nature of political debate, the size of the political elite, the traditions of the jurisdiction, and particular aspects of demography or geography also had important effects on reform. Cibulka (1991) shows clearly how assessment reforms took on very different characters in three US states because of differences in political processes, structures and cultures. Even the most popular reforms are rarely adopted by as many as 80 per cent of states (Mintrom, 2000). In Australia, states have swung sharply back and forth in their policy orientations, moving from extensive decentralization to more central control and back again. In Canada, many provinces have recently reduced the number of school districts, but several provinces, including at least two with many small districts, have chosen not to move in that direction. Even in Britain, as Glatter *et al.* (1997) note, the impact of decentralization and choice depends very much on the geography, demography and history of school provision in particular local areas.

These differences draw attention to the ways in which context mediates the flow of ideas across and within national boundaries. As Whitty and Edwards put it, "This process is perhaps less a matter of direct policy exchange than of mutually reinforcing versions of reality which reflect shared reference groups and assumptive worlds" (1998, p. 223). Perhaps more importantly, differences in jurisdictions make it clear that policy choices can be made, and that there is no inevitable adjustment that everyone must make to accommodate globalization or economic competitiveness. People can set their own directions through their own political systems if they wish to do so. The options may not be unlimited, but they do exist.

Influences on Origins – Some Conclusions

Kingdon's three streams – problems, proposals and politics – are all important in each setting. In no case can one understand the origins of education reform without paying attention to individual actors, streams of influence and political processes, as well as to underlying ideas. However, the interplay of the elements is different in each case. In light of these cases, what can be said about some of the main elements of reform?

All governments used similar arguments about economic competitiveness and the need for higher standards to justify their policies. A relatively coherent rationale for reform – what might be called an ideological position – was most explicitly articulated in England and New Zealand, but much less so in the other settings. The less that there was such an explicit rationale, the more reform depended on the particular people and circumstances. Key individuals played a particularly vital role in Manitoba (Minister Manness) and in Minnesota (several "policy entrepreneurs" and legislators) compared with the other three settings. Specific political events were vital in Alberta (commitments made during an election by a new premier) and Minnesota (Governor Perpich's need to carve out an education policy niche).

The dynamics of the political process affected reform in important ways in all five settings. The timing of elections and the government's sense of its mandate were always important. Clayton Manness's retirement from politics at the 1995 election meant that he did not have enough time to advance his agenda as much as he wanted to. The British government made education an important issue in the 1987 election, and the New Zealand government shifted its attention to social policy after its 1987 re-election. Shorter-term political processes were particularly important in Minnesota because in the other four settings governments with parliamentary majorities were able to act more independently once elected. In most settings the civil service was much less important in shaping policy, the exception being the role of the Treasury and State Services Commission in New Zealand. In Manitoba the staff of the Department of Education were involved to some degree with Minister Manness in determining the nature of the reform program. In Alberta many of the reforms were consistent with long-standing approaches of the Department of Education

The role of other influence groups also varied across the settings. Policy groups within the Conservative Party in England played an important role in shaping policy options, but party interests do not appear to have been vital in any of the other settings, supporting Kingdon's view that individual politicians are more important in shaping policy than are political parties. External interest groups of various kinds were especially important in Minnesota. In both Minnesota and New Zealand, large businesses organized specifically to influence education policy, though with mixed success. In Alberta and Manitoba there is no evidence that the shape of the reform program had been substantially influenced by particular lobbies or individuals outside government, although the reforms were certainly consistent with much of the agenda advanced by business.

5 Adoption

Theoretical Framework

For the purposes of this study, adoption is the process of moving from an initial policy proposal to its final form in an approved piece of legislation, regulation or other vehicle. Implementation, taken up in the next chapter, has to do with trying to get policy translated into practice. While there is a substantial literature in education on issues of implementation, much less has been written about the political process of adoption of education reform, and there are few useful conceptual frames available for looking at this aspect of reform. Commentaries on the ideas behind reform or on its effects on schools are much more common.

Yet the process of adoption is important in its own right, and seldom smooth. As noted in the last chapter, policy proposals most often have their origins in the political realm. Typically this means that they have been developed only at a very general level. The promises in party election manifestos, for example, are often couched in quite abstract terms. Many critical elements may not have been thought through in any detail. Opposition parties have particular difficulty in framing campaign promises because they do not have access to the detailed administrative understanding that is sometimes necessary to design workable approaches. It is often difficult to anticipate the impacts of multiple policies on each other. Changes in separate areas such as financing, curriculum and governance will all affect each other as implementation proceeds, making the policy design task extraordinarily difficult. In many cases compromises have to be made during the political process to secure approval.

For all these reasons, proposals do get altered as they move through the political approval process. In general, more controversial policies will have a more difficult time, but the path is seldom predictable, and sometimes what seems innocuous can become contentious while issues that looked as if they would be difficult turn out not to be.

In the adoption process several elements collide. What began as a slogan or a concept – school choice, local management, open enrolment, provincial testing, charter schools – must be turned into a detailed scheme in the form of legislation, regulations or policy guidelines so that it can actually be put into place in a large and complex system. Both administrative and political issues can result. Many important policy initiatives begin as ideas that are not fully developed, so turning them into something workable may involve quite a bit of debate as to what the intentions originally were and how they can best be realized. The debates can be political, in that opponents of reform in and out of government may revisit their concerns as the details are worked out. At other times the issues will be administrative as the system tries to work out detailed procedures for managing large-scale changes.

Much of this discussion takes place in a public political arena in which conflicts over both intent and implementation are debated. The latter may include the "official" debate in parliament or a legislature as well as the debate that goes on in public, through various consultation processes, the media, and with various interest groups. Through the entire process, proponents and opponents of reform are trying to advance their position and counter opposing arguments, so reforms are frequently accompanied by intense political disagreement. Although all of these processes may be intertwined and often occur simultaneously, the following discussion considers them under the headings of internal political debate, bureaucratic accommodation and public political debate.

Internal political debate

The announcement of a policy intention is rarely the end of the political debate, even within a government. One reason is disagreement within government as to whether a given policy is the right one to pursue. Any political party or cabinet will contain a wide range of views on policy issues. Even after an idea is adopted, disputes will continue because people have different ideas about what the idea could or should look like in practice. Those supporting a particular conception must take into account the source and vehemence of alternative points of view. The development of detailed plans or the requirement to approve budgets or legislative proposals can reopen internal disagreements about how strongly or how far a policy should be pursued. Proposals will often be altered as they are developed to be more appealing, or at least less objectionable, to those inside the government with divergent views. It is not always easy to know which people are going to be key to a policy's fate. Certainly heads of government are vital, but they are not necessarily the only essential actors. Ministers of finance and their deputies can be especially important if a new policy has financial implications – as they almost always do. Heads of other units may be important if they see a policy as affecting their own programs or plans or if their co-operation is needed to move a proposal forward.

Typically, an important program will be reviewed politically on several occasions –before it is first announced, and then again as various details are worked out. Each time this happens, those who see the program as ill advised for any reason can renew the internal debate. In the world of government, things are rarely final; changes in circumstances can easily put issues that were considered to be resolved back on the agenda.

Nor is the debate always substantive. People working together in a government may actively dislike each other and take steps to oppose proposals not because they necessarily disagree with their substance but because they want to make things more difficult for a political rival.

A second element of political debate inside government involves the government's sense of what is politically possible or desirable. People who agree on the merits of an idea in principle may disagree sharply on its political merits or timing. A proposal may be opposed for any number of reasons other than its substantive value – because the timing is wrong, because more pressing issues take priority, because it is too close to an election, because it costs too much, because key elements of the party or electorate are not seen to be sufficiently supportive. This kind of analysis is a fundamental part of the calculus of governing, and no major proposal will be approved unless enough of the right elements are in place to satisfy at least a sufficient number of the key people. In the course of these internal political discussions, changes are often made in proposals – for example, to make them more acceptable to a key constituency group or to fit with other central commitments of the government.

All these processes of compromise are quite common, but the result, especially when policy processes are so often rushed and the subject of rather cursory discussion by key decision-makers, may be a policy that tries to be many things to many people and therefore contains important inconsistencies. Indeed, it would be surprising to find important policy initiatives that did not contain at least some loose ends or seemingly contradictory elements.

In public, once a policy is announced governments tend to feel that they need to stay committed to its main thrust, even if the actual development reveals many unanticipated problems. The classic discussion of this phenomenon in organization theory is work by Staw (1976) on the US commitment to military intervention in Vietnam, which describes how the United States' commitment intensified even as doubts about its value grew. For a variety of reasons it remains very difficult for governments to extricate themselves from commitments even when almost everyone doubts that the commitment is a useful one. A policy strongly advocated by some within a government and strongly opposed by others can prove a political lightning rod if later events suggest it was ill advised yet there is already a strong public commitment to it. Again, opposition parties may have particular difficulty here, as they are inevitably making policy commitments with less detailed knowledge of what is required for successful operation.

Bureaucratic accommodation

The greater the political element in a proposal, the less likely that the bureau-cracy has had a role in shaping the proposal and the more concerns any given proposal is likely to engender from the standpoint of the system. Politicians and administrators live in quite different worlds. Politicians, as described earlier, tend to be sensitive to the symbolic impact of their pronouncements and with the extent to which proposals are consistent with government programs and political realities. The political process of adoption often leads to policy proposals that are vague or even contradictory. Politicians may lack any experience or depth of knowledge in a substantive policy field, so may not understand the complexities of existing organizations, the impact of other competing agendas, or the difficulties that inevitably arise in the attempt to move from a general idea to a specific set of procedures.

Civil servants, on the other hand, as Wilson (1989) points out, are concerned to make the system work as smoothly as possible. They may have no personal commitment at all to a government's purposes, but they do have to think about the procedures in detail – what could go wrong, who will administer or manage the policy, how exceptions will be handled, what timelines are possible – all the things that form no part of an attractive political vision. They must be concerned with the potential difficulties and uncertainties in any proposal that they will eventually have to manage. It is the job of civil servants to anticipate problems, which is not always what their political masters wish to hear about.

In the end, every policy idea has to be turned into a set of detailed proce-dures. A commitment to student assessment has to be translated into specific tests for specific populations at specific times with specific marking and reporting schemes. A commitment to an increased parent role in school governance must be specified in terms of the bodies to be created, their constitution, their powers and limits on their powers, and their relationships with other existing institutional structures. All of these details and many others must be worked out, and sometimes their working out interferes considerably with the original intent. This rubbing away at new policy proposals is doubtless one of the reasons that politicians see bureaucrats as so resistant to change, and why newly elected governments often want to put their own supporters into key administrative positions.

As a policy proposal moves towards adoption and implementation – or, as Fitz and Halpin (1991) describe it in their study of grant-maintained school policy in England, "from a sketchy policy to a workable scheme" – the various and not always consistent concerns of the bureaucracy will come to bear. On the one hand, where difficulties are foreseen there will be attempts to reduce the scope and impact of proposals, to rub off the sharp corners of policy that will create the most difficulty and to try to make new policies at least partly consistent with existing policy and procedures.

On the other hand, civil servants may also use political proposals as vehicles for other purposes. For example, they may see a political commitment as an opportunity to move in a direction they have previously supported but for which they have been unable to get political commitment. Civil servants may well have their own views about what is desirable policy and may work to promote those where possible. Political direction will typically apply to only a few aspects of policy that are seen as most vital, leaving many other elements to be developed by the bureaucracy and therefore considerable scope for bureaucratic initiative. A new proposal can also gain civil service support because it provides new resources for their unit, or increases their responsibility or prestige vis-à-vis other departments.

The way in which the civil service influences policy depends not only on the skills of individuals but also on the institutions and practices in a given setting. There is a large difference between the tradition of an independent and professional civil service in parliamentary countries and the American practice of changing the administrative leadership when political leadership changes. However, even within parliamentary systems there are important differences. In Britain, political appointments to key civil service positions, even by a new government, are very unusual. In Manitoba, it has long been practice for a new government to make some changes at the senior levels. Alberta, on the other hand, with only one change of government in the last fifty years, has no tradition in this regard. However, in a long-standing government close ties inevitably develop between politicians and the civil service leadership.

The bureaucratic process is also affected by institutional structures. Sometimes central agencies such as finance or government management units play key roles in shaping policy, whereas in other cases the line departments are pivotal. Some governments may have weak processes for managing internal bureaucratic conflict, which can lead to delays and inconsistencies in adoption. The degree of rivalry among units of the administration can vary greatly.

Size of the jurisdiction matters, too. In a relatively large country such as England, most civil servants will have no direct contact with the political arm of government. In a much smaller setting such as Manitoba, Alberta or New Zealand, small size means that a much larger proportion of the civil service will have political contact with ministers and their staffs, which tends to reduce the independence of the bureaucracy.

In practice, the administrative apparatus almost always has an important role in determining what a political commitment will actually look like when it comes into practice.

Political opposition

Government programs of almost any kind create opposition. For one thing, political systems in democratic countries have opposition built into them. It is the role of opposition parties to oppose what a government does, and this usually involves trying to make the government's intentions or actions or both look bad. This effort is often supported by the media, not necessarily because they have a position that is opposed to a government's actions, but because they tend to cover what is interesting to people, and political conflict is interesting. It is also the case that policy changes usually involve gains for some and losses – real or perceived – for others. Ever since Machiavelli, political theorists and politicians have been aware that the fear of loss is often a more powerful political motive than the possibility of gain. Over time, some policies that were once hotly opposed become generally accepted, as has happened with compulsory seatbelt use, or prohibitions on smoking, or many others. However, at the outset opposition to almost any government initiative is to be expected from at least some quarters.

These standard elements of conflict have been exacerbated by more recent development in education. As policy-making in education has moved away from a system of consensus among the major participants, the politics of education have become more confrontational (Macpherson, 1996), with the result that most of the main reforms considered in this book were also the subject of intense public political concern. In some cases positions are so strongly held that parties are almost entirely unwilling to compromise, resulting in a win/lose atmosphere that is difficult to manage (Cody *et al.*, 1993).

Political opposition can come from a variety of sources. First on the list, though not necessarily most important in practice, are opposition political parties. It is their obligation to raise concerns about government actions, and they will almost always do so, though their degree of involvement and effectiveness varies considerably. The kinds of arguments that opposition parties make can also be revealing in terms of the ways in which opponents characterize the weaknesses in a given reform.

The second main source of opposition comes from organized groups of various kinds. Just as a variety of lobby, pressure or interest groups can be sources of ideas or support for reform, so other groups can be important sources of opposition. Given the dominant agendas in education reform in the cases considered here, business groups have been either neutral or supportive. Because many reform programs have sought to diminish the influence of those within the education system – teachers, administrators and local districts – these groups have been the strongest single source of opposition, with teacher unions constituting the largest, best-organized and best-financed opposing body.

In many ways the reform process has proved a difficult issue for teacher organizations. One problem has been how to position themselves in the public eye so as to avoid falling into the characterization of teachers by governments as being entirely self-interested. Reforms have in many cases made teachers' working situations more difficult – for example by reducing support services or increasing public scrutiny of schools. Yet a critique of reform based entirely on the interests of teachers would inevitably be seen as self-interested. Teacher groups have therefore often sought to frame their opposition to reform in terms of support for the quality of education and the interests of students. A second problem for teacher groups has been to reconcile divergent views within the membership about many aspects of reform. While teachers are often united on issues of salary and working conditions, they are not necessarily of one mind on many educational questions. Many teachers, especially in secondary schools, may be supportive of initiatives such as increasing assessment of students or more stringent academic requirements.

Parents are another key element of the political process in education. Parents are increasingly spoken of as having very important – sometimes the most important – interest in education reform. Their interests, and those of students, are often appealed to by both proponents and opponents of reform. Proposals to introduce elements of market forms to education, for example, rest on a view of parents (seen as consumers) as being the final arbiters of quality. Formal consultation processes are often seen as a way to ascertain the views of parents.

While their views and interests are often appealed to, in most cases parents are insufficiently organized to play an explicit and independent role in the political process. Nor is it likely that parents are of a single view on very many issues. However, parents have either mobilized themselves or been mobilized in various cases to be more active participants in the political process. Some important changes in schooling have occurred largely because of ongoing efforts by parents. Greater accommodation of students with disabilities is a good example of an issue where the impetus came largely from parents, often over the objections of the school system. In other cases, opposition by parents has scuttled proposed reforms, especially where the reform calls for an approach to teaching and learning with which parents are unfamiliar (Tyack and Tobin, 1994). On more recent issues of reform, parental political activity has most often been in opposition to particular reforms, though parent groups have also formed to press for changes such as school choice, charter schools or more academic curricula.

As mentioned, political dispute often arises within government as policies are being adopted. Part of this internal debate has to do with the stance a government wishes to take on external political opposition. Although governments are highly cognizant of opposition, a government with a clear majority or a high level of popularity can override almost any opposition if determined enough, and in some cases a government may use strong opposition as evidence of its commitment to its principles no matter what.

Consultation processes

Formal consultation processes have become an increasingly frequent and important part of the policy adoption process. In various ways governments seek both to gauge and to influence public opinion on their ideas before committing fully to implementation. Many different vehicles can be used for this purpose. In the settings in this study, consultation mechanisms included the issuing of policy papers with an invitation for response, the holding of various consultative events to seek public input, and the organization of working groups comprising some key stakeholders.

The existence of a consultation process may mean that a government is really interested in learning more about an issue and in hearing what those consulted have to say. Commissions of enquiry, for example (sometimes called Blue Ribbon in the US and Royal Commissions in Commonwealth countries) are often used by governments facing an important issue and unsure what to do about it (Mazzoni, 1994; Ginsberg and Plank, 1995). Public debate and discussion can be a way of building understanding about complex issues such that some consensus can be developed on how to address them. However, at other times consultative processes are designed more to impress people with the government's openness than as genuine occasions for debate and dialogue that might actually lead to change in what has been proposed. As already suggested, the more committed a government or key politician is to a course of action, the less inclination to look seriously at changing it in response to different views. In this regard, consultation may sometimes better be viewed as one of the strategies governments use to sell their ideas or proposals.

Consultation also clashes with the desire governments often have to move things forward quickly. Political horizons are short, and the pressure to have implementation as soon as possible may be very great. In other cases, as in Roger Douglas' famous dictum in New Zealand, moving reform forward as quickly as possible is a way to avoid giving the opposition too much time to mobilize. Where opposition is expected to be strong, governments have an incentive to avoid too much consultation.

Public consultation is becoming an increasing element in policy-making in most spheres. A more educated public, and one increasingly organized into many different groups, often demands a greater say in policy development. Such vehicles as environmental reviews and citizen forums have been developing as responses to this demand. These developments present new issues and challenges for governments, as both political and administrative structures must learn how to work in a world in which policy-making is more public. Governments are only beginning to think about the challenges for policy-making that will be brought about by signi-ficantly greater public involvement.

The nature of the political debate

All parties to the debate about education reform make efforts to shape the discussion to support their own positions. This process is ongoing at all times, from the inception of policy through its introduction, adoption and implementation. Governments are constantly trying to convince voters of the rightness of their plans while opponents attempt to do the opposite.

One theoretical lens for understanding this kind of political debate comes from the sociological concept of "framing" –"the tactical tailoring of shared understandings to promote certain perceptions of injustice and social solutions" (Davies, 1999, p. 4). Framing suggests that parties to a debate attempt to promote their ideas and proposals in a way that is most sympathetic to broadly held public views. Another approach can be found in work on the idea of discourse. Discourse analysis builds on the views of Edelman and others about the symbolic aspects of politics and the importance of defining the basic ways in which people think about issues. As Ball puts it,

> Discourses are ... about what can be said, and thought, but also about who can speak, when, where and with what authority. Discourses embody meaning and social relationships, they constitute both subjectivity and power relations ... Meanings thus arise not from language but from institutional practices, from power relations, from social position.
>
> (1990, pp. 17–18)

Ball has developed these ideas further in other work (1998), arguing that concepts once thought to be extreme have gradually become mainstream or even dominant, at least in part through well-orchestrated efforts by particular political groups to make them so. For example, the privatization of public services such as health and education has moved over twenty years from being an idea on the fringes to being a very strong component of public policy in many countries.

Discourse is shaped by various forms of argument. People may either try to construct arguments to show that their positions are self-evident, or they may use various forms of evidence to support their position, or they may simply loudly assert their own views and dismiss those of others. In general, as political debate about education has become more acrimonious, all parties have become more sophisticated about and paid more attention to the management of discourse, sometimes called "spin doctoring."

Decisions about how to frame arguments are often tactical. In some cases – for example as an election draws nearer – governments may seek to avoid looking too confrontational in public. In other cases they may be not only prepared but anxious for a public political row that can establish their bona fides with their supporters. For example, a number of conservative governments have been quite willing to have confrontations with organized labor as a way of establishing their commitment to pro-market policies.

In attempting to shape debate and public opinion, governments use all the apparatus of office such as parliamentary committees, white papers, advisory groups, formal consultation processes and public statements by ministers. Advertising may be used extensively in some cases. In education, governments have increasingly provided information directly to parents through publications of various kinds. Governments often poll the public to gauge the level of support for their proposals as well as how best to present them. Communications has become an increasingly important part of the government apparatus, and communication strategies a standard part of just about every policy proposal system. Mazzoni describes the process of issue creation in the United States during the reform ferment after 1983:

> many activist governors engaged in high powered "issue campaigns" to arouse popular sentiment. Conducted like an election campaign, these usually consisted of "a campaign organization, a campaign kickoff, a series of campaign speeches, a campaign tour, and a panoply of campaign slogans, endorsements, advertisements and materials."
>
> (cited from Beyle, 1993, p. 96)

The increasing attention in government to managing communications likely contributes to increasing public cynicism about government, and hence in the longer term may be at least partly self-defeating.

Governments are not, of course, the only parties to be making calculations of political gain and loss; all participants in a policy debate will be doing so. Each opposing organization will have to decide how much opposition it can afford politically at a particular time. Opposition groups also have to decide how to put forward their views in a way that is most likely to garner public support or convince vital stakeholders to agree with them.

Opposition groups use many of the same means as government, such as issuing official statements and press releases, advertising, polling, and the citing of authorities. They also have some of their own devices, such as demonstrations and the media's interest in conflict and controversy, to get their views across. Public distrust of government is itself a weapon that can be used by opponents. In Canada and the United States, opponents have also sometimes used the courts to attack elements of various reform programs.

All sides may appeal to the views of supposedly neutral or objective third parties. Research is often used in this way in political debate as the different sides cite studies and experts are trotted out to bolster differing positions.

Of course, the resources brought to the process of political persuasion are far from equal among the various parties. Those with money and expertise – typically governments, large businesses and to a lesser extent other organized groups – have far more ability to put their ideas on the public agenda than do the rest of us.

The result can certainly be processes that are more misleading than helpful. It is easy to cite examples of ideas that became commonly believed even though there was no real evidence to support them. Various political "scares" arose regularly in the twentieth century, even though in many cases a few years later almost everyone would have admitted that they were entirely unjustified. It is easy to be highly cynical about the very possibility of useful political debate, given all the efforts to shape opinion, which is one of the reasons for the "flight from democracy" (Plank and Boyd, 1994) and interest in other ways to shape policy, such as markets.

Charles Lindblom's analysis provides a useful counterpoint to this cynicism. Lindblom is not naive about political manipulation, noting that "In the history of humankind there is nothing quite like this institutionalization of deliberate, planned, carefully calculated impairment through sales promotion, institutional advertising, and the use of the same techniques in campaigning and political advocacy" (1990, p. 114).

However, with all its weaknesses there is no apparent substitute for public debate as a vital process of social learning. Lindblom also suggests that "There would seem to be more hope for good policy in the contestation of partisan participants, each aided by social science, than in policy-making by an inevitably partisan single decision maker falsely perceived or postulated as above partisanship" (1990, p. 265).

Evidence From Our Cases

Although the literature on education reform has a great deal to say about the problems inherent in various reform proposals, very little empirical work has been done on the politics of opposition to reform in education. Most of what is reported in this chapter is derived from official records of legislative debates, newspaper accounts, documents such as those issued by teacher organizations in the various settings, and interviews with participants. One exception is work that looks at the stances of teacher unions towards various reform programs (e.g. Robertson and Smaller, 1996).

Internal debates

Evidence on the extent to which governments were internally divided on matters of education reform is hard to come by, since insiders often remain silent about these matters. However, it seems likely that most of the reforms in these cases were a matter of at least some internal disagreement.

Several British politicians have given their own accounts of the reform processes. Although these accounts do not agree in many respects, it is clear that British government policy was the result of compromise at almost every turn among the different elements of the Conservative Party and government. It is known that Kenneth Baker and Margaret Thatcher had some serious differences of opinion on the Education Reform Act. For example, they gave quite different versions of and appeared to have very different levels of commitment to the goals of the grant-maintained schools policy

(Fitz *et al.*, 1993). An unverified story is that at one point they disagreed over two important elements of the proposed Act. Thatcher would not agree to support both, and let Baker choose the one he wanted. Lawton (1994, p. 60) believes that Kenneth Baker made important compromises on the National Curriculum in order to make it acceptable to disparate views within the Conservative Party. During the 1992 debate on the legislation to establish Ofsted, there were heated debates within the government about whether inspection should be privatized or retained in government, and whether local authorities should have some role in the process (Wilcox and Gray, 1996).

Any caucus of more than 300 members, as the Conservatives were in the 1980s, will have divisions. Former Prime Minister Edward Heath, for example, spoke strongly against the Education Reform Act in parliament, calling the provisions for choice "a confidence trick" (1 December 1987). However, Thatcher had a strong hold on her caucus, so the occasional dissenter did not threaten the overall direction of the government.

In New Zealand, also, the reforms in education and more generally were the subject of considerable debate within the Labour government and the Labour Party. Eventually the party split over its social policy, with a group of MPs leaving Labour to set up their own political party. In Lange's first term, 1984–7, the cabinet appeared to have considerable agreement on the main lines of reform. By 1987, however, when the reforms in social policy, including education, began, Lange was less enamored with the fervency of Roger Douglas and his supporters. By Lange's own account, he took on the Education portfolio as an attempt to forestall the same kind of approach in education that his government had already implemented in other policy fields (Lange interview). Certainly, his later critical comments about the role of the Treasury suggest considerable ambivalence, at the least. In late 1987, Lange forced Douglas out as finance minister, only to resign himself the following year.

In Minnesota, the disagreement over the choice proposal in 1985–7 is well documented. The idea did not come out of the Democratic Party apparatus or the civil service, and Governor Perpich was not able to put together a legislative majority for it until, after two years of discussion, the idea gained support of some key legislators, both Republican and Democrat. The problems in putting together such a coalition are well described by Roberts and King (1996) and Nathan (1996). They include rivalries between the governor and the legislature as to who initiates policy, rivalries in the legislature between political parties, personal dislikes or alliances among legislators and with the governor, and, of course, individuals' views on the particular issue. The chief sponsor of Governor Perpich's initial education reform legislation was actually the House Republican majority leader, Connie Levi, whose interest was drawn by a relatively minor feature of Perpich's program that would allow high school students to attend post-secondary institutions. Levi had been trying to advance a similar policy for a couple of years. Although the Democrat's Senate leader supported school choice, he did so knowing that many of his colleagues in the party opposed it (Roberts and King, 1996). The 1991 charter school proposal was even further removed from the official political apparatus. Lobbyists worked hard to convince the legislature to support it in the face of much opposition from the educational establishment. One strategy used was to bring students to the legislature to testify to the benefits that school choice had brought to them (Nathan interview).

In neither Manitoba nor Alberta is there evidence of serious dissent in cabinet or the Conservative Party over the 1994 reforms. However almost any important policy will have at least some skeptics in cabinet, as Manitoba Education Minister Manness admitted.

Bureaucratic accommodation

On the whole, in these cases bureaucracies shaped and modified political reform proposals rather than providing very much direction to them. There were tensions in all cases between the politicians and the civil service over these issues. However, the role of the civil service varied, not only across jurisdictions but within each jurisdiction, depending on the specific policy issue.

One common difficulty concerned timelines. The introduction of policies and programs often took longer than originally intended as the system tried to work out the details and fit them into the overall organization of education. The more complex the proposal, the more likely it was that additional time would be required. There were frequent collisions in most of the settings between civil servants and politicians on this issue, as the latter sought to maintain momentum and the former tried to make implementation timelines feasible.

However, other stresses between civil servants and politicians were more fundamental as civil servants tried to inject their own sense of goals and priorities into reform programs at the same time as they were carrying forward the government's agenda. In Manitoba, some of the senior civil servants spoke of themselves as trying to pursue an educational agenda beyond what the political level had actively supported.

In Britain, the civil service role varied depending on the particular reform, keeping in mind the Conservatives' overall level of suspicion about the civil service. Inevitably, the process of moving from rather general political proposals to all the detail needed for a very large and diverse school system gave the civil service an important role. Fitz *et al.* (1993, p. 26) note efforts by "civil servants to temper the worst excesses of the keenest advocates of GM status" in 1987, even while they note that the whole idea of GM arose outside the civil service. They go on to say:

DES civil servants had to reconcile the philosophy and differing ambitions of the advocates of opted-out schools, while securing the smooth running of the existing system. What emerged was a policy framework which *enabled* rather than *encouraged* schools to opt out of LEA control.

(1993, p. 26, emphasis in original)

There were many difficulties in the administrative work around various reforms in England. The development of the National Curriculum and its link to student assessment proved an enormous – and enormously difficult – task that eventually led to a number of political problems and a substantial revamping of the entire plan in 1993 and 1994.

The most unusual relationship between the bureaucracy and the political level occurred in New Zealand, where the main lines of public sector reform were, as has already been noted, developed in the civil service by the Treasury and the State Services Commission. Both the Picot Report and (even more) *Tomorrow's Schools* moved some distance away from the ideal Treasury model of agency theory. In the spring of 1990, the Labour government commissioned the Lough Report to review the status of the education reforms, partly, it appears (Dale and Jesson, 1992) because of concerns within the Treasury and the SSC about the limited nature of what had been done so far. The National government that was elected later in 1990 substantially accepted and implemented those recommendations. Although education in New Zealand never adopted all the features of agency and contract theory that were promoted by the Treasury and SSC, it moved increasingly towards many of them over the decade after *Tomorrow's Schools*.

The work of the civil service on the New Zealand reforms was made much more difficult because the Department of Education was itself being dramatically restructured at the same time as it was trying to move forward the government's proposals for school administration. The change from a large Department of Education with an administrative focus to a small ministry with a policy focus was a wrenching one. A substantial number of civil servants ended up working on these plans knowing that their own jobs would disappear as a result. The accounts of the process in New Zealand by civil service insiders make it clear just how difficult the entire exercise was (Butterworth and Butterworth, 1998).

Senior civil servants in Manitoba said that much of the initiative for the reforms came from within the service rather than from the political level, and that *New Directions* was really a continuation of earlier policy initiatives. However, this was not the perception of the educational interest groups, or of Minister Manness.

After the adoption of *New Directions* there was a huge amount of activity in the bureaucracy to try to move the reforms forward, including new curricula, provincial guidelines on a host of issues, working parties, professional development and other steps. A stream of policy documents were then issued by the Manitoba Department of Education and Training in support of these proposals. Assistant Deputy Minister Loeppky spoke of 191 different deliverables that emerged from *New Directions*.

At the same time as advocating and defending *New Directions*, the civil service was also trying to make the reform program more manageable for schools. Schools found it very, very difficult to keep up with what was being asked of them in addition to meeting their ongoing obligations, especially given the concomitant reductions in budgets that were occurring. The proposals ran into a variety of difficulties and had to be modified several times. Timelines for the development of new curricula and assessments had to be adjusted several times. Deputy Minister Carlyle said that one of the key problems with implementation was the realization that

> the pace of implementation had to be slowed down to build ... accep-
> tance because one thing that was surely killing acceptance was the fact
> that it was so much so fast that people couldn't cope with it, or did not
> want to.

> (Carlyle/Loeppky interview)

In another case, the province issued revised timetable allocations for elementary schools that turned out to require more time than actually was in the school day. Minister Manness suggested at one point deleting recess from the school day to create more instructional time, a proposal that led to such a storm of opposition that it was soon withdrawn.

In Alberta, much of the reform initiative was quite consistent with the strongly interventionist stance of the Department of Education. Indeed, the deputy minister of the time took the view that the 1994 reforms were really a logical continuation of a process that had started much earlier and that was substantially driven by the department as much as by the politicians (Bosetti interview). School districts and school administrators in Alberta were used to receiving and implementing directions from the province, leading to less opposition on many of the issues. Difficult timelines on some issues, such as the reduction in the number of school districts, were met. The deputy minister felt that in general the 1994 reforms, even those that reduced salaries for teachers, encountered relatively little opposition (Bosetti interview).

In Minnesota, the State Department of Education played very little role in developing either the issue of choice or that of charter schools. Adoption issues were simpler because the reforms were single reforms rather than large-scale programs. On the whole, the introduction of open enrolment and school choice went relatively smoothly, partly because the policy was phased in over several years. In the case of charter schools, the restricted number of schools at the beginning meant that the adoption process could be worked out gradually. Over time Minnesota increased the number of charter schools allowed, however, and abolished restrictions on the number in the late 1990s (Nathan interview).

Political opposition

Opposition parties

Opposition parties opposed reform in all the settings, of course. In Minnesota, as in other US states, there is no official opposition in the parliamentary sense, so legislative opposition and support runs across party lines. In the case of the choice policy of 1985–7, Democratic Governor Perpich's legislation was championed by a number of key Republicans, and otherwise would likely not have passed. In 1991, too, both support and opposition for charter schools were bi-partisan.

In England, the Labour Party was strongly opposed to all the major elements of the Conservative program in education, including choice, local management of schools, national testing and grant-maintained schools. Labour's strongest criticisms were that the bill gave too much power to the Secretary of State at the expense of local authorities, and that the effect of choice would be to favor a selective system over a comprehensive one. As Labour Shadow Secretary Jack Straw said in responding to the bill,

> That success [of comprehensive education] has never fitted with the prejudices and fantasies of the Conservative right. So, from the Prime Minister downwards there has been a constant campaign to instill a distrust of state education ...
>
> It is to the Secretary of State's eternal shame that he has brought forth a Bill that will divide: that will set child against child, class against class, parent against parent, school against school, race against race.
>
> (1 December 1987)

The Liberal Democrats, in the difficult position of a small third party, supported the principles of choice and improved standards, but took the view that the Reform Act would not actually bring them about. They objected particularly to the increase in the powers of the education minister.

Labour's opposition had no impact on the reform program since the Conservatives had a comfortable majority in parliament and were quite prepared to use it. During the debate on the Education Reform Act the government itself made many amendments to the bill but accepted none of those offered by the Opposition. Probably the most important amendment was the decision to abolish the Inner London Education Authority, and this came from Conservative cabinet ministers, not from the Opposition. Despite vigorous debate in parliament in the late fall of 1987, the bill was easily passed into law early in 1988.

The same process occurred with the 1993 Education Act. The government itself introduced hundreds of amendments (suggesting that the bill had been prepared in considerable haste), and more amendments were made in the House of Lords by Conservative peers. However, only three of seventeen amendments offered by the Opposition were accepted. Morris *et al.* conclude that the bill

> exemplified what the report [of the Hansard Society] found wrong in our system: lack of pre-legislative scrutiny, haste in the presentation of Bills, no legally recognized arrangements for ... supporting ... papers; time-wasting by Opposition Members in the early days ... followed by expressions of outrage at the imposition of a guillotine on debate; insufficient public access to the process.
>
> (Morris *et al.*, 1993, p. 125)

Because the other reform programs were not justified by governments in terms of a set of ideological commitments, and generally used much softer rhetoric, the parliamentary debate was also less focused, though often quite vituperative. In New Zealand the National Party's comments on *Tomorrow's Schools* lacked any central focus. For example, in an initial speech during a debate on the first announcement of *Tomorrow's Schools*, National Party MPs defended centralization in the New Zealand system and suggested that greater decentralization could threaten both equity of provision and standards of achievement. One speaker (Mr McClay, *Hansard*, 9 August 1988) raised doubts about review and audit, and suggested that the government pay more attention to the views of the teacher unions – ironic in light of National's stance once in government!

In the two Canadian provinces the Opposition focused on specific elements of the reforms rather than on grand critique, not surprising since the reforms themselves did not have a grant narrative to be critiqued. In Alberta the Liberal opposition challenged the 1994 reforms primarily as a power grab by the provincial government at the expense of school boards, as well as criticizing the size of the cuts in spending. Discussion of school choice and charter schools was almost entirely absent from the debate. However, facing a government that had just won an election, their concerns were easily overridden.

In Manitoba the political debate over *New Directions* also focused less on its overall intent than on a number of the specific elements in it. The opposition New Democratic Party expressed concerns about some of the changes in curriculum, the increased powers of the minister, and the provision for teachers to be able to suspend students from their classes.

Other opposition groups

Teacher unions were a main source of opposition to reform in every setting, but other groups within the system, parents and academics were also sources of opposition to some of the reforms.

Links between teacher unions and political parties vary across the five settings. In Britain teacher unions have been quite closely tied to the Labour Party. In New Zealand it was Labour who brought in the reforms. Teacher unions were officially non-partisan. In North America teacher unions have tended to be politically unaffiliated, though several provincial unions have in recent years linked themselves — often unsuccessfully — to efforts to defeat incumbent governments that had introduced reforms to which they objected.

In New Zealand the Post Primary Teachers' Association (PPTA) has traditionally been more militant than the elementary teachers' union (NZEI). However, both unions publicly opposed the Treasury report on education in 1987 and *Tomorrow's Schools*, especially in regard to the plan to shift the responsibility for teacher pay and hiring to individual schools. Opposition from teachers led the Labour government to abandon plans for this system of "bulk funding," in which, as in Britain, schools have the total budget and make decisions on what staff to hire and how much to pay them. New Zealand's two teacher unions argued that such a system would eventually destroy collective bargaining and single salary scales. Bulk funding was implemented in some schools in the ensuing decade, but resistance to it meant that it never became a national practice.

In Manitoba the reforms occurred during a time in which the provincial government was making efforts to limit the role and strength of the Teachers' Society, as with labor unions generally. The Manitoba Teachers' Society was partially excluded from formal consultations around the *New Directions* reforms. When Advisory Councils for School Leadership were proposed for each school as a limited form of parent involvement, initially parents who were also teachers were prohibited from serving, though this ban was later rescinded. More significantly, the government made a number of legislative changes that limited teachers' rights in collective bargaining, and towards the end of its term commissioned a report — never acted on — that would have made very significant changes in the way in which teachers were paid.

The Alberta Teachers' Association did organize to oppose the Klein reforms. For example, while the Alberta government organized a series of consultations in the fall of 1993 to look at how to reduce spending, the ATA organized its own series of counter-consultations to put a pro-education position in the public domain (Taylor, 1996).

In England, the ability of unions to oppose reform had been substantially reduced by the government in the early 1980s through legislation that effectively ended collective bargaining and also greatly limited political action

(Busher and Saran, 1995). Although British teacher organizations had been deprived of many of their legal protections, action by teachers (though not initially led by unions) was responsible for one of the major setbacks to the Conservative reform program. In 1993 teachers were so upset by the assessment requirements of the new curricula that large numbers of them, often supported by their school governing bodies, refused to implement the government's testing program for 7-year-olds, arguing that it was too complex and educationally unjustifiable. The widespread resistance led the government to back down on its plans and to appoint a commissioner, who recommended simplifying substantially assessment requirements for teachers and students. In other respects, the British unions attempted to moderate various aspects of the reforms, for example by working hard on the development of the National Curriculum (Bangs interview).

Minnesota's two teacher unions were both strong political forces. Both were very opposed to the Perpich choice plan in 1985, and lobbied heavily to have the legislation defeated when it was first proposed. Mazzoni concludes that teachers, especially when they worked with other groups of educators, "did have substantial impact as a blocking or moderating force," but that "this impact, though formidable, did not constitute anything like an absolute veto" (1993, p. 370). As a result of the defeat of his proposals in 1985, Perpich convened a Governor's Discussion Group that spent nearly two years looking for some consensus on a reform program. The choice laws that were eventually passed were weaker than originally intended, due to opposition from teachers and others. The same story was replayed in the charter school debate of 1991. Teacher organizations were strongly opposed. Though the bill eventually passed, teacher opposition was instrumental in leading to important modifications on numbers of charter schools and the role of teachers in their initiation.

Although teacher unions in all the settings opposed the reform programs in many respects, they always did so with some trepidation. Teachers were worried about being seen as motivated only by self-interest and as being anti-change. The use by several governments, especially in Britain and New Zealand, of a rhetoric of "provider capture" or other accusations of self-interest illustrated that these fears were accurate. As one Minnesota teacher union lobbyist said, "strenuous opposition would have won us the title of 'opposition to education,' opposing reform, unfriendly to change, so we muted our opposition ... It was dangerous to oppose the governor and dangerous to always be in the opposition to choice" (Roberts and King, 1996, p. 193).

Local authorities in Britain and school boards in Canada and the United States also opposed many provisions of reform, but generally with little effect. In Britain the reduction in the powers of the local authorities was a prime goal of the Conservative government, so LEA opposition was anticipated and disregarded. In Manitoba the government backed away in 1994 from plans to amalgamate school boards, perhaps because many of the small boards that would have disappeared were in rural Manitoba, which is the Conservative political heartland. In Alberta, amalgamation of school boards did take place, and funding was centralized in the hands of the province, but the Catholic boards in Edmonton and Calgary, the two main cities, were able to use the threat of court action to block some of the provisions in the reforms that would have reduced their financial authority significantly. The government also backed off on its plans to require Department of Education approval before boards could hire superintendents.

Ironically enough, the local school governing bodies set up in England and New Zealand also proved quite resistant in many cases to the plans of central government. As Munn put it, "Having created a parental lobby through the establishment of school boards and through parental choice, government has had to live with the consequences of that lobby being used in opposition to its own policies" (1993, p. 88). New Zealand school governing bodies consistently opposed bulk funding, for example, and British governing bodies made representations against a number of the later Tory reforms. However, the 2,700 governing bodies in New Zealand and the more than 20,000 in England are much harder to organize in collective protest than were the much smaller number of regional bodies, especially since the school bodies began with no national or regional organization to support them.

Parents have probably played the strongest organized role in the United States, where religious groups especially have organized to support some reforms and oppose others. For example, Boyd *et al.* (1996) describe the way fundamentalist groups blocked outcomes-based education in Pennsylvania. The problems encountered in Minnesota around outcomes-based education are also partly linked to opposition from parent groups, though Minnesota has a smaller fundamentalist Christian presence than do many other states. In the other settings, small groups of parents did organize to oppose particular features of reform, especially cuts in funding and increases in student testing, but these groups appear to have made little difference to the process. Even more than in the case of school governing bodies, organizing parents for effective political action is an enormous task for which there is almost no established infrastructure. A partial exception is in Britain, where groups such as CASE (the Campaign for State Education) have had a consistent if not necessarily powerful presence in the education debate.

In several cases opposition groups worked together in efforts to change or defeat reform proposals. In Minnesota in 1985 the two teacher unions, the school boards' association and the school administrators' association created a formal coalition (the 6M Group) to oppose Perpich's plans, which led in part to the two-year delay in their adoption. In Manitoba and Alberta teachers, boards and administrators also tried to co-ordinate efforts, though less formally.

Academics provided another source of opposition to reform programs, though some academics also supported various reforms, as in Minnesota. In England and New Zealand articles in the popular media and in academic publications attacked reform proposals vigorously. In both countries academics conducted studies, the results of which questioned some of the benefits of reform. In Alberta and Manitoba there was less academic comment, though what there was tended to be critical of reform. However, whether such opposition had any significant political impact, at least in the short term, is doubtful.

Opposition groups had varied success. In none of the settings was the opposition able, over the longer term, to prevent a determined government from moving ahead with key elements of its plan. Mass protests by opponents, for example, seemed to be an ineffective strategy, or even one that strengthened government positions in some cases. Rallies in front of the legislature in Manitoba and Alberta appeared to have no impact at all, and both the Klein and Filmon governments were re-elected despite strong opposition from teacher unions.

Determined opposition was able, however, in most of the settings, both to delay or to modify government proposals. Where opposition was strong enough, some features of reform were postponed or altered to be more acceptable, at least for the short term. With the exception of England, political opposition led to important changes between government's initial proposals and what was eventually put into practice.

In New Zealand Labour backed off several key aspects of the Picot plan. In Alberta the government gave up on a number of proposals that would further have limited the powers of school boards. Legal action by Catholic school boards in Alberta did lead to the Klein government's backing down on its attempt to remove taxation powers from these boards. In Manitoba a number of measures around school councils, curriculum and assessment were also altered in response to public concerns. In Minnesota opposition led to substantial delays and then to passage of much weaker measures than had originally been proposed. Even in England, the boycott by primary teachers of the Key Stage 1 tests in 1993 led to very large changes in curriculum and testing.

The impact of opposition should not be exaggerated, however. Determined governments were able to turn their proposals into law in each case, and to gain most, if not all, of what they originally sought. Moreover, opposition to many initiatives tended to decrease over time and governments in England and New Zealand pressed their reforms forward over a number of years. For example, open enrolment generated growing public support in Minnesota between 1985, when the idea was first proposed, and 1992, when it was standard practice across the state (Roberts and King, 1996, p. 189).

Consultation processes

All the reform processes in this study involved public consultation processes of one kind or another, but there is little evidence that most of these were really intended to be a meaningful part of constructing policy. Public consultations were often either rushed or manipulated. The potential of public discussion to build knowledge and understanding about education and its possible improvement was not used to any great extent.

In Britain the Conservatives did use a number of consultation devices, but generally appeared to have made their minds up in advance on most issues. In 1987, following their re-election, they issued a discussion paper on the major features of the proposed Education Reform Act, but the period for input occurred during the summer when schools were closed, and was in any case very short given the scope of the proposed reforms. Their approach reflected the Conservative view that education had been captured by teachers and administrators and that consultation would just give these groups another opportunity to vent their opposition. Criticisms of their proposals were largely ignored. Fitz *et al.* describe the consultation in 1987 on the proposals for grant-maintained schools as "leading to an avalanche of negative responses" (1993, p. 10), including many critical reports in the popular education press and two polls showing "ambivalent support" among parents. However, the bill "moved towards the legislative stage with little serious discussion" (p. 25), partly because of Kenneth Baker's view that speed was important precisely in order to minimize the build-up of opposition. The 1993 Education Act was introduced before public consultation had even concluded (Ranson, 1994).

In New Zealand there was very substantial public input into the Picot Taskforce, which made many visits, received briefs and held public hearings. The Taskforce did, it appears, take this input very seriously in formulating its proposals. Once the Picot Report was published, further comment was invited and a substantial amount was submitted. However, the government released *Tomorrow's Schools* within four months and implementation began almost immediately, even before the necessary legislation had been passed, so it is hard to believe that this latter phase of consultation had very much impact.

In Manitoba most of the public consultations were managed by restricting participation to those with invitations and by strictly limiting the participation of teachers and school boards. On the other hand, Minister Manness in Manitoba did work quite intensively for about a year with a group of representatives of the major educational organizations on issues related to *New Directions*. It was clear throughout, however, that while the group could give opinion and advice, the minister and the government would always determine what steps they would actually take (see box on p. 100).

In Alberta, several public consultation processes preceded the 1994 reforms (Taylor, 1996). In the fall of 1993 Alberta Education organized a series of Basic Education Roundtables to address the question of what were the essential elements of public education. Participants were selected by the government and the consultations were seen by many, including some of those who attended, as having a predetermined outcome (Lisac, 1995). The document *Tough Choices* was distributed as part of the discussion on possible funding reductions. Following the announcement of the 1994 reforms, five teams of MLAs were established by Minister Jonson to provide a contact between the government and the public on implementation of the reforms. Opponents were highly critical of these processes, contending that they were packed events intended to provide a show of support for what the government had already decided to do.

Minnesota was the only setting, it appears, in which government worked hard to enlist various groups in support of its program, because that was the only way to create pressure for passage of legislation. After the defeat of his proposals in 1985, Governor Perpich created a large Governor's Discussion Group (GDG) on education reform which included all the main education stakeholders as well as business and other representatives. This group met for about eighteen months. According to Roberts and King, key policy entrepreneurs in Minnesota worked with the State Education Commissioner, Ruth Randall, to help shape the Group's work and keep some of Perpich's key themes, which they had earlier promoted to him, prominent in the discussions. The work of the GDG, which did eventually agree on a limited choice plan, was also quite high-profile publicly, being the subject of frequent newspaper articles and editorials. This was no doubt a major reason that the choice provisions passed the legislature in 1987.

The nature of the political debate

In each setting, the reforms to education were controversial. The way in which the political debate was constructed depended on a number of factors. Each government adopted a strategy for neutralizing opposition, which in turn depended on the political culture of each jurisdiction as well as on the nature of the reforms themselves. In some cases, such as England, the approach was confrontational, while in others, such as Alberta or New Zealand, a softer strategy was used.

Both proponents and opponents of reform sought to link their positions to some key social values, including both excellence and equity. By and large the reformers placed more stress on the former, and many opponents of reform on the latter. Government rationales for reform tended to focus on economic needs and the consequent requirement for higher levels of achievement in schools. Opponents of the reforms tended to focus on the human costs and the dangers that reforms would increase inequality. Governments also tended to argue that education required more control from the outside – whether by parental choice, testing or other means – while opponents of reform placed more confidence in professionals to run the schools.

In England the basic stance of the government was to treat all opposition as misguided at best and more often narrowly self-interested. They portrayed their policies as "common sense" and those who opposed them as "the loony left" or else as entirely self-interested. Ball (1990) described their approach as "the discourse of derision." The Conservatives were particularly distrustful of professional educators and university academics, whom they characterized often as supporting the kind of "progressivism" that had created serious problems in education. Their strategy in education mirrored their broadly combative approach to government generally.

In the other settings governments were less aggressive in dealing with opposition, and more inclined to alter their proposals to try to allay some of the criticisms. In New Zealand the National government turned out to be more aggressive in its approach to criticism than Labour had been, suggesting again the ambivalence in Labour about its reforms. However, the relatively soft political language in the education debate in New Zealand has to be put in the context of the wider discussion of social policy in which terms such as "provider capture" were used frequently to describe the position of defenders of the status quo. Inevitably, such terms take on a symbolic significance that is well beyond their literal meaning and become rallying cries for friends and foes of specific proposals.

The reforms were the subject of considerable media attention in all settings. However, in most settings this coverage was quite superficial and focused on the political aspects of the changes (see box on newspaper coverage in Alberta, page 139). For example, stories discussed who was in favor or opposed to particular changes without saying very much about how the reforms were actually intended to work. The situation was somewhat different in Britain, where the existence of vehicles such as the *Times Educational Supplement* meant that there was much more weekly media coverage of reform issues. The main British newspapers also provided extensive and relatively sophisticated comment on education issues – much more so than is typically found in North American newspapers.

Research results played differing roles in the debate. Where research on the reforms was done, it often provided grounds for public debate and criticism. In England, although the government was largely uninterested in research about its reforms, a number of studies of particular policies were done and the results of this work did often receive a considerable amount of public and media attention. The New Zealand government commissioned two sets of studies of the impact of its reforms (Mitchell *et al.*, 1993; Lauder *et al.*, 1999), both of which turned out to be quite critical of the reforms in many respects but seem to have had little impact. In Minnesota the legislature commissioned a number of reports on the impact of school choice that turned out to be generally supportive of the policy. Neither Alberta nor Manitoba did any formal research on their reform programs.

Polling was another vehicle often used by opponents of reform to strengthen their position. Teacher groups in Alberta, Manitoba and Minnesota commissioned and released a number of polls of public opinion intended to show public opposition to the reforms and support for more spending on education. However, majority public support for a position may not be enough to change policy. Governments gauge not only the nature of public opinion but also the salience of any given issue. People have opinions on many things, but relatively few of these opinions will lead to direct political action or have a decisive effect on voting intentions.

It must also be noted that many of the reforms did have considerable public support, or at least a willingness to try a new approach. Moves to decentralize authority to individual schools and to give parents more control over schooling are broadly consistent with many other social trends. Declining public faith in all large institutions created fertile ground for proposals that would move authority away from school systems that were seen as large and sometimes unresponsive bureaucracies (Apple, 1996). The reforms embodied ideas of individual and family responsibility that many people found appealing. Providing more information and a greater role to parents was popular among many people. The emphasis on standards and accountability through testing and inspection appealed to the preference of some for social policies that promoted excellence and to others for policies that punished failure. Educators in England and New Zealand, while critical of many aspects of the reforms, were also supportive of some aspects, and few thought that a return to the status quo ante would be desirable even if it were possible. For example, there is strong support in both countries for the idea of local school management (Wylie, 1997).

Media Coverage of Reform in Alberta

Many people get their picture of public policy from the mass media. Some sense of the way in which print media reported reform is in the following headlines and lead sentences from coverage of reform in the *Edmonton (Alberta) Journal*, the main newspaper in Alberta's capital city.

8 January 1994, front page: "City public schools to lose $51M"

Edmonton's public school board will lose at least $51 million in provincial grants by 1996 because of the government's proposed 20 per cent funding cutbacks, says board chairman Dick Mather ... Ultimately the cutbacks will spell larger pupil teacher ratios and lower-quality programs because layoffs of unionized staff are virtually impossible, says Mather.

21 January 1994, front page, part of a series called "Understanding the cuts": "School trustees perturbed as Klein grabs the funding"

Ralph Klein says he's trying to emancipate poor school districts and create an equal education system. Trustees say the premier is sounding the death knell for local school autonomy. Some call his government's move "ludicrous" and "fascist."

The province's decision this week to seize control of all funding of Alberta's $1.93 billion education system is a fundamental change for the way Alberta's school system operates.

26 January 1994, front page: "Jobs gone, salaries cut in $32M school shortfall – the cuts crisis"

Teaching jobs will disappear and salaries will be rolled back in Edmonton public schools next year as the board grapples with a $32 million shortfall caused by provincial government cuts.

Trustees decided Tuesday to try to negotiate some kind of salary roll-back with its [sic] 4,100 teachers and 2,300 other unionized staff as one of many tough, new tactics to try to keep financially afloat. Starting September 1, each school's budget will also take a nine percent cut.

During a packed, tense meeting, trustees worried that despite their new strategies, the government cuts will still force a terrible decline in education.

27 January 1994, page B3, a series of articles on funding changes with the following headlines:

"Big changes at schools expected – 9 per cent loss of funding hurts"
"Schools prepare for slashed budgets – demoralized teachers will be pressed to do more work in less time"
"What will be left of schools? – would be teachers"

31 January 1994, page B1: "$13M short, board to seek salary cuts – Catholic schools to talk to unions"

Salary rollbacks and the possible loss of 175 teaching jobs will hit Edmonton Catholic schools next fall due to a sudden $13 million shortfall caused by provincial government cuts.
Preschool chaos predicted in fall – Private firms expected to offer early education service – Parents fume at education cuts.

3 February 1994, page B1: "One school's budget dilemma – a report on the impact of budget cuts on an Edmonton elementary school"

5 February 1994, page B1: "School boards team up to address funding cuts"

21 March 1994, front page: "Church joins fight against school reform – Parents urged to write premier"

The Roman Catholic Archbishop of Edmonton has joined the opposition to the Klein government's plan to restructure school boards. Last week Archbishop Joseph MacNeil sent a letter to Edmonton priests, asking them to mobilize their parishioners in a fight for the independence of Catholic school boards.

27 March 1994, page C3: a whole page of articles on charter schools

Conclusion

On the whole, adoption processes did result in some changes being made to government proposals. One set of changes occurred in the process of developing details. The attempt to move from general announcements to detailed policies and programs inevitably led to changes in the nature of the policies as well as their timing. However, these adjustments were chiefly at the margins of a particular policy intention, involving timing or scope rather than purpose.

Political opposition did exist in each setting and did have an impact, though primarily outside the formal legislative process. Each government made some modifications in its plans in the face of strong opposition. Even determined opposition did not always lead to change, however. The power of opposition seemed to make a difference only when it involved a political threat that a government either could not or was unwilling to ignore – for example, because it involved important government supporters or because it came from some other highly credible source. Where governments were sufficiently determined and committed, they were eventually able to carry through most of their plans.

6   Implementation

Theoretical Framework

This chapter considers issues of policy implementation – the work that is done to move from policy to practice so that policies take the desired form and have the desired results. Research on implementation goes back more than thirty years, with many tracing its origins to work on the implementation of US federal government anti-poverty programs in the 1960s (Pressman and Wildavsky, 1973). Since then, a large body of research has accumulated in education and other policy fields, with the general finding that moving from policy to practice is a very uncertain business. A whole series of difficulties – some of them generic to policy implementation and others particular to schools – stand in the way of policies being put in place as intended (McLaughlin, 1987). Although the problems of implementation are well known, governments have tended to give relatively short shrift to these issues in the policy process.

Early research on implementation was concerned with describing the range of barriers and the reasons why so many policies seemed to have implementation difficulties. Gradually, attention shifted to research aimed at improving the fidelity of implementation, addressing the kinds of policies or practices that would support effective translation of policy to practice. Not everyone has shared this view, however. A dissenting view sees organizational life as inherently a struggle among competing ideas and powers. New policies are one of the vehicles through which these struggles take place. Resistance to change, rather than being something to be overcome, may be something to be understood and even celebrated. Where policies are seen as misguided, resistance to effective implementation could be desirable.

Another perspective, that of organizational learning, tries to combine elements of these approaches. From an organizational learning perspective, a given policy change is not so much something to be faithfully implemented or definitely opposed, but an opportunity to engage in a process of building understanding and moving an organization towards widely shared goals.

Governments have primarily been concerned, of course, with having their policies put into effect as planned and having the desired outcomes. To this end they have available a variety of tools, referred to in the literature as policy levers or policy instruments.

Thinking about implementation

Schools are often described as organizations that are especially resistant to change. At the same time, they are also sometimes criticized as being prey to every passing fad. The reality would seem to be that many of the basic structures and approaches to schooling have remained remarkably stable even though there have been many attempts to change them, often with a great deal of initial enthusiasm. It is easy to think of a large number of innovations in education that have been initiated with great fanfare only to disappear over a number of years with hardly a trace left behind. At the same time, some changes have had great and lasting impact, such as the recognition of increasing diversity, the development of mass secondary schooling, or changes in legislation and attitudes towards students with disabilities.

Most of the early work on the implementation of change in schools described the problems in creating change that is both substantive and lasting, leading to the oft-heard lament that schools are almost impossible to change at the same time as endless efforts are made to change them. As David Tyack put it, "The utopian impulses in recent decades to reinvent schooling have often been shooting stars, meteors that attracted attention but left little deposit" (Tyack 1995, p. 209).

The list of potential difficulties in implementation is long. Fullan (1991) considers the barriers to change in terms of the *characteristics of the change* itself, the *setting* where implementation is to occur, and the wider *context*. Under the first heading are features such as the clarity, complexity and degree of difficulty of a proposed change. The second heading addresses aspects of the school as an organization. These include the level of commitment by important actors (for example, school principals), the skills of those involved, the resources of various kinds allocated to support change, and the extent to which a given change fits the existing culture and structure of the system. The third category includes the various other pressures either supporting or inhibiting implementation. These might include the nature of the support system, competing demands on schools, or levels of community support for change.

Characteristics of the change – clarity, complexity, difficulty

As has been noted more than once, policies that emerge from the political process are rarely clear and unambiguous. However, implementation takes place in specific settings, where the confusions are likely to be multiplied as people try to sort out what a change might mean in their own particular school or school system. When a policy change reaches a school or school system, questions inevitably arise about both purposes and means. The more a policy is designed to appeal to a variety of interests – which is frequently the case – the less clarity there may be about its purpose in a given setting. However, even a policy that seems relatively clear when thought of at a national level can raise many questions in a particular school. For example, creating school councils seems straightforward until one starts to work through questions of the roles of all parties, the relationship of parent governors to their own children's teachers, problems of conflict of interest, and other such matters. What, exactly, does an advisory role for such a council mean? What happens when the advice is not taken? What happens if parents and teachers are related in some way?

Clarity is often reduced where reforms are more complex. A reform such as decentralized governance has so many aspects and ramifications that it will inevitably raise a large number of questions about what its drafters had in mind and how schools are actually to proceed with it. Some reforms seem straightforward in basic intent, but their implementation still raises many issues of detail. Testing of all students seems unambiguous until one starts to think about which students are actually to be included in a particular school, what will actually be tested, how tests are to be scored, and the myriad of other details that have to be managed. Changes in teaching practice are among the most complex changes in schools, as discussed a little later.

In the cases in this book, multiple changes were occurring in a short period of time, or even simultaneously, which made the implementation much more difficult for all parties. All the problems of implementing single changes are increased enormously when multiple changes are involved. The attention that can be given to any single requirement is naturally reduced. Time, energy and expertise have to be spread more thinly. Multiple changes may also, as suggested in Chapter 2, have interactive effects such that moving forward on one makes another more difficult. For example, increased assessment may make teachers more reluctant to attempt to alter their mode of instruction. Unhappiness with one reform may spill over into general opposition to all.

The setting – commitment, skills, culture, resources

Several features of schools make implementation more difficult, even if the change is reasonably clear and straightforward. School systems are large, diverse and often decentralized. In the end, the success of policies depends on the actions and interpretations of school administrators, teachers, parents and students.

Some regard this kind of discretion as an inherent feature of human action. Some take the view that discretion is highly desirable and indeed fundamental to what "education" means. Still others wish that human action could be controlled much more effectively. But whatever one's philosophical position on the matter, the fact is that every organization does involve a considerable degree of discretion on the part of those who inhabit it.

The steps from a government policy to an individual school or classroom are many. Since districts, schools and teachers may all act with considerable independence and are not subject to very much monitoring in regard to their day-to-day practice, the interpretation of policies is especially dependent on people's understandings, skills and commitment. New curricula present an interesting example. In many cases, governments focus on having new curriculum documents developed and distributed. But impact occurs only when teachers use the new curricula in meaningful and effective ways, and this is both much harder to bring about and much harder to assess (Elmore, 1995).

In federal states such as Canada and the United States, yet another level of partly autonomous actors is added. David Cohen (1992) has pointed out that the decentralized governance of education in the United States makes it much more difficult to move policy into implementation in that country. The intent of the federal government may be altered by the states, and further by local school districts, and then again by schools, and finally by individual educators within the school. State policies, too, have to move through several levels of implementation. Given all these levels it is perhaps surprising that practice on the ground ever looks much as policy intended it should. Even in unitary states such as Britain or New Zealand there will often be quite a bit of disparity between national policies and local practices.

In a large and decentralized system there will inevitably be quite varied understandings, as well as differing levels of commitment to any given policy. Both understanding and commitment are critical to effective implementation. Some people may like a policy but not know how to implement it. For example, teaching for higher-order skills may require teaching repertoires that most teachers do not possess, and access to the necessary supports may be difficult precisely because the skills needed are not common. Organizations often underestimate the difficulty people may have in putting new kinds of practices into effect, even when they are predisposed to the practices.

Some actors may not like a policy and may look for ways to subvert it or ignore it. In the case of new curricula there are many stories of such documents remaining unopened and unread on teachers' shelves. Others may like parts of a policy but may modify it in practice to suit their own preferences. The greater the degree to which policy changes involve discretion in interpretation, the greater variability there will likely be in implementation.

The skills and attitudes of teachers would seem to be an absolutely critical factor in implementation. As Cohen put it in discussing efforts in the US to implement more challenging programs of instruction and learning:

> Teachers are the problem policy must solve, in the sense that their modest knowledge and skills are one important reason why most instruction has been relatively didactic and unambitious. But teachers also are the agents on whom policy must rely to solve that problem.
>
> (1995, p. 13)

In his view, policy-makers have not taken this issue very seriously, and most policy emulates precisely the kinds of didactic and unmotivating strategies that teachers are being asked to change.

A number of efforts have been made to deal with the effects of teacher discretion through very tight specification of policy that would leave less room for interpretation. The problem with this approach is that education is not an activity that is amenable to standardization across subjects or settings. The students are different, the communities are different, curriculum areas are different, teachers differ in style. All of this means that what matters most cannot be specified in detail, and effective education must rely on the discretion of those who practice it.

People make choices about their response to policy on the basis of several factors. One is practicality. Whatever people may think of a policy in the abstract, they have to see it as workable in their own situation in order to accept it. What teachers are willing to do depends in large measure on their sense of what is workable in a classroom. Some reforms, such as mainstreaming of special needs students, may be seen by teachers as desirable in principle but unworkable in practice, in which case implementation is likely to be weak. Practicality is in turn affected by skills. People who do not know how to do something are likely to see that something as impractical even if other people can do it. Teachers who do not know how to undertake new teaching strategies will tend to see those strategies as unworkable.

Acceptance of change is also strongly affected by the degree to which a policy is consistent with existing practices and culture. A policy that does not fit is likely to be resisted even with clearly established evidence of better results. To put it another way, the main reason people usually do things in a given way is because that is the way things were done last time and the time before. Legions of examples can be cited where practices with strong evidence to support them were rejected because they did not fit with common practice. For example, navies refused to carry fresh fruit on ships to prevent scurvy, doctors resisted the practice of washing hands in hospitals to prevent infection, and many people refused to wear seatbelts to protect against injury in auto accidents.

Schools are subject to the same forces. Indeed, many structural and cultural features of schooling have been with us since the beginning of mass public schooling. Examples include one teacher working with a class of students typically of the same age; the day organized into standard chunks of time; the division of the curriculum into a standard set of subjects; the five-day week and the ten-month school year; and the awarding of marks and the decision to pass or promote students at the end of each course.

> The basic "grammar" of schooling, like the shape of classrooms, has remained remarkably stable over the decades. By the "grammar" of schooling we mean the regular structures and rules that organize the work of instruction ... Continuity in the grammar of instruction has frustrated generations of reformers who have sought to change these standardized organizational forms.
>
> (Tyack and Tobin, 1994, p. 454)

The history of schooling is also full of examples of practices that were at one time seen as necessary even though most people eventually came to regard them as foolish or even harmful. Examples include the separation of students with disabilities, placement through IQ testing, or streaming of students on the basis of race or gender. Nor are schools now in a situation where every practice can be justified on a basis other than past practice and tradition. Increased testing of elementary students is resisted by many teachers because it does not fit with their image of elementary schooling. However, secondary teachers are more open to testing because it has always been a more important part of the way secondary schooling has operated. The involvement of parents in an advisory capacity is something many educators are comfortable with, but giving individual schools a great deal of autonomy and turning school principals into managers of enterprises requires a much greater adjustment on the part of many people.

In the absence of careful thinking about all the dimensions of implementation, debates often turn on arguments about whether enough money has been allocated to support change. Those within the system tend to be particularly concerned about having additional resources to meet new, external demands. Resources are, of course, an important part of creating change. Even where governments rely on legislation or policy direction, they do so on the assumption that these changes will themselves trigger reallocations of time, attention, people and money to the new priorities. One of the problems of recent education reforms is that they have been put forward at the same time as overall financial resources for schools have been static or even declining. However, it has been increasingly difficult for educators to make a convincing political case that all change requires additional resources, given the changes that many other organizations, including governments, have had to make with declining resource levels. Reallocation, whether desired or not, has become a way of life in school systems, as in other sectors. Recent work on the financing of reform also suggests that quite a bit of restructuring can be accommodated within the existing resource levels of many schools through effective reallocation (Odden and Busch, 1998).

The context –demands, system, community support

Several aspects of school context are important to understanding issues of implementation. Government mandates are by no means the only contextual pressure operating on schools. Many other external factors may be pushing schools in directions other than those being proposed through government reforms. Probably the most important pressure is simply the requirement to get through the day-to-day work in an institution with large numbers of young people. Whatever governments may have in mind, teachers and administrators have to cope each day with the needs and problems that students (and staff) bring to the school.

In recent years schools have had to cope in some fashion or another with increasing population diversity and demographic shifts, the impact of information technology, changing patterns of youth employment, changing gender roles, concentrations of urban and rural poverty, changing attitudes and requirements in regard to disability, and so on. All of these bring immediate pressures to bear on educators that have to be dealt with regardless of what reforms governments have initiated.

Public expectations, particularly those of parents, are also powerful influences on schools. Even though schools are often chided as being insufficiently open to parent views, in many ways the ideas that parents hold about schooling do have significant influence. Reforms such as whole language or multi-graded classrooms have run into difficulty partly because they do not fit with the image many parents have of appropriate schooling.

Paradoxically, all these pressures are usually strongest in those schools that are also the prime target for reform. Schools with high levels of poverty or high proportions of minority students are often the focus of reforms because of concerns about their achievement levels. Yet these are the same schools that are most buffeted by day-to-day pressures from their students and communities, and where parents may in some cases be very resistant to departures from conventional schools practice, even where such practices are not currently serving them well (Metz, 1990).

Schools have also been affected by changes in the larger educational system. At one time, for example, high school graduation was an important lifetime credential with significant labor market value. In the current era of mass participation in post-secondary education, that is no longer the case, raising important questions about the role and nature of secondary schooling. Increasing attention to the importance of early childhood development has also changed the way elementary schools think about their role. Schools are less independent institutions than they used to be.

Another important contextual factor is the overall political situation around schooling, which, as described in Chapter 1, has been quite negative for some time. Schools have been subject to continuing criticism from many public groups. Funding has been cut back in many cases. All of this tends to create a defensive atmosphere in which people in the school system worry about public support and perhaps lack the sense of confidence required for effective implementation of significant changes.

A further point about contextual pressure is that changes in context will affect the way a reform is viewed over time. For example, as teachers become more experienced, they will also have gone through more periods of reform and may become more cynical about each succeeding proposal almost regardless of its merits. In a number of countries the period of reform in the 1980s and 1990s collided with a veteran teaching force. Similarly, proposals from a new government may be met with greater enthusiasm than new proposals from a government that has already been in power for some time and has a history to overcome.

Implementation and resistance

Not everyone agrees that implementation is primarily about the adoption of reforms from elsewhere. Another school of thought, instead of emphasizing the development of consensus and common vision, stresses the contested nature of organizational life and sees implementation as an ongoing struggle over the nature and control of an organization.

Those who are critical of particular reforms may see acts of resistance not just as understandable, but as heroic. Teachers who want to fail students may be seen by some to be upholding standards in the face of permissiveness, or – from another point of view – those resisting increased testing may be seen as upholding professionalism in the face of a narrow accountability. These debates about motives are a further indication of divided views over the values that ought to inform both schooling and reform.

Borrowing from postmodernism, some analysts arguing this view see policies and programs as texts that will be "read" by various actors in different ways depending on their location and interests. As Ball (1997, p. 270) puts it, any policy can be seen as posing a problem that people will address or solve in their own contexts. In this sense the response to policy direction always involves some kind of creative social action.

Those who emphasize the professional nature of teaching argue for the importance of teachers having more control over their practice. Professionals would expect to have an important role in shaping and sometimes resisting reforms that are seen as inappropriate.

Resistance need not always be overt. School administrators and teachers have many ways of either advancing or inhibiting the goals of a policy, just as students have many ways of resisting teachers' demands, not all of which involve active opposition. New curricula are left substantially unused, new teaching practices are not adopted, subtle messages are given to students or parents that are not what government intended. All of these can be seen as forms of resistance.

A substantial amount of implementation research has looked at the ways in which policies are modified or transformed in schools. The conclusion is that the intentions of reformers are often modified very substantially, and are sometimes abandoned altogether (Cohen, 1995; Elmore, 1995; Wilson *et al.*, 1996).

Overt resistance, on the other hand, is rare. Aspin and Chapman conclude that the typical response of schools to mandated change has been acceptance.

> Our evidence suggests, however, that in facing and coping with all this change and the consequences of restructuring, the part played by school-based educators has often been of a reactive kind: their response to reform has been one of managing the practicalities of introducing a series of changes, the origin of and impetus for which came largely from outside influences, embedded in wider political commitments and economic concerns, in the shaping and control of which the school-based members of the education profession have had a less important part to play.
>
> (1994, p. 114)

Implementation as learning

Over time the literature on school change and on policy implementation has given increasing attention to the idea of implementation as a form of individual and organizational learning (Fullan, 1995). Several more general intellectual developments have influenced this shift. In education, there has been increasing acceptance of constructivism – the key role of the learner in shaping and forming knowledge – as the central dynamic of learning (Prawat and Peterson, 1999). This has paralleled the development of ideas of organizational learning within the field of organization theory (e. g. Senge, 1990). Both sets of ideas focus on the ways in which people within an organization think about and understand their work, and on the need for organizational processes that encourage people to get better at what they do by learning more about it.

From a learning perspective, implementation becomes a much more difficult task. It cannot simply be a matter of promulgating ideas and assuming these will be put into place. In fact, the more novel or difficult the idea, the less likely it is to be implemented without learning on the part of the people involved.

In an organizational learning framework, support for implementation must involve attention both to how people think and to the material conditions of their work. Among those working to improve implementation, a consensus has gradually emerged that learning is supported by a combination of external pressure and support (Fullan, 1991), or what economists call appropriate incentives. What this would actually look like in schools is far from clear.

New standards and frameworks offer persuasive or even inspiring visions, but at most they sketch directions and commitments, principles and aspirations. They do not provide guidance for the specifics of minute-to-minute – or even week-to-week – practice ... We can see that most teachers would have to learn an enormous amount to make the reforms workable but we are only beginning to understand how that learning might be accomplished.

(Wilson *et al.*, 1996, p. 475)

The current literature on school improvement (see Hargreaves *et al.*, 1998) includes a number of elements as being key to developing meaningful and lasting change. These typically include involving all parties in the improvement process; building in time to talk and think about what is changing and why; gathering and analyzing data to guide improvement; and providing extensive, workplace-based staff development (e.g. Macpherson, 1996). Perhaps just as important is an attitude that values learning as the key to improvement.

At the same time, understanding itself will not necessarily produce lasting change either. Individual commitment is important, but lasts only as long as the same individuals are there with the same commitments. Lasting change cannot rest solely on the commitment of exceptional individuals. Changes in elements such as work roles, compensation systems, accountability systems and management structures may also be necessary to provide the appropriate institutional structure within which effective learning and institutionalization can occur.

One important indicator of an organizational learning approach would be the use of research and evaluation as a means of assessing the impact of change and of making adjustments to programs and strategies as required. The use of data to support discussion and learning among all parties is an essential part of a true organizational learning strategy.

The idea of organizational learning, as noted in chapter two, is not without problems. One problem is what we mean by speaking of an organization as learning. Many views of organizational learning focus on process concerns, framing a learning organization in terms of the ways data are gathered, problems are analyzed and discussed, and so on. However, there can be a tremendous amount of analysis and discussion without anything much changing as a result, and one would presumably be reluctant to speak of this as learning. Indeed, one of the problems of the organizational learning approach may be its requirement for people to rise substantially above common practices. As Argyris and Schon (1978) demonstrated years ago, people generally find it very difficult to behave in accordance with the values they publicly espouse. An idea that depends on making unusual behavior the norm is likely to run into difficulties!

The focus on process also obscures the matter of results. What does it mean to say that an organization has changed as a result of learning? Is this something different than the people within the organization learning? Presumably an organization learns when it encodes new ways of doing things. When, though, can we say this has happened? When some teachers have changed their practice but others have not, has the school learned? When some practices change for a time but then return to old modes, has there been learning? At least to some degree all organizations are constantly taking in information and adjusting practice in one way or another. Could there be, then, an organization that was not learning? Sometimes organizational learning becomes a normative term; organizations are learning when they make change A, but not when they make change B, because somebody else has decided that A is a good change while B is not.

Policy levers

In seeking to have their policies put into effect, governments have access to a variety of instruments, sometimes called policy levers. A number of different classification systems for policy levers exist (Howlett, 1991). Ranson (1994), in discussing the history of the British Department of Education, uses the categories of persuasion, pressure and accountability. Howlett and Ramesh (1995) use a classification system of voluntary, mixed and compulsory instruments, with increasing state involvement from the former to the latter. Voluntary instruments include the use of market mechanisms and the assignment of responsibilities to families or community groups. Mixed instruments include the provision of information, exhortation and persuasion, as well as subsidies of various kinds such as grants, loans and tax incentives. Compulsory instruments include regulations, legislation, public enterprise and direct provision of services. It should be noted, however, that "voluntary" instruments are only voluntary in a limited sense. The assignment of social tasks to markets or citizen groups can itself be an act of compulsion.

The choice of a particular category system for analytic purposes is largely a matter of convenience. For this book I use a modification of a categorization system developed specifically in regard to education by McDonnell and Elmore (1987). They place policy instruments into four categories: *mandates, inducements, capacity-building* and *system-changing*. I add a fifth category, called *opinion mobilization*. Mandates rely substantially on legal authority and include such measures as legislation and regulation. Inducements include strategies intended to promote attention to policy goals, often through some form of additional funding. Capacity-building rests on the belief that policy adoption requires a set of institutional skills and systems that must consciously be built and supported through means such as training. System-changing focuses on changes in structures to support particular policies. Opinion mobilization refers to efforts by governments to change the way in which actors see the system, and thus affect its practice through non-mandatory external pressure.

Each strategy can involve a variety of activities. Mandates typically involve legislation or regulation or policy directives that change the official rules in some fashion. Inducements involve funding, other resources, or various forms of recognition of accomplishment. Capacity-building involves various forms of training or skill development.

Some activities, however, can support more than one strategy. Consultation is one example. Although consultation processes are used most often in the process of introducing reforms, they can also be a part of the implementation process. Governments can engage in a variety of kinds of consultation as a way of building understanding, improving commitment or of trying to deal with particularly difficult aspects of implementation, all of which are forms of capacity-building. Consultation can also be used as a political device to put pressure on the system by showing the degree of external support for change. This is a form of opinion mobilization. Consultation processes in these cases will also vary in their sincerity. If there is genuine desire to learn how to move forward, consultation can be a useful way to gather information and promote real learning. On other occasions, however, it may be simply a way of trying to defuse opposition.

Another example of a practice that fits more than one category is student assessment. Assessment is often treated as a mandate. However, the results of assessment are used as inducements – either rewards for good performances or penalties for poor performance. Governments may also use assessment results as a form of opinion mobilization, to put pressure on schools to improve performance. Finally, assessment results can be used to support capacity-building if schools treat them as a way to assess the efficacy of current strategies.

A recent development has been the use by a number of governments of outside organizations to implement and support reform. These third parties may be created by government itself or by external bodies that are supporting reform, such as charitable foundations. They may have statutory authority or operate entirely on a voluntary basis. Whatever their form, they represent a new element in the attempt to implement reform, and one that has not yet been studied very much.

Each implementation strategy embodies a set of assumptions about how the desired result can best be brought about. For example, the use of inducements such as grants assumes that capacity exists but needs to be mobilized, whereas capacity-building strategies imply that the required skills do not exist and must be developed. Reforms also differ in regard to the target for change. New curricula clearly require understanding and commitment on the part of educators. However, changes in governance may be aimed much more at parents.

The five strategies can also be seen as in some respects complementary and in other respects contradictory. Mandates tend to be antithetical to capacity-building unless they are explicitly accompanied by efforts to improve capacity, such as support for new teaching practices. However, opinion mobilization or inducements of various kinds can work well with a capacity-building strategy.

The range of available strategies raises the question of why a government would choose a particular approach to implementation. Policy instruments vary in many ways, including cost, complexity, visibility, precision of targeting, autonomy granted to local actors, and political acceptability. Some instruments are more intrusive while others are more user-friendly. Some instruments involve substantial spending, while others do not. Some instruments require a bureaucracy to implement, while others do not. Some can be put into place quickly while others take long-term attention.

Implementation vehicles are also themselves political statements, so their choice is affected by the same range of considerations as any other policy choice. For example, governments promoting market-based reforms would be highly unlikely to see direct provision of service or public enterprise as a viable instrument. Governments committed to reductions in spending are less likely to use additional funding as an implementation strategy, and may choose to rely on low-cost strategies such as mandates or opinion mobilization. If a reform strategy has been advocated as being common sense, it would be contradictory to then argue that it required substantial capacity-building.

Other strategies may be unattractive for other reasons. Legislation may not be possible because of other more important legislative commitments or because it will generate significant opposition. Capacity-building may not be possible because the required infrastructure to build capacity is itself not available, or it may simply be too expensive. State bureaucracies that have been primarily concerned with regulation of local systems may be unequipped to move into a new role as builders of local capacity.

As with other aspects of the political process, the characteristics of the setting including constitutional features and political culture will also affect the attractiveness of various policy instruments. For example, the decentralization of authority in education in the United States has made reform at even the state level quite difficult, while the strong American ideological preference for individualism has acted in some cases – though by no means all – to limit the attractiveness of legislative mandates.

Even though implementation is increasingly recognized as difficult to do, most of the debate in education is over policy concepts rather than over their implementation. Governments do not seem to have taken to heart the idea that implementation issues require careful attention from the outset. Instead, they are often seen as details to be left to the bureaucracy once the important work of defining policy has been done. As well, the literature on implementation suggests that effective implementation of complex reforms will require a range of policy instruments. Mandates and sanctions may be an important part of a reform strategy, but are unlikely to be sufficient.

Evidence From the Cases

The most striking feature of these five cases is how little willingness governments exhibited to invest in implementation. Mandates, opinion mobilization and system changes were the primary vehicles, with some attention to inducements but little or none to capacity-building. In almost every case, reforms were announced, turned into legislation or policy, and largely left to work their effects. On the whole, measures to support implementation, where they occurred at all, tended to be piecemeal and small in scale. In some cases additional funding or some modest level of training was provided, but in many cases almost no support was given, especially considering the scope of the changes. Few steps were taken to assess the effectiveness of policies, either. Where particular reforms did not seem to be working well, governments did sometimes make adjustments in policy, but seldom within a longer-term implementation strategy.

The lack of attention to implementation when reforms were being developed created considerable difficulties later. Civil servants often did understand the importance of implementation and made efforts to support it, but political support for implementation was often lacking. The result was to make the reforms less effective than they might otherwise have been. In some cases, such as Manitoba, timelines could not be met and had to be adjusted, which itself fed cynicism about reforms within the school system. In other cases, such as New Zealand, local schools were left with no official guidance as to what they were supposed to do, leading to considerable inconsistency in actions. Certainly the stress on educators and local policymakers was substantially increased by the relative absence of supports.

Why was implementation given such short shrift? Several reasons can be suggested. First, at the political level, where policies and resource allocations get made, governments tend to be focused on the creation and promotion of policy. Attention goes largely to what is to be done rather than to how it will actually work. Policies get made quickly, often without nearly enough time to think through how they will work in practice. Political horizons tend to be short-term, so where implementation is a long-term consideration it may lie outside the time-frame that is of concern to the political world. Policy-makers may be quite ignorant about the realities of the organizations they are trying to change, with limited understanding of their cultures and capacities. Effective support for implementation may be seen to require significant additional resources that governments are unwilling to commit or simply do not have. For example, supports to help people take on new practices are often simply not available just because the practices are new. Finally, where governments are changing policy because they do not trust the system, they are unlikely to want to use strategies that require greater investment or a high degree of trust in that same system.

Even if there had been greater willingness to pay attention to implementation, the results might not have been very different. Both governments and school systems generally lack capacity to support organizational learning effectively. For example, systems for gathering and analyzing evidence on the impact of changes are weak or non-existent. People's skills in using evidence to inform policy and practice are often limited. Bureaucracies set up for one purpose – such as funding schools or controlling their practices – have a very difficult time turning themselves into the very different sort of organization that would be needed to support capacity-building and learning.

Mandates, system-changing and opinion mobilization

All governments used legislation and formal policy as the prime means of implementing reforms. Typically, legislation was used for changes in governance whereas curriculum or assessment changes were more often the result of regulations or policy statements. The extensive use of mandates and system-changing strategies highlights the extent to which governments relied on a view of change as being driven by structural elements. A basic assumption seems to have been that changing system parameters would result in changes in school programs, teaching, learning, parent involvement, and eventually improved student and social outcomes.

In England the massive legislation of 1988 and 1993, as well as several less significant bills, was supplemented by a large number of policy circulars from the Department of Education and, in some cases, from other government departments. An example of the latter is the requirement imposed by government for LEAs to entertain competitive bids for various school services such as maintenance. In New Zealand the legislation implementing *Tomorrow's Schools* was altered in some respects by later National Party legislation and regulations produced not only by the Department of Education but also later by the New Zealand Qualifications Authority. In both Alberta and Manitoba the provincial governments passed legislation putting in place some parts of their program, while others were introduced through regulations or policy statements. In Minnesota the choice program of 1985–7 and the charter school provisions of 1991 were both the result of bills passed by the legislature.

Several of the governments also made extensive use of opinion mobilization as a way to put external pressure on schools. Governments launched public advertising campaigns to explain their reforms and build public support for them, whether the education system agreed or not. The New Zealand government used radio and television ads to promote *Tomorrow's Schools*. The British government used a variety of communication strategies to support its various reforms. In all the settings ministers, premiers, governors and other change promoters went on speaking tours. Pamphlets were prepared and distributed and, in more recent years, World Wide Web sites provided another vehicle to build public support for reform.

Another strategy involved the provision of information (as distinct from advertising or promotion) to parents and the public. Most of the governments in this study used a variety of publications and other vehicles to try to provide more information to parents about schools. This mechanism was used most extensively in England with such devices as the Parents' Charter – a statement of the rights of parents in connection with schooling. Schools in England were also required to provide more information to parents through brochures, annual reports (which had to contain information on achievement results) and compulsory distribution of Ofsted inspection reports. This approach was quite consistent with a stance that saw parents and students as consumers who required more information to make choices about schools. The Manitoba government issued a whole series of documents in support of the *New Directions* reforms, including a number of publications designed largely for parents. Schools were to develop and publish annual development plans, although this provision was not widely practiced. Alberta Education issued an annual Business Plan that described its goals and provided quantitative indicators of progress on them. Alberta school boards were also required to prepare and publish business plans. ERO reports in New Zealand were made public in various forms, and schools were required to produce public annual reports.

Third-party organizations were important features of reform in England and New Zealand. The British government created the Schools Curriculum and Assessment Authority (SCAA, later renamed) to manage curriculum change and student testing, and also created the Teacher Training Agency (TTA) to be responsible for initial and continuing teacher education. School inspections were given to yet another agency, the Office for Standards in Education (Ofsted). Although all of these were government creations they had varying degrees of autonomy from the Department of Education. Ofsted, as one instance, reports to the prime minister rather than the education minister.

New Zealand, as part of its attempt to implement contract and agency theory, tried to turn its Department of Education into a small policy unit while giving operating responsibility to other agencies such as the Education Review Office (ERO) which did school inspection, and the New Zealand Qualifications Authority (NZQA) which was given responsibility for school and post-secondary qualifications. The School Trustees Association was given a contract to provide training to the new school governing bodies in 1988 and 1989.

In Manitoba a charitable foundation set up, with support from the government, the Manitoba School Improvement Program (MSIP), an autonomous agency intended to foster change in secondary schools. MSIP was not, however, part of the *New Directions* process, and in some ways acted as a counterweight to some aspects of those reforms.

Although third parties did not play an important role in implementation in Minnesota, interventions by foundations have been a feature of growing importance in education in the US in recent years. The Annenberg Challenge, for example, is channeling hundreds of millions of dollars into educational reform through third-party organizations in large urban school districts.

Inducements

Financing

In considering financial support as an implementation vehicle, it is necessary to consider both the provision of additional funds to schools to support reforms and the additional spending that governments needed to make in their own operations in order to implement their commitments. The analysis of financing is made very difficult by the lack of standard figures on school funding in several of the jurisdictions and by the serious problems of comparison across jurisdictions.

In Alberta and Manitoba and to some extent in England, the reforms in this study were introduced at the same time as budgets for education were being cut, so additional funding to support reforms in the schools was either non-existent or very limited. The Labour government in New Zealand did provide additional funds to schools during the first year or so of the implementation of *Tomorrow's Schools*, although there was some controversy about whether the infusion was actually significant (Ward interview). The National government was much more committed to austerity in funding for schools, and limited funding during its first several years in office. Alberta cut funding to schools by 12 per cent beginning in 1994, and Manitoba had five consecutive years in which funding to schools was either reduced or frozen. In Minnesota funding levels can fluctuate quite considerably from year to year depending on state revenues, but there was no formal austerity program during the time under consideration here.

In England, though general funding for schools was decreasing in real terms during the period of the Education Reform Act, the government did provide additional funds for some initiatives, such as grant-maintained schools, City Technology Colleges and the Office for Standards in Education (Ofsted). However, the size of these additions was smaller than the amount cut out of regular funding of LEAs in regard to schools, and the money was targeted to particular schools and programs. In New Zealand the Department of Education was dramatically downsized after 1989, and the Education Review Office was also reduced quite significantly soon after its establishment. Manitoba and Alberta both cut their provincial Departments of Education significantly, though Manitoba later added a considerable number of staff to support *New Directions*, notably in the area of assessment.

The main way in which finance was used as an inducement was through the rewards built into competition for enrolment. Wherever choice schemes came into play, schools that attracted more students received more government financing. Schools that lost students would lose money and hence have to reduce staffing and services. In England and Minnesota this competition for students was highlighted as a main element of reform. In the other jurisdictions, though competition was not stressed publicly, schools were very aware of the impact of enrolment changes on their budgets.

Government also added funding in support of particular policies. The British government offered substantial additional funds to schools that opted out of their local authorities to become grant-maintained. The National government in New Zealand offered schools additional money if they chose to accept bulk funding of teachers' salaries, and if they decided to put their principals on independent employment contracts. In Manitoba and Alberta schools or districts that chose to pilot particular policies of interest to the government were eligible to receive some additional funding in support.

In all the discussion of funding, surprisingly little attention was given to the reallocation of resources. There was presumably an assumption that schools would devote time, energy and money to government policy directions. Yet very little effort was made to track such changes, and few incentives were provided to support resource reallocation.

Recognition

Another form of inducement used in some settings was a combination of public recognition of what was regarded as success and public blame for what was regarded as failure in terms of inspection and testing results. This approach is most evident in England, where the publication of school-by-school assessment results clearly labeled some schools as "good" and others as "failing." The issues of newspapers reporting these results sell a very large number of copies each year.

Publication of school-by-school scores, either on national tests or on state assessments, is a routine event in many parts of the United States including Minnesota, where the newspapers and electronic media report the results with considerable interest. The publication of school-by-school test results is also done in Alberta and Manitoba, though Manitoba has had a very limited number of tests for this purpose.

Ofsted inspection results provide another public measure of English schools. The 1993 legislation gave the government the right to declare some schools to be officially failing and to step in to give them new management and make other changes. British newspapers happily publish lists of schools in rank order, and government officials make public statements about so-called "failing schools" in what has come to be known in England as "naming and shaming." These practices have been continued and even extended since the 1997 election of Labour.

New Zealand has had some of the same measures. The Education Review Office has issued a number of reports that identify specific schools as failing and in need of special measures (Thrupp, 1998). These reports are widely circulated and are available on the World Wide Web. However, the strong ethos of local school authority in New Zealand has made it quite difficult for the government to intervene in schools. Also, New Zealand has not had, except at the senior secondary level, a national assessment that can be reported on a school-by-school basis.

In both England and New Zealand the inspection agencies (Ofsted and ERO) have made very public comments on school quality issues. Both agencies have published reports identifying issues they regard as important for further attention – such as the neglect of phonics teaching in England. The heads of the agencies – Chris Woodhead in Britain and Judith Aitken in New Zealand – have been quite outspoken personally in raising what they consider to be problems with school attainment levels and teaching practices. Both the reports and the comments of the agency heads have received a great deal of media attention in both countries.

Capacity-building

In contrast to extensive use of mandates and some use of inducements, there is little evidence of a capacity-building strategy in any of the reform programs. On the whole, the training provided to schools to assist them in implementing reforms was minimal.

Changes in governance, although central to reform strategies, were accompanied by limited, if any, assistance to the new governors. Legislation in England and New Zealand gave school governing bodies very significant new powers in managing their schools, including responsibility for staffing, buildings, budgets and many aspects of program. In England almost no training was provided to these groups to help them manage the new responsibilities.

In New Zealand some effort to support training was made. In mid 1989, after the first governing bodies had been elected but before they had official status, two days of training were provided for two people from each region, who were then to run training sessions in their own regions. Partly because this was simply an inadequate amount and partly because of the paucity of information as to just how the new boards would work, the training proved largely useless (Ward interview). However, the New Zealand government also funded the School Trustees Association to provide support to the new boards. It took the view that school budgets included funds for training, which schools were now free to purchase from any provider they wished. Indeed, a number of organizations and consultants did set up training services. However, the take-up was relatively small, partly because schools were used to receiving such support services at no cost, and in the early years of reform boards and principals were struggling to understand what their budget would or would not support. A particularly interesting feature of reform in New Zealand is that the teacher unions, especially the NZEI, ended up providing quite a bit of support to schools in the implementation of the reforms, even though they had opposed many of the reforms in the first place. In doing so they were responding to the needs of their members, especially school principals, who were struggling to cope with the new conditions and simply required assistance wherever they could get it.

Nor were the elected board members the only people in need of support. The creation of governing boards changed the work of school administrators quite dramatically, but little support was provided them in their new roles. The introduction of inspection in England and New Zealand added further challenges to the work of governing bodies and school administrators, again with minimal support. The Manitoba government, mainly for financial reasons, reduced the very modest support it had previously given to an education leadership organization.

Curriculum changes, as already noted, can be very challenging for teachers. However, efforts to provide training and support to teachers and administrators to assist in the introduction of extensive new curricula were quite modest. The introduction of the National Curriculum in England was not accompanied by very extensive professional development, even though it involved enormous changes for many teachers. In Manitoba one of the main complaints of educators about *New Directions* was their inability to keep up with the flood of new curricula and policy documents, let alone to devote adequate attention to the implementation of each of these.

When Ofsted inspections began in England in 1993, schools were not given much help in understanding the inspection process or learning how to make it more useful to them. In the early 1990s the Major government did take several steps to provide some additional training for school administrators, but this was well after most of the reforms had already been introduced.

In Manitoba and Alberta governments did provide training to support new curricula, but the primary support for implementation was through the development of a wide range of documents and resource materials, and a limited amount of professional development for teachers. In Minnesota neither choice nor the introduction of charter schools was accompanied by any form of training or ongoing support. And in almost all cases, where training was provided by governments, it was generally in support of compliance rather than as an encouragement to learning and adaptation.

An interesting comparison to the approach to implementation in these cases is the strategy used by the Labour government in Britain in 1998 and 1999 to support its national literacy and numeracy strategy. Millions of pounds have been allocated to allow the hiring of a network of supporting consultants, to develop high-quality teaching materials, and to finance an extensive program of professional development for governors, administrators and teachers over several years. Capacity-building, though within a framework of clear targets and expectations, is a central component of these programs.

Implementation as adaptation and resistance

The way in which various reforms were "taken on board" was clearly affected by the factors listed earlier in this chapter, although to different degrees in different places and circumstances. On the whole, what is striking is the degree to which leaders in the education system tried hard to make reforms work, or at least to make them manageable, even when they disagreed with them. Grace's description of England would be true in most other settings as well: "The great majority of primary and secondary school head teachers adopted a response of compliance-mediation and were apparently prepared to take on the role of cultural managers of the new arrangements" (1995, p. 112). In Manitoba civil servants felt that school concerns about many of the reforms gradually shifted from active opposition to a concern about how to manage a large number of wide-ranging changes in a short time (Carlyle/Loeppky interview).

Opposition to the reforms has been discussed in Chapter 5. Once reforms were put into legislation or policy, however, there was not very much overt resistance. The most striking example of resistance across all the cases was the rejection by English primary teachers of national testing of 7-year-olds, discussed briefly in Chapter 5. Teacher unions in all the settings continued to oppose various aspects of the reform programs. A number of parent organizations – in England and Manitoba for example – continued to argue against testing programs. However, most educators tried to make the reforms work, at least to some extent.

Adaptation occurred in many different ways. For example, some schools in England continued to collaborate on enrolments rather than competing as intended (Woods *et al.*, 1998). There are many stories in several jurisdictions – though not necessarily very much good empirical evidence – about schools taking steps to improve assessment results by controlling which students actually wrote the tests and by spending more time preparing students for them. Many other instances of adaptation are described in the discussion of outcomes in the next chapter.

Organizational learning

If capacity-building was seldom used, implementation strategies that modeled organizational learning were even more rare. One reason was because the reforms were based on distrust of people in the system, which did not lead to a desire to extend their role in shaping reform. However, it also seems to be the case that political requirements are seen to call for certainty about solutions, which is antithetical to the kind of open search for problems and opportunities that would be part of an approach based on ideas of organizational learning. Reluctance to make information widely available and to encourage debate is not unique to formal politics, either, but is often a feature of the internal politics of organizations.

In New Zealand the problem of implementation was made even more difficult because the Department of Education was being totally reshaped at the same time as the schools were becoming independent. Schools had always looked to the department for support and direction, but now found that this support was not available since the department was itself in considerable confusion. As well, nobody really knew what the new system would look like when established. It is hard to provide technical assistance on a task that nobody has done! School trustees and school administrators in New Zealand were tremendously frustrated because they received directions from Wellington only to have the directions countermanded by new directions within a short time, while all the time being unable to get either definite answers on policy or advice on implementation. When change is as far-reaching and as compressed in time as that in New Zealand, this kind of frustration is almost inevitable.

Minnesota was the only jurisdiction that chose to invest any significant amount in research or data-gathering about the impact of reform or ways of improving implementation. In Minnesota, formal evaluation was built into the law that created school choice, so the state commissioned a number of studies of the impact of the program (see Nathan and Ysseldyke, 1994). The New Zealand government did provide financial support to two sets of studies of the reforms (Mitchell *et al.*, 1993; Lauder *et al.*, 1999), though in both cases the initiative for the research came from outside the government (Mitchell interview). In terms of the size and scope of the New Zealand reforms, the research effort could only be described as very modest. The British Conservatives, being highly skeptical about the academic venture in the first place, seemed largely uninterested in any research on their reforms. Alberta did have a history of department support for policy research, but did not directly finance any studies of the 1994 reform program, whereas Manitoba had no history of education policy research and did not attempt to do any in this case either.

In none of the settings is there any evidence that research or collection of data affected policy in any noticeable way. Where research on reform was done, whether funded by governments or elsewhere, it did sometimes generate a public and media interest but seemed to have little or no impact on subsequent policy. Various studies in New Zealand that pointed out problems in the reforms, including those supported by the government and others by the New Zealand Council on Education Research, were essentially ignored. Some of the studies in England of various policy initiatives did get some media attention but were of no interest to the British government, which tended to deride university research on education generally.

Conclusion

Implementation is known to be a vital part of any reform. Yet in these cases it was the neglected element in the reform process. Governments gave relatively little attention to how reforms would be implemented. They used a narrow range of implementation vehicles, and were on the whole not much interested in learning about how reforms were working and adjusting them accordingly. This lack of attention can be seen to arise from a variety of political and administrative reasons. Lack of attention to implementation could be seen as an indication that governments were more concerned with the symbolic import of reform than with its real effect on schools and students. Alternatively, governments may lack the understanding, capacity and sense of commitment that is required to sustain attention to reform over time and across contexts. Reforms were clearly modified in some ways as they moved into schools, although on the whole school systems did make serious attempts to fulfill the new objectives set for them. The opportunity to use reform as a way for governments, educators and the public to learn more was largely wasted. The net effect of the lack of attention to implementation was likely to reduce the impact of reforms.

7   Outcomes

Theoretical Framework

Education policy is always proposed on the basis of the outcomes it will produce, even though it may be suspected that in some cases the commitment to outcomes is more a matter of political posture than of substantive belief. When policies are introduced there is often, as has been described, a great deal of debate about the outcomes they might generate, whether positive or negative. Proponents stress benefits and minimize problems; opponents tend to do the opposite. Ongoing and careful attention to real outcomes of policies is much less common.

This chapter begins by sketching a potential set of outcomes for education reform. It goes on to consider the difficulties in defining these outcomes more clearly and in assessing the extent to which they have been achieved. All of this sets the stage for an examination of the available evidence on the outcomes of the reforms in the settings in this study.

What are the outcomes of policy?

Policies are intended to achieve goals. A review of the various arguments that have been made for and against the education reforms discussed in this book indicates a number of main outcomes that can be described as falling within three levels. One set of outcomes is concerned with what happens to students. A second focuses on policy impacts on the education system itself. The third looks at the broad social outcomes of education policy. Within each of these levels several more specific outcomes can be distinguished.

Student outcomes

The most frequently cited reasons for education reform have to do with impact on students. Although the greatest focus has been on academic achievement, other student outcomes are also of considerable interest and importance.

1   Academic achievement. The most common outcome measure for schooling is some form of assessment of students' skill or knowledge in the various curriculum areas. Such assessments take many forms, ranging from the common use in the United States of standardized tests, to scores on subject examinations, to a variety of other measures of academic skill and knowledge, including proportions of students achieving or failing to achieve certain target levels.

2   Other school-based student outcome indicators. A variety of outcome measures beyond academic achievement have also been used to assess the impact of education policies. These include graduation rates, attendance rates, numbers of disciplinary problems, and rates of referral to special education.

3   Satisfaction. Students' assessments of the quality and value of their schools experience are an important if seldom evaluated outcome indicator, if only because they say something about motivation, which is absolutely critical to all other outcomes.

4   Life chances. Since many of the most important purposes of schools have to do with what happens to students after they leave the institution, a number of outcome measures concern post-school activities. These are wide-ranging, but could include such indicators as post-secondary education participation rates, employment outcomes, interest in lifelong learning, income, and citizenship indicators (such as propensity to volunteer, voting behavior or criminality).

School outcomes

Although education reforms are often framed in terms of student outcomes, the approach to changing student outcomes usually involves attempts to alter the way that schools work as institutions. Impacts on schools and school systems are frequently identified as important outcomes of reform, especially the following areas.

1   Work of teachers. One of the most frequently assessed aspects of reform is its impact on teachers' work and their attitudes towards their work. Outcomes related to work might include hours, time in and out of the classroom, attention to individual students, professional development activities, skill levels or teaching practices. Indicators in regard to attitude include teachers' sense of effort, efficacy, satisfaction and stress, among others.

2   Work of administrators. Reform is held to have had different effects on administrators than on teachers, partly because governance changes have altered the work of administrators in important ways. However, indicators are similar to those used for teachers.

3   Parent involvement. Greater involvement of parents has been a goal of most reform programs. Parents' active role in school governance and in their children's education, as well as their sense of satisfaction with the school and their part in it, have been assessed.

4   Programs. Some reforms are intended to affect school programs. Changes in curriculum or graduation requirements are obvious examples. School choice is also often proposed on the basis that it will lead schools to diversify and improve programs.

5   Teaching and learning. Reform programs have by and large not given very much attention directly to teaching and learning practices per se, with the possible exception of efforts to extend the use of educational technologies. However, teaching and learning practices are clearly central to the achievement of all school outcomes and so should be a key part of assessing any reform.

6   School organization. Although changes in school organization, such as devolution of authority, are usually argued as means to achieve other more important ends, they could also be considered to be outcomes in themselves.

Social outcomes

1   Economic outcomes. Insofar as reform has frequently been justified on economic grounds – that is, on the contribution of schooling to economic success – societal economic outcomes would be important indicators of the success of reforms. Such outcomes could include labor force participation rates, employment rates, earnings, and productivity growth, not only for students but more generally.

2   Equity outcomes. Many critics and some proponents of the reforms discussed in this book have been concerned about the potential of reform to increase inequity in society. An important outcome measure is thus the extent to which reforms act either to reduce or to increase the gaps in outcomes in society due to socio-economic status, ethnicity, gender, or other demographic factors.

3   Social cohesion. A related issue, also the subject of much debate in most of the cases discussed in this book, is the degree to which reforms serve to build or reduce an overall sense of community among people. Schooling has often been seen as a vehicle for building strong societies by, for example, giving people a better sense of their national heritage or an appreciation of their system of government, or a desire to contribute to the social good. Efforts to assess social cohesion have included measures of ethnic segregation, citizen participation, and attitudes such as tolerance.

The reforms programs considered in this book were broad and were justified on the basis of a range of outcomes. In some cases the reforms were tied to specific outcomes such as increasing standards of achievement. In other cases commitments were made to outcomes as a way of fending off criticism, such as the commitments to equity outcomes in a number of settings.

Assessing outcomes

Assessing policy outcomes is difficult, for a number of reasons. The range of desired outcomes is broad, including everything from student achievement in particular skills to general impacts on society in the long term. Various outcomes may not be entirely compatible with each other. Many outcomes are very difficult to assess, sometimes for technical reasons and sometimes because people disagree as to what would actually constitute evidence of progress on a particular outcome. It is rarely clear that an outcome has been the result of a particular policy, because so many other factors act to shape outcomes. Moreover, one cannot focus only on the desired outcomes, since policies often produce unanticipated outcomes that may be just as important.

An important difficulty in thinking about the outcomes of reform is that the goals and purposes of education are multiple, broad and sometimes inconsistent. We want our schools to produce skills in reading and writing. We want students to learn science and history. We want them to become proficient in technology, knowledgeable about work, believers in good citizenship, and environmentally aware. We hope they will be committed to healthy ways of living, including physical fitness, avoidance of drugs, and good parenting practices. We expect schools to give students a range of skills for work that go well beyond curriculum knowledge, such as teamwork and critical thinking but also habits of hard work and the willingness to follow instructions. We also want every student to achieve all these goals.

This list is ambitious enough. However, our goals for education go well beyond student achievement. We also expect schools to play an important role in developing a strong economy, supporting social mobility and alleviating social problems.

Our goals for schools are not only multiple and very hard to achieve, but they may also involve inconsistencies and contradictions. Can we teach critical thinking and obedience at the same time? Can we simultaneously encourage competition and a belief in the value of teamwork and a supportive community? Can we have success for all in a system that involves differential and limited rewards?

These trade-offs are rarely discussed. We tend to assume that all the goals of education can be achieved concurrently. But as every teacher knows, time is limited, and the resources devoted to one purpose cannot also be devoted to another and quite different purpose.

A further difficulty in thinking about educational outcomes is that they have both short-term and long-term dimensions. Consider student achievement. Most assessment of achievement is quite short-term, yet presumably our real interest in learning is long-term. We want students to learn history not so that they can pass a test in Grade 8 (leaving aside the question of what knowledge or skills such a test would actually measure), but so that their lifelong perspective on their world will be enriched. We assume that the former will lead to the latter, but have only weak empirical evidence that this is so. The same is true for other aspects of achievement. For example, Walberg (1987) found that the association between academic grades and various measures of lifetime professional accomplishment was essentially zero. Better grades in professional school did not predict later professional achievement. In the case of schools, too, evidence suggests that the predictive power of grades is less than we might wish (H. Levin, 1998).

The same short- and long-term considerations apply to other outcomes as well. In the short term, for example, it may be possible to increase productivity in schools by increasing workloads or reducing resources. In the long term, however, such policies could be self-defeating by leading to increased turnover and reduced commitment among teachers. In the short term we can all go a few days without eating, but in the longer term we either eat or die.

Short-and long-term considerations are even more difficult when we consider societal outcomes. Take the issue of equipping students with appropriate skills for the labor market. When could we conclude that this had been done successfully? At the point of first entry into the labor market? Ten years later? After a lifetime of work? When do we know that students have developed skills of critical thinking or citizenship? Is this a matter of assessing knowledge, or must it depend on people's long-term behavior? If the latter, can we ever know how well schools have done?

Although most people would agree that long-term outcomes are more important, it is short-term outcomes that receive most attention. This is understandable, if contrary. Short-term measures are easier to carry out, more likely to be connected to the particular policy, and more likely to command attention. It is difficult to introduce or defend a policy on the basis of data that will only be available ten or twenty years later, and just as difficult to show that today's circumstances are clearly the result of policies of ten or twenty years ago. Was higher unemployment in the 1990s a result of problems in schooling ten years before? Is today's lower unemployment evidence that something suddenly changed in schools decades before?

Even the most straightforward outcomes are not necessarily easy to measure in a reliable and valid way. Consider student achievement. The raging debates about how to assess student achievement are evidence that discovering how much students have learned is fraught with technical problems. Every method of assessment, from standardized tests to curriculum-based testing to authentic assessment, has its advocates and its critics. For many years there has been a recognition that much assessment in education focuses on the learning of discrete pieces of information, leading to attempts to give more attention to measuring the development of conceptual understanding and application. This has turned out to be very difficult to do, even in well-defined content fields such as mathematics or science. When one moves to goals that are less defined and longer-term, the problems of assessment become much greater.

In part the debate about assessment is linked to a debate about the meaning of knowledge. What does it mean to say that a student knows history? Is that a claim about ability to state facts, about conversance with broad underlying themes and processes, about an understanding of how historians work, about a sense of how the past has shaped the present, or about all of these? Is a test of factual knowledge a true indicator of a student's understanding of some subject, let alone her or his ongoing interest in that subject? Does a student who can recite the capitals of countries understand geography? Could a student who does not know any capitals understand geography? These are difficult questions.

On every one of the outcomes listed, there is an equally active debate about forms of assessment. Opinion polls to measure satisfaction are subject to bias depending on how the questions are framed and ordered. Measures of attitudes do not necessarily predict corresponding behavior. Measures of employment depend greatly on definitional issues. Even when we can agree on what to measure, how to do so often turns out to be very difficult.

Assessment of the outcomes of policies is further complicated because policies are not the only things that shape outcomes. The most important outcomes of education are all greatly influenced by factors outside the school. Abundant research shows that social factors such as family background, parents' education and neighborhood resources are very strongly related to students' outcomes (Levin, 1995; Thrupp, 1999). This is true of academic achievement and even more so of other life outcomes such as earnings or health. Schools alone cannot fully compensate for other aspects of society that may be working against desired outcomes. If many social factors are, for example, pushing students towards unhealthy ways of living, then it is quite unlikely that schools will be able to turn the tide single-handedly. If macro-economic conditions turn sour, all the education in the world will not prevent higher unemployment or dropping outputs.

Various efforts have been made to try to measure outcomes taking students' initial status into account – something that has come to be known as "value-added measurement." Statistical controls of various kinds are used to try to parcel out the effects of schools from the effects of family, upbringing and prior achievement. The debate on these matters is complex and highly technical. It involves not only difficult statistical issues but also a set of assumptions about the ways in which and extent to which background does actually influence achievement. Without entering into these questions, it is clear that producing value-added measurement that is widely accepted and reasonably understandable is very difficult (Linn, 2000). On the other hand, that is not necessarily a reason to give up the effort. Public indicators have become widely accepted in other fields that involve similar difficulties. The complexities of determining "seasonal adjustment" of unemployment rates, or price and inflation indices, or the measurement of Gross Domestic Product (GDP) have not prevented these indicators from being widely used and broadly accepted.

Confused purposes

Policies are linked to goals by a set of assumptions about cause and effect. A given policy measure embodies, whether explicitly or not, a theory about how one or more goals of education can be attained. A proposal to increase testing assumes that testing will increase students' or teachers' efforts, thus improving achievement. A proposal to change curricula supposes that the new curricula will lead to more or deeper learning. A proposal to change governance assumes that a new form of governance will lead to some other desired outcomes, and so on.

In practice, the links between policies and outcomes are rarely so clear and explicit, for reasons that have been discussed at length in earlier chapters. The nature of the political process is such that many measures end up being amalgams of ideas so that the link to outcomes is often quite unclear.

Links across levels are also complicated. Student achievement, for example, is valued partly in its own right but partly for larger purposes, such as its presumed link to economic growth or higher employment or social cohesion.

There is increasing evidence that what really matters to education outcomes is not primarily the organization, structure or governance of school systems. As Elmore puts it, summing up the views of many who have studied education reform, "Changes in structure are weakly related to changes in teaching practice, and therefore structural change does not necessarily lead to changes in teaching, learning and student performance" (1995, p. 25).

Unintended outcomes

Assessment of the intended outcomes of reform is clearly problematic. However, this is only part of the problem of evaluating reform. Schools, like other social institutions, can usefully be thought of as ecologies in which the various elements are connected in many ways, so that a change in one element often leads to changes in others as well. While reform programs tend to look at elements such as curriculum or finance or governance as being separate domains, in fact they are not. The results of changes in governance, for example, may be strongly affected by concomitant changes that affect governance issues, such as changes in financing or in the working conditions of teachers. The work of governance is more difficult if staff feel beleaguered than if they feel optimistic and supported. A little room in the budget can make changes much easier, while the need to cut spending has the opposite effect. Changes in curriculum may affect the way that parents make choices about schools, which may in turn affect finance and governance. Changes in tertiary education can have important consequences for schools, as was the case with the changes in sixth-form practice in England. These patterns of interaction are very difficult to predict, or even to assess.

Another consequence of this interrelation is that policies usually produce outcomes in addition to or other than those that were intended. A policy intended to lead to X may lead to Y and Z either in addition to or instead of X. Unintended effects arise because systems are complex and because the motivations for human actions are multiple and hard to predict, especially where action is affected by a large number of policy variables. As March (1984, p. 28) put it, "A system of rewards linked to precise measures is not an incentive to perform well; it is an incentive to obtain a good score."

Examples of such unintended effects abound. For example, a wage subsidy intended to encourage employers to hire young people may lead them to eliminate permanent jobs in favor of temporary subsidized jobs. Competency tests designed to encourage students to work harder may lead them to drop out earlier. Providing additional funding for students with high levels of need may lead schools to try to identify more students as having high needs. And so on.

Education reforms may also produce changes beyond the school. For example, desegregation efforts in the United States in the 1970s are held by some to have resulted in changes in residential patterns as some parents tried to leave desegregated districts.

These difficulties are not being outlined as a way of suggesting that assessing the results of policies is impossible. Despite the difficulties, assessment of the outcomes of schooling goes on all the time. The measures are imperfect, to be sure. They should be – and are – the subject of frequent reassessment and heated debate. But the task of trying to determine the results of reform policies is an important one.

The need to look at multiple intended and unintended consequences of several different kinds of reforms suggests a matrix approach (see Table 7.1). One dimension relates to the areas of reforms, using the framework of changes in governance, curriculum, assessment and choice. In other words, this analysis starts with the reforms and their intentions. The second dimension looks at the entire range of impacts of reforms taken as a whole and is intended to reveal both the ripple effects and unintended consequences of reforms.

Table 7.1   *A framework for assessing the outcomes of education reform*

Outcome (can be assessed in the short term or the long term)	*Governance – local management, parent involvement*	*Curriculum – traditional, math/science focus*	*Assessment – national testing, publication of results, inspection*	*School choice*
Students – impact on achievement satisfaction other school-based life-chances				
Schools – impact on teachers administrators parent relationships programs teaching and learning practices school organization				
Society – impact on economy cohesion equity				

Evidence From the Cases

The nature of the evidence

This study relies entirely on data about reform outcomes that have been collected by others. The body of evidence is, not surprisingly, uneven in distribution and in quality. In some areas there is quite extensive data and in other areas almost none. Many of the reforms discussed in this book were controversial, leading to strong predictions about their impacts from supporters and opponents, but often no data have been gathered to assess the validity of these predictions. Quite a bit of the political debate has been, and continues to be, based on anecdotal evidence – stories about a school here or a student there. The mass media tend to use such stories widely, presumably because they evoke reader interest, but they are no substitute for carefully gathered, representative evidence. Some interest groups have gathered data through polling and surveys in trying to make their cases for or against particular reforms.

Governments themselves have produced relatively little data on the outcomes of their policies, for various reasons that have already been discussed. The only areas where data on outcomes are regularly made available are around student achievement in testing programs and, where they exist, the results of school inspections. However, these data have not been intended to evaluate the effectiveness of policies so much as to make judgements about the effectiveness of schools. As mentioned in the last chapter, governments themselves sponsored very few studies on the impact of their reforms. The best evidence on policy outcomes is available where academic researchers have been most interested and conducted research. Such work has been largely concentrated in a few areas of interest, and is discussed in Appendix 1. Other areas of reform have been the subject of much less attention. In general, issues of teaching and learning have been given short shrift, both in the reforms themselves and in the research on their impact. We simply do not know very much about what teachers do and how this has changed under reform. However, the same is true of many other important outcomes, so that in general judgements about the efficacy of reforms rest on rather slender evidence.

Missing almost entirely from the base of evidence are the views and experiences of students. Although the whole system of education is supposedly set up in the interests of students, very little work looks at schooling from their viewpoint (Levin, 2000). Much more attention has been given to the views and practices of teachers or administrators than those of students. As Fullan (1991, p. 182) puts it, "we hardly know anything about what students think about educational change because no one ever asks them."

Governance

The comments that follow on governance must be read in the context of reductions or limitations in funding in most of the jurisdictions under study. Budget reductions meant that administrators and governing bodies inevitably had to devote very substantial amounts of time and energy to finding and allocating resources. One small but relevant piece of evidence is that in New Zealand by 1996 parents reported spending about \$500 per child per year for additional school costs, about 250 per cent of the figure reported in 1991 (Wylie, 1999, p. 18). It is quite possible that the picture around school governance would have been quite different had resources been increasing at the same time.

Local management

Local management has two elements to it – the administrative and the political. Administratively, local management is justified on the grounds that those closest to the operation are more knowledgeable about what will work in their context. Local management is therefore thought to lead to improved efficiency, as those on-site make better decisions about programs and resources (Brown, 1990). However, local management can also involve shifts in the balance of political power, not only between levels of the system but also between professionals and the clients of the system, particularly parents. Here the argument is that parents are better able than professionals to know what their children need. Giving parents more control will break the professional monopolies that critics alleged were stifling schooling.

Several different elements of reform have embodied elements of local management of schools. In England and New Zealand, control of many aspects of schooling was moved from central or district authorities to school governing councils. England also allowed schools to opt out of local authority control and become grant-maintained, or entirely self-governing. In Alberta and Manitoba, school councils with parent majorities were created but were given only advisory powers; traditional governance structures remained intact. Minnesota did not change school governance structures.

The evidence suggests some guarded support for the achievement of administrative efficiencies through local management. Studies in North American by Brown (1990) and in Britain by Levačić (1995) and by Thomas and Martin (1996) all suggest modest improvements in schools as some resources were reallocated. However, all the studies also agree that these changes tended to be at the margins of practice and had little effect on the organization of learning. Levačić's conclusion stands for the other studies as well: "There is therefore little evidence from this sample of schools of local management stimulating any significant changes in the way schools operate with respect to their core technology of teaching and learning" (1995, p. 105).

Some practices associated with decentralization, such as the requirement in England to tender for some school services, or the constant pressure in New Zealand to make support services "contestable" (that is, competitive) actually may have produced inefficiencies. Levačić (1995) notes that governing bodies found that having to tender services such as cleaning resulted in more expensive and poorer-quality work.

The analyses agree that local management has changed the work of school administrators substantially. It has required them to take the main responsibility for matters such as budgets and staffing that were previously largely managed by districts. Principals have had to pay attention to marketing their school, to the impact of enrolment changes on staffing levels, and to managing the work of governing bodies or advisory councils. Administrators report that their workloads have increased significantly as a result, and that it is more and more difficult for them to pay attention to issues of curriculum and teaching. One impact reported in England, linked to the much-increased flexibility in job roles and pay schedules, has been the creation of senior management teams in larger schools, where management work is centered.

A number of researchers have suggested that local management has increased the power of school principals at the expense of teachers and parents. The gap between school managers and teachers appears to have grown. This pattern has been found in England in regard to grant-maintained schools (Fitz *et al.*, 1993), and in schools generally (Levačić, 1995; Thomas and Martin, 1996). However, at least one study (Bell *et al.*, 1996) did not find that elementary schools in England have been polarized between teachers and administrators.

Although decentralization may have increased workloads for school administrators, a strong finding in both England and New Zealand is that principals generally like the new system and would not want to return to a more hierarchical approach.

Teachers, on the other hand, are less positive, reporting lower morale than school administrators, and generally seeing many reforms as making their work more difficult while simultaneously seeming to blame them for any shortcomings in student outcomes.

A consequence of the shift in governing authority to individual schools has been a decline in interschool collaborative mechanisms, including shared support services and ongoing professional dialogue across schools. In New Zealand and in England, teachers and principals report that they are now less likely than before the reforms to share ideas with colleagues in other schools (Bottery, 1998; Wylie, 1999). This is partly because the connections between schools through districts have been broken, and partly because of competition among schools for enrolments, discussed more fully later.

Support services in areas such as curriculum implementation, special education or teaching and learning were in the past provided by local authorities. In New Zealand and England, where local authorities were eliminated or had their powers substantially reduced, the availability of support services declined sharply. Alberta limited the proportion of budget that school districts could spend on central administration, which resulted both in reductions in district staff and in changes to the way such functions were coded on budget sheets.

In New Zealand, the regional boards disappeared after 1988, and the effort to replace them with various sorts of regional services did not work. "Clustering" – the idea that groups of schools would join together for administrative efficiency – was never taken up by schools, with the result that many very small schools are required to organize the full range of management services themselves. Support services provided by the Department of Education were moved to colleges of teacher education as a temporary measure, but have remained there now for a decade. At the same time, ongoing efforts to operate these services on a fee-for-service basis subject to demand from schools have made them very unstable. Teachers and school administrators in New Zealand have consistently complained about the lack of support on a regional or national basis.

In England the transfer of responsibility for more than 90 per cent of all spending to individual schools led to a system in which schools bought support services either from LEAs or from other providers. Many LEAs reduced quite substantially the numbers of support staff that they employed.

On the whole, the evidence suggests that the move to much greater school-level control has had the predictable effect of increasing attention to school-level issues at the expense of cross-school or regional concerns. Attention will be directed to the level where political institutions operate.

Local management does not seem, in general, to have led to greater diversity in schools or to significant changes in teaching and learning practices in most schools. The provision in New Zealand legislation to allow different kinds of schools to be established was not used at all in the first several years after its adoption. In England, Halpin *et al.* (1997) concluded that the grant-maintained schools they studied made relatively few curriculum changes, and tended to focus on changing their image through such vehicles as school uniforms, stricter discipline codes and extensive public relations efforts. Part of the reason for the lack of change is that schools did not take steps to seek out the views and preferences of parents or pupils, concentrating instead in most cases on improved marketing of what they were already doing. As West and Hopkins put it,

> the research functions of marketing, the analysis of needs, the design of "products" to meet the identified needs are scarcely to be found. It appears that the most common response of the school in the market place is to attempt to "sell what it can make," rather than to "make what it can sell."
>
> (1995, p. 19)

Insofar as greater local autonomy did not lead to more focus on school strategy, it is not surprising that school strategies did not change.

An important exception to this general finding, however, is the development of schools targeted to particular ethnic groups, as discussed later in the section on school choice. Private school enrolment has also grown in all the jurisdictions, though this growth may not be directly related to the reforms.

The evidence on teaching practices is somewhat limited, but it also suggests that most schools and teachers did make significant changes to their approaches during the reform period (Wylie, 1999).

Parent involvement

Local management was justified not only for reasons of efficiency, but also as a contribution to democracy by involving more people in decisions that affected their community. Whether it has achieved this objective is uncertain. Despite their considerable powers under legislation in several settings, parents' role in school governance seems to have remained quite modest. A detailed analysis of governing bodies in England (Deem *et al.*, 1995) concluded that they tended to be dominated by well-educated professional men not necessarily representative of the school's community. Governing bodies spent little time on educational issues in comparison with budgets and facilities, were not very knowledgeable about educational issues, generally deferred to the views of head teachers, and saw themselves more as managers than as representatives of all parents. The dominance of head teachers over parent governors has also been noted by many others (Thomas and Martin, 1996; Levačić, 1995). Quite similar results were found in New Zealand (Wylie, 1999).

Annual meetings of school governing bodies, which are considered in both England and New Zealand to be a major vehicle for accountability, are in general not well attended and generate very little discussion of education policy issues. Willingness of parents in New Zealand to stand for election to school governing bodies has decreased over the last decade, suggesting that more experience with governance will not lead to greater interest. In 1998, the fourth round of New Zealand trustee elections resulted in more than 30 per cent of schools having either a shortage of candidates or an acclamation (Wylie, 1999). Wylie concludes that parent involvement in schools in New Zealand actually declined in the ten years since the reforms began, although she cautions that the decline is not necessarily a result of the reforms. She also notes that involvement is highest in schools with higher socio-economic status.

On the other hand, while some feared that increased parent control of school governance might lead to excessive parochialism, on the whole governing bodies appear to have discharged their responsibilities competently. Very few local boards in either England or New Zealand have run into serious management difficulties. In fact, a number of people in New Zealand and England suggested in discussion that participation in governing bodies had helped develop more skills in local democracy and political action.

The move to increase parent authority was seen in part as a way of increasing lay control over professional educators. However, on the whole governing bodies have supported professionals. On a number of issues, governing bodies have allied themselves with professionals in opposition to government proposals, such as the resistance to bulk funding of teachers' salaries in New Zealand or to assessment practices in England. As more than one commentator has noted, in many cases the changes in governance have actually strengthened the role of professionals (Wylie, 1999; Deem *et al.*, 1995).

Policies that assumed parents were anxious to take control over schools appear to have mistaken the degree of interest parents have in playing an active role in governance or their support for a consumerist model (Vincent, 1996). Only 3 per cent of New Zealand parents surveyed in 1998 reported an active role in school policy-making, primarily because they did not want such a role (Wylie, 1999).

At the same time, parents do seem to have an increased interest in being actively involved in their own children's education, and this trend does have important impacts on the work of teachers and administrators (Epstein, 1995; Levin and Riffel, 1997). In education, as in most other professions, citizens are more and more circumscribing the autonomy of professionals and moving towards a model that is closer to co-management. Yet the emphasis on parents as governors or consumers may have diverted attention from more important opportunities around parents as educators and supporters of their children's progress.

Changes in curriculum

The base of evidence on the actual impact of curriculum change is very limited, with few studies looking in any sustained way at how reform has actually changed time allocations, students' course-taking patterns, teaching practices or learning outcomes. Nor have there been careful assessments of the actual quality of new curricula. Nonetheless, some conclusions can be drawn.

Changes in curriculum have had some contradictory elements. On one hand, in several countries there has been a reversion to traditional subject divisions, such that the 1988 National Curriculum in England was described as being very similar to the 1904 curriculum (Aldrich, 1995). English secondary education maintains its traditional narrow academic focus on A levels despite several attempts supported by some powerful Conservative ministers to move to a broader curriculum model.

Another development has been the increased emphasis on so-called "core" subjects such as language, mathematics and science. More time has been allocated to these, and they are also the central elements of assessment programs. The result, not surprisingly, has been to limit attention to other subject areas, including not only the arts but also more traditional subjects such as history. In Manitoba, for example, Minister Manness attempted to make history an optional subject after Grade 10, an effort he eventually had to reverse because of protest. In elementary schools also, the increased focus on literacy, mathematics and science is reported by teachers to have diminished the time and attention given to other subjects and activities.

A greater emphasis on tracking or streaming of students can also be noted, in England particularly. The Conservatives took a number of steps to differentiate programs and schools more sharply, including favoring selection of students, re-authorizing grammar schools and, later in their time in office, officially endorsing "setting" (ability grouping) as a main element in school organization.

Many of these developments seem quite out of step with other efforts to strengthen connections between schooling and work, or to foster the supposed new workplace skills such as problem-solving and teamwork. The result has been a rather contradictory approach, in which one set of measures makes the curriculum increasingly traditional while another set attempts to make it more relevant to a certain view of the modern workplace and society.

The rapid change in curricula in several settings certainly led to a great deal of pressure on schools and teachers. In England after 1988, as in Manitoba after 1994 or in Minnesota in the 1990s, a flood of new curricula led to strong complaints from teachers that they were not getting enough time or support to understand the new programs or to translate them into effective teaching practice. As the evidence in Chapter 6 shows, changed teaching practice does not follow automatically from new curriculum documents. In fact, the greater the change in curriculum, the less likely it is that classroom practice will reflect the new goals and intentions. Since the resources and effort devoted to supporting new curricula were modest in most of the jurisdictions, it is likely that teaching practice did not change as much as reformers had hoped, although evidence on this point is quite limited. It does seem clear, however, that changes in curriculum, especially when coupled with changes in assessment, did create stress for teachers (Harold *et al.*, 1999).

The big question – whether students' academic achievement has improved – is also one on which there is limited evidence. In England the relevant indicators – proportions of students passing their GCSE and A-level exams as well as proportions completing secondary school – have been increasing steadily for more than a decade. However, Britain's rates of school completion as of 1988 were very low by international standards, so it is not clear whether the increase was a result of reform or part of an inevitable move to adapt to changing educational requirements for work. (This is precisely the kind of question that is unlikely ever to be determined in a clear way because of the many intervening variables.) In New Zealand, the consensus of opinion is that the reforms have had no noticeable impact on student achievement (Wylie, 1999; Butterworth and Butterworth, 1998). Alberta's evidence on learning outcomes since 1994 shows no consistent trend. Manitoba has no consistent evidence on this point.

If evidence on short-term achievement is lacking, even less is known about the impact of reform on longer-term outcomes such as post-secondary enrolment and completion, employment skills or work outcomes. Given the length of time before these outcomes could be assessed, and the many other intervening variables, it will be very difficult to draw any meaningful conclusions as to the impact of education reform on these matters.

Student assessment and publication of results

From the point of view of students, testing and assessment have always been an essential element of school life. The increase in state, public assessment makes relatively little difference to the school lives of individual students who, unlike educators, are used to having their performance publicly assessed and attributed to their own deficiencies. Indeed, there does seem to be some inconsistency between educators' concerns about the inimical impact of public evaluation on their work and their own willingness to do just about the same thing to students with relatively few qualms.

Nonetheless, increased state assessment was an important feature of reform in England, Alberta and Manitoba, while Minnesota made enormous, though not very successful, efforts to move to an outcome-based education model. England had always had national testing in secondary schools, but introduced a program of tests at ages 7, 11 and 14. English and mathematics are tested at all three levels, and science at the latter two. Manitoba planned to test language (English or French), mathematics, social studies and science in Grades 3, 6 and 9, and language and mathematics in the final year of high school. Alberta maintained its diploma examinations in Grade 12 and tested language and mathematics in Grade 3, as well as language, mathematics, science and social studies in Grades 6 and 9. New Zealand has a program of testing at the end of secondary schooling, but no other national testing program. Minnesota planned statewide tests in reading and mathematics in Grades 3, 5 and 8 as well as a competency-based high school graduation requirement.

The testing programs proved controversial, complex and expensive. The model first developed in England was rejected by the government (Black, 1994; Gipps, 1995). Testing was changed again later in response to teacher concerns about the time it required. Manitoba began with a plan to test several subjects in each grade, but the high costs led to very considerable simplification of these plans so that by 1998 only language and mathematics were being tested at most levels. In all settings these tests have proved a lightning rod for criticism of reform more generally, though expanded testing certainly also has many supporters.

The research on the effects on teachers of increased testing is limited with, as in so many areas of education policy, much more rhetoric than evidence, as indicated in a careful review of evidence by Mehrens (1998). In some studies teachers report increased attention to those skills and subjects that will be tested externally, including spending extra time on material that may be tested and using practice test exercises. Teachers also report changing classroom practice to include fewer activities such as student projects or discussions (Wideen *et al.*, 1997; Wylie, 1997). However, these studies tend to rely on teachers' self-reports, and self-reports are always of doubtful validity. Certainly, teachers tend to feel heightened anxiety as testing dates draw nearer. Assessment may also bring workload concerns, increased stress and the possibility of cheating. In Manitoba, concerns about the time that teachers would be absent from teaching in order to mark the new provincial tests generated considerable friction between school districts and the Department of Education, and in England, as noted already, testing of 7-year-olds brought a full-scale teacher revolt.

Proponents of assessment argue that changes in teaching are precisely what they are seeking, that the whole purpose of high-stakes testing is to push instruction to address the key learning outcomes that are being tested. However, Mehrens (1998) also concludes that the evidence about the impact of external testing on students is too limited to draw any real conclusions. Bishop (1994), using results from the 1991 IAEP assessment, concludes that Canadian provinces with more extensive provincial examinations had better results. The ability of assessment to drive appropriate changes in instruction depends not just on having tests, but on the tests actually doing a good job of measuring important learning outcomes, on teachers seeing the tests as having that validity, and on teachers having both the skill and the material conditions to alter instruction appropriately. None of these conditions can be taken for granted; indeed, the evidence suggests that they are quite difficult to bring about, especially given the limited attention paid to these issues in most of the reforms under discussion here (Linn, 2000). An OECD report took the view that "Simply making schools 'accountable' (whether to the State, parents, the community, or to others) is unlikely on its own to lead to improvements in standards of performance" (1996, p. 20), and that monitoring was only useful if set against a clear set of criteria and defined ways for schools to improve their performance.

The main impacts of assessment at the school level are related to the publication of results and their potential impact on school image, enrolment and resource allocations. These issues are discussed below under the heading of "choice."

As noted earlier, a great deal of controversy has surrounded the publication of assessment results because of concerns about both validity and impact. Given the powerful effect of socio-economic status on school outcomes, it is no surprise to learn that in England and New Zealand (and in areas of the United States where similar measures have been introduced) schools designated as failing are almost entirely in areas characterized by high levels of poverty. A debate has ensued as to whether and how background should be taken into account in thinking about achievement. Some argue that background should not become an excuse for low levels of achievement (e.g. Barber and Dann, 1996), that it is important to have high expectations for all students regardless of their starting points. Others (e.g. Thrupp, 1999) argue that the effects of socio-economic status are so powerful that to leave them out of consideration in judging achievement is to place impossible burdens on schools. Both sides may end up defending positions that are difficult to maintain – either that schools make no difference or that they can make all the difference.

Inspection

England and New Zealand have both developed systems of external inspection of schools. In England the inspections are organized by the Office for Standards in Education (Ofsted) and carried out by teams who bid for particular inspection contracts. The inspectors use a public framework developed by the agency, spend a considerable amount of their time in classrooms, and also report on various other areas of school policy and life. There is a very detailed set of instructions for inspection, and a series of numerical rating scales leading to summary comments. The Ofsted reports on schools are made public and the school is required to issue a public response to any recommendations for improvement. The agency also issues various national summary reports on its view of various aspects of the state of education.

A number of studies have examined the impact of inspection on English schools. The consensus of opinion seems to be that the inspections engender a great deal of stress among educators, and involve a large amount of time in preparation and follow-up. On the whole the impacts on schools seem to be modest, with the exception of schools that receive very negative reports. Fidler *et al.* (1998) report that most schools found their reports "somewhat useful." Wilcox and Gray (1996) conclude that most findings were "broadly accepted" (p. 57), and heads used them to promote their own plans for the school. However, few inspections resulted in really substantial changes in the school, and many inspection findings were not really implemented even a year later. School action was least likely where the findings dealt with the most difficult but important issues, such as quality of instruction. Ouston *et al.* (1998) point out that one impact of inspection has been that schools monitor themselves to make sure they are in compliance with the inspection requirements, which would naturally reduce the degree to which inspections produced significant findings.

Looking at inspection in England from a US point of view, Grubb is highly critical.

> As it has been implemented since 1993, inspection in elementary and secondary schools has become stressful and punitive. Its benefits, only grudgingly admitted by teachers and administrators, are hardly worth the costs, and the conversation about teaching it has engendered is limited and awkward.
>
> (1998, p. 2)

A further complication in England is that the results of Ofsted inspections are not always consistent with test results. In at least one case to this author's knowledge, a school that rated in the top hundred in the country in published test scores had at the same time failed its Ofsted inspection, raising the question of the validity of either or both measures.

School inspections in New Zealand by the Education Review Office are very different from those done by Ofsted in that they focused primarily on the degree to which schools were in compliance with national policies and guidelines (Thrupp and Smith, 1999). The inspections paid much more attention to policy documents than to classroom observation. ERO has been studied by Robertson *et al.* (1997) and by Thrupp (1998). Both studies are critical partly because of its focus on policy compliance rather than teaching and learning.

Although the inspection agencies in both England and New Zealand officially disavow socio-economic status as a reason for school failure, in practice their reports have drawn attention to socio-economic issues precisely because most "failing" schools are in poor communities. In New Zealand the declaration by ERO that schools in South Auckland were failing has led to a significant investment of additional resources in these poor communities. In Britain, also, the fact that failing schools were so often in poverty-stricken communities has prompted more attention to the problems that poverty creates for educational attainment – a good example of unanticipated consequences

Choice

The impact of school choice has probably been the object of more research than any other single reform policy. Many studies in England, New Zealand and Minnesota have looked at the various impacts of choice on students and schools, and the general literature debating the merits of choice is enormous and growing.

One conclusion that emerges from this body of work is that the impact of choice depends greatly both on the nature of the choice scheme and on the particularities of local context. In regard to the former, there is clearly a big distinction between a plan such as Minnesota's, in which choice is optional for students and families, and the arrangements in England in which every student must make a selection of a secondary school to attend. Choice in an inner city will be very different from the situation in a rural area where few schools may be reachable.

Much depends on the nature of the local community and the existing set of schools. Woods *et al.* (1998) describe these as "local competitive arenas." For example, in a setting in which schools are already seen as being of quite different levels of quality and in which most schools are readily accessible, choice may exacerbate the distinctions. This was the case in some English communities, where grammar schools had traditionally ranked at the top of the hierarchy and choice acted to reinforce this ranking. However, in other communities where schools did not have the same reputational differences, the impact of choice was also very different. The larger the disparities in schools in terms of image, facilities and resources, the more important choice may be.

Where choice is voluntary, as in Minnesota, relatively small numbers of students have moved out of their home district. In Minnesota, five years after school choice was introduced, about 5 per cent of students were attending a school outside their district of residence. However, actual transfers are not the only measure of impact, since the Minnesota evidence also suggests that many more students transferred within districts and that some schools that felt vulnerable to out-migration did take steps to try to retain students, which is one of the points of a choice program (Nathan and Ysseldyke, 1994).

Although advocates of choice speak as if school choice was always made by parents, the reality appears to be more complicated. In many families children play a decisive role in choosing a school. In Britain, children of working-class parents were more likely to choose a school themselves, whereas middle-class parents either made the choice for their child or worked carefully to guide the child towards a choice they supported (Carroll and Walford, 1997). Other work (Smrekar, 1996; Ball and Vincent, 1998) suggests that choices are strongly influenced by parents' and students' local networks rather than formal information, though this may depend in part on how much information is actually made available to parents, and in what form.

Choice is often defended as a way of improving school achievement, so it would seem to follow that parents would choose on the basis of schools' levels of achievement. However, academic results are only one of the factors parents use in making decisions about a school. Academic achievement may not even be the most important element. A feeling that the school is a warm and caring environment is also very important for many parents. Proximity to home and attendance by the child's friends are also influential.

> The data ... incline us to the view that the more important of fundamental values for parents tend to be child-centered ... "Product" – including emphasis on academic success – is important, but its importance appears from our data so far not so consistent, and it is not, generally, given priority above child-centered factors.
>
> (Glatter *et al.*, 1997, p. 21)

In Minnesota, Lange (1996) concluded that contextual factors such as socio-economic status or proximity to a larger and richer district were stronger factors in affecting choices than any actions by the schools themselves.

Although most of the research looks at the impact of choice on schools, it is also clear that the requirement to choose has implications for students and families. A decision must now be made, and its consequences faced, where earlier no decision was required. For some this will be a positive experience leading to a heightened sense of responsibility and a feeling of greater control over one's future. For others, however, the opposite may be true. Having to choose can create considerable anxiety. Parents and children may disagree over what choice to make. Either or both may be quite uncertain as to which choice is best. These difficulties may be compounded because in England and New Zealand – and to some extent in Manitoba – students and parents know that their choices are constrained by the student's prior performance. Research indicates that families will limit their own choices, based on what they think are the real possibilities for acceptance (Ball and Vincent, 1998; Lauder *et al.*, 1999). Students will not choose schools that they think are highly unlikely to accept them. Even then, a substantial number of students will not be admitted to a popular first-choice school, and so have to face a form of rejection. In England (Sofer, 2000) and in New Zealand (in Annual Reports of the Ministry of Education) the number of students expelled from schools increased quite dramatically after the introduction of choice. Moreover, in both countries those excluded came disproportionately from visible minority groups, suggesting that schools were less tolerant of students who did not fit in.

Choice has important and complex community consequences around issues of diversity. Several studies in England (reviewed in Tomlinson, 2000) and New Zealand (Lauder *et al.*, 1999) have concluded that choice plans lead to increased segregation along lines of social class. These researchers conclude that more affluent parents are more likely to pursue active choice, and that schools that are in demand will tend to select students with higher levels of academic attainment, which is itself linked to socio-economic background. In New Zealand the growth of private and integrated schools has also been cited as problematic (McGeorge, 1995).

Ethnic composition of schools can also be a factor. Lauder *et al.* (1999) also found that choice in the area of New Zealand they studied led to greater concentration of Maori, Pacific Island and Caucasian students in specific schools. Wylie (1999) reports that Maori parents in New Zealand were more likely to feel that they had not been able to access their first-choice school. In England, the proportion of minority students was a factor some parents considered in choosing a school for their children (Gewirtz *et al.*, 1995; Woods *et al.*, 1998). However, these relationships are not simple, especially for minority groups. Some minorities prefer to be in schools with many people of the same ethnicity, but others may see high minority population schools as of lower quality and so opt to move.

In Minnesota, choice did not significantly change the nature of ethnic concentration in schools, partly because the take-up was relatively small. In fact, choice in the US has been used as a vehicle for racial integration as well as increased segregation. Choice plans in the US vary dramatically in nature, so it is impossible to generalize about their impact (Fuller *et al.*, 1996). Some studies have found that magnet schools tend to attract families with higher socio-economic status, even among minorities (Citizens' Commission on Civil Rights, 1997).

Concerns have been expressed that charter schools, which are another form of choice provision, may increase racial segregation. As with school choice, outcomes depend very much on the nature of the charter school provisions. The first charter schools in Minnesota actually had high levels of enrolment by minorities and by students with special needs (Nathan, 1996). Several US studies (Fuller *et al.*, 1996) suggest that the impact of choice plans on ethnic segregation depend greatly on the design of the plan and the safeguards it includes against segregation. However, there is very little evidence to suggest that choice has had a significant positive impact in promoting integration.

Not all the evidence points to greater segregation, however. Recent work on the socio-economic composition of secondary schools in England (Gorard and Fitz, 1998) concludes that schools overall are actually less segregated on the basis of socio-economic origins than they were a decade earlier, before choice was introduced. Evidence in the United States and Canada on the impact of choice on equity is also mixed, depending greatly on the particular provisions and context (Fuller *et al.*, 1996). Ethnic or religious groups may choose separate schools even though these have overall lower socio-economic status or poorer resourcing.

Competition among schools to secure enrolments has led to a decline in collaboration across schools. Bottery (1998) reports comments from teachers and administrators to the effect that they would no longer share good ideas with other schools for fear of losing competitive advantage. However, this trend was not universal. Woods *et al.* (1998) note that in some areas schools collaborated to share the market and continued to support each other professionally. Collaboration depended on very strong commitment by school leaders, and was also linked to the degree to which a set of schools already had clear "market niches" and so saw the competition between them as limited.

The effects of choice on school programming are, in England and New Zealand, tied in with decentralization, already discussed. In Minnesota, where there has been no similar decentralization, teachers and principals reported little effect of choice on their instructional practices, though parents did tend to report changes in school programs as a result of the choice policy (Lange, 1996). Lange reports that in the first few years of the Minnesota choice program, schools marketed primarily to existing students and parents rather than to outsiders. In Manitoba, school choice has led to increased competition for enrolments, especially among secondary schools. Schools have used advertising of school programs and program changes aimed at attracting new students, such as advanced academic programs, science and technology programs and, recently, the introduction in a few schools of a kind of school uniform. In both Minnesota and Manitoba, the number of students changing schools has been relatively small, but their impact on the attention of school managers has been substantial because these students represent important marginal revenues.

Choice may also have implications for the way schools work with ethnic diversity. In New Zealand, schools with a Maori focus developed (although all schools were required, in the initial stages of the reform, to give attention in their charters to Maori issues). In England, some schools have positioned themselves competitively by targeting particular audiences. All-girls secondary schools have been a particularly popular option (though all-boys schools have not, leading to concerns about gender selection issues). In areas with high ethnic concentrations, some schools have marketed themselves as particularly interested in, for example, Muslim or South Asian populations. In Manitoba, though their existence predates the 1994 reforms, two Aboriginal schools have been created, and other school programs are aimed at attracting groups such as Ukrainians, Germans or Jews through special language options.

An unexplored consequence of choice may have to do with neighborhood relations. In many communities people get to know each other because their children attend the same school. Where students from the same neighborhood may be scattered across many schools, some community bonds may be weakened. Research from the US on magnet schools indicates that these schools do not generally produce a strong sense of community among the families who attend them (e.g. Smrekar, 1996; Goldring, 1997). However, this is an issue on which there is currently little empirical evidence.

The social impact of reform

The arguments around the equity and social cohesion effects of school reforms are subtle and complex. Some have worried that reforms will cause Balkanization of schools and communities on grounds of class or ethnicity. Others have argued that allowing people with like values to control their own schools is the only way in which we can avoid a "lowest common denominator" school system.

In looking at broad social outcomes it is impossible to sort out the impact of school reform from other social changes. School reforms were not the only or even the most important social changes in these societies over this period of time. England and New Zealand underwent far-reaching changes in many aspects of social and economic policy. All four countries in this study have seen increasing inequality in incomes, and high levels of poverty (Cox, 2000). Economic deregulation and restructuring have fostered greater social uncertainty and in general a more atomistic approach to life. Under these conditions, it is not surprising to find at least some evidence of increasing social, ethnic and economic segregation in schools, whatever education policies may have been in place.

The longer-term impacts of schooling are, as already noted, very difficult to assess, and the patterns differ across countries. The United States and Canada, for example, have had very different experiences with returns to post-secondary education in recent years, partly because of different demographics and partly because of different policy choices. It is probably fair to say that education in itself has only modest effects on economic and social outcomes for a society, and that changes in earnings, employment or other life outcomes are driven much more by macro-economic events and policies than by what happens in schools.

Nonetheless, it is hard to find evidence suggesting that these reform programs have had any positive impact on social cohesion or on equity. Private school enrolments have increased. Schools with high populations of disadvantaged students often have poorer resourcing – less funding, or less qualified teachers, or fewer extra resources from the community. More critically, performance of students from low-income families or from some ethnic minorities continues to lag seriously behind national averages.

Conclusion

The empirical evidence on the impact of reform in these five settings is quite limited, and almost non-existent in some cases. The available evidence is largely focused on a few parts of the reforms, especially those that were most highly charged. Changes in teaching and learning have not been the subject of very much study.

The picture that emerges from all the evidence reviewed is that these reforms have had relatively modest impact, especially taking into account the enormous effort involved. They have changed some relationships in important ways, including giving individual schools much more autonomy in some settings. They have changed the work of administrators in significant ways, and certainly intensified pressures on teachers. They have increased the importance of parents in a number of ways. They appear on the whole to have had small impacts on student achievement levels. Their effects on social outcomes are difficult to measure but hardly appear to have been very positive. Most notably, the evidence on the impacts of reform is remarkably scanty, raising the question of why so little is known about policies seen to be so important.

8   Reconsidering Education Reform

What can we learn about education reform from the experiences in these five jurisdictions? Given that schools are unlikely to disappear from the political gaze in the near future, are there suggestions that might be put forward for governments, educators and researchers to consider in thinking about large-scale reform?

The discussion of conclusions and implications from the study is in three parts. The first is a brief synopsis of the main conclusions of the study, focusing on the picture of education reform that emerges from the work. This is followed by comments for those directly involved in reform – governments and educators. What might governments do better or differently in trying to improve schooling? How might educators think about reform in ways that are more productive for them? The third part of the chapter is addressed to researchers, and looks at the implications of this work for thinking about and studying reform. The three discussions do overlap. Politics is at least partly analytical, and research is at least partly political. The process of reform embodies a conceptualization of education, so suggestions for researchers are also potentially useful to educators and governments. The reverse is also true, since researchers' work needs to take into account the realities of political and educational life.

Understanding Education Reform

Education reform is a complex phenomenon – a melange of ideas, politics, institutional structures, history and culture. Many of the portrayals of reform treat it too simply (Power, 1992), often as a straightforward matter of powerful people putting their well-developed ideas into practice. In fact, putting together a program, having that program adopted and then having it put into practice so as to produce the desired outcomes is extraordinarily difficult and almost never occurs in a straightforward way. So many factors come into play, many quite unpredictably, that we should be surprised when efforts succeed rather than when they fail.

Reform programs grow out of a variety of sources. As political commitments, reforms are influenced by party policies, the characteristics of individual politicians, and the overall climate of political ideas. Groups outside of government, both lobbyists and think tanks, can have an important influence on political ideas. Policy ideas also come from the civil service and from those engaged directly in education.

Which particular proposals get adopted is a matter both of power and of circumstance. A determined leader can have a great deal of influence on what happens, but in other cases policy commitments are driven by all sorts of circumstances that may be far removed from a careful consideration of ideas. The creation of political programs is always affected by such matters as election timing, personal and organizational conflicts within government, and the presence of crises or other unusual circumstances. Political programs are not necessarily carefully crafted or coherent.

Ideas do matter, of course. As these cases evidence, some proposals for reform were frequently put forward while other possible options were rarely mentioned. Ideas that seem common sense at one point in time can gradually come to seem ridiculous, and vice versa. People and organizations work hard to get their particular policy options on to the political and public agenda and to reduce the likelihood of alternative ideas being adopted. Success in this struggle is partly a matter of resources, organization and persistence, but also partly a matter of whether one's ideas resonate in a given political and cultural moment.

But while ideas are important they are far from omnipotent. All policy ideas are ground through the mills of practical politics and institutional structures. Governments have to balance their prejudices with their sense of possibility, and most of the time the practical wins out. That is, governments do what they think is possible, even if that is not what might have been their first choice. Modern societies do contain a variety of official and unofficial checks and balances. These affect not only what policies are adopted, but even more what happens to policies in the move from adoption to implementation.

Policy proposals often get modified between initial suggestion and eventual adoption. The civil service tries to alter political proposals so that they fit better with existing institutional aims, resources or patterns. In other cases governments change their ideas in the face of opposition, though a determined government can usually push forward if it has the political clout.

Because so much of politics has to do with image and impression in the relatively short term, and because public policy agendas are so crowded with so many issues, governments tend to give much less attention to issues of implementation and outcomes for any given policy. Education is a relatively decentralized activity in that its actual practice rests on the actions of thousands of people who may have little or no interest in, let alone commitment to, a reform program. Quite a bit has been learned in the last twenty years about how policies get worked out in schools and school systems, but government practices have not yet caught up with that knowledge, and the short-term pressures on governments have, if anything, intensified.

The actual outcomes of policies are often, it seems, of less public importance than is the debate around purposes. Governments are not necessarily anxious to look carefully at the real impacts of their policies or to maintain an open mind as to whether a given policy has been successful. Since there are so many other intervening variables, it is rarely possible in any case to draw direct links from a particular policy change to specific outcomes.

All of this might leave the reader feeling rather cynical about politics and policy. If everything is about image and about short-term political gain, then is there any chance for a real discussion of substantive educational issues? Many educators, already suspicious of politics, might see the evidence in this book as suggesting that the only hope is to try to avoid the entire political game. Although I can understand people feeling very negative about politics, I do not think that such a thoroughgoing cynicism is justified.

In fact, there have been some positive trends in policy-making in recent years – not so much in the substance of what has been done but in the changing nature of the political process. Three particularly important developments concern the growing importance of public debate, the growing importance of research and evidence, and the growing understanding of the importance of implementation and adaptation. More people today are more insistent on having a voice on political issues than used to be the case. This is no doubt at least in part a result of more people having more education. There are more interest groups and they are better organized. The result is that governments generally have to pay more attention to public opinion than they used to, and cannot so easily dismiss firmly held views. There is no guarantee that any particular view of education will be well founded, but increased public debate does offer the opportunity for everyone to learn more about the issues. This potential is far from being fully used, but may become more so as societies learn more about how to conduct political argument in a constructive way. We are only at the beginning of this process.

The growing importance of public discussion of issues coincides with increased interest in research and evidence as contributors to policy. In some policy fields, such as health or training, few debates now take place without at least some attention to empirical evidence. Education lags these fields by quite a bit, with in some cases astoundingly little attention to evidence, but here, too, the pattern is changing. Even some of the most vitriolic education debates, such as those over reading methods or choice or testing, have made extensive use of evidence of various kinds. Some might argue that the evidence is only brought forward to support previously held opinions, but over time evidence can begin to assert an independent effect on what people take to be true. Insofar as more evidence is gathered and made public, people will also get increasingly used to evidence as a part of debate, which would itself be a positive development.

Finally, an increased attention to issues of implementation and adaptation makes it more possible for those directly involved with education reform – especially teachers, parents and students – to have a real and acknowledged share in shaping the way reforms actually work. As thinking moves from reform as mandates to reform as capacity-building, leaders will have to pay more attention to what those "in the field" think, because in the end it is their commitment that will shape the success of most initiatives.

One might, of course, turn all three of these trends around and argue that they could just as easily support even more manipulative processes of change. In such a view, the increasing debate just adds noise and confusion for most people while disguising the true interests of governments. The increasing body of evidence is designed to bolster a priori positions, and the attention to implementation is intended to push people to do things even if those things are not in their interest.

Governments do have massive power to coerce, but on the whole there is reason to be an optimist on these points. The trends seem to be pushing towards a wider, not narrower, distribution of political influence, even if such influence remains highly unequal. How one sees these developments must depend on one's particular context. It would be both incorrect and naive to suggest we are marching steadily towards some utopia of political participation. Much also depends on one's time frame; the events of a decade may give a very different impression than would a fifty- or hundred-year time scale.

In any case, improvement comes primarily from people's efforts to shape what they take to be a better world. A pessimist has little to say except "I told you so." An optimist can offer suggestions and recommendations, even some that seem rather unlikely. Such suggestions take up the remainder of this chapter.

Suggestions for Governments and Educators

Reform is a complicated business. Getting it right, either in terms of what is proposed or how things actually develop, is far from easy. To my mind, any suggestions arising from this work cannot be too far removed from the realm of the possible. In an ideal world, perhaps, policy would only be made with extensive consultation and considerable research, and research would always be motivated by the desire to understand and improve practice. However, such a world is not likely to exist any time soon. Our political and social institutions have always been quite imperfect. Greed, ambition and perversity are in constant struggle with idealism. There is no point telling people to do things differently in situations when they do not see an option of that kind. On the other hand, some improvement is possible in every situation. The fact that we cannot change everything does not mean we can or should do nothing. Dror (1986) provides the right combination of realism about human limitations but also optimism about improvements that might be made. Gramsci expressed it as "pessimism of the intellect; optimism of the will" (1992, p. 12).

Propositions that policy-makers and educators might consider in attempting to improve education reform could include the following:

1   Goals for reform, at least in the short term, should be modest. Promises of great things in a short time are almost always going to lead to disappointment.
2   The design of reforms needs to take account of changing social context.
3   Goals should focus on those things that have a real chance to make a difference in outcomes for students.
4   To have any chance of lasting impact, reforms need to have careful and extensive processes to support effective use.
5   Reform should be seen as an opportunity for learning.
6   Research and evidence should play an important role in the reform process.

Modest goals

What is planned is not necessarily what is implemented, and what is implemented does not necessarily produce the intended results. In none of the settings discussed in this book could it be said that the results of the reforms were substantially as predicted by their promoters. On the whole, reforms appear, even after a decade or more, to have had less dramatic impact than was anticipated. They were rarely as successful as their proponents predicted. Achievement levels did not increase dramatically. Choice was not taken up by huge numbers of students or parents, and did not lead to significant increases in quality or diversity. Decentralization did not change school practices very much. Parental involvement is difficult to increase, and does not seem to have very large impacts on schools in most cases. Changes in curriculum did not necessarily translate into changes in teaching or in learning. Changes in student assessment may have altered instructional practices, but not necessarily for the better.

On the other hand, the worst fears about reforms also do not appear to have come about. Education systems have not yet been atomized into competing enclaves based on social class or ethnicity, or at least not much more so than they were before the reforms. Levels of inequality among schools have increased somewhat, but probably less than inequality generally in the same societies. Competition among schools has decreased collaboration, although it is not evident to what extent this is really a problem. In the vast majority of cases parents have not taken over governance from professionals and insisted on making unreasonable decisions – in fact, parental involvement in governance may have strengthened the role of professionals. The work of teachers and administrators appears to have become more difficult, but the experience of students does not seem to have changed very much (Levin, 2000).

All this suggests that our goals for reform might benefit from being more modest. Modesty is important because our capacities are so limited. Modesty in intentions does not mean that we cannot have great hopes and dreams; it has more to do with realizing how difficult such dreams are to bring about, so that we truly do start the journey with small steps. Moreover, modest intentions are more likely to generate some sense of success and increasing confidence instead of the spiral of grand plan followed by grand disillusion. This is an approach that many good teachers understand and use every day with learners – building on small successes to reach big objectives over time.

Taking into account social context

The horizon of politics is short, but changes in large institutions take a long time. This contradiction is fundamentally important to thinking about reform. Many policy changes in education have had fleeting effects, if any. In North America such important reforms of the 1970s as open-area schools, team teaching, differentiated staffing and alternative schools have disappeared with hardly a trace.

Other changes, however, have had important and lasting effects. Changes in the education of people with disabilities have actually grown stronger over time, such that a reversion to the practices of the 1960s is unthinkable in this area. Attention in schools to the needs of minority groups generally has improved significantly, even though social inequalities remain very large – and have increased in a number of countries.

The difference between reforms that disappear and those that last lies in the relationship of the reform to the larger social context. In general, changes that have had a lasting impact on schools have come from outside the system (Levin and Riffel, 1997). Changes in demographics, in social mores, in labor markets, in views of human rights and capacities, in legal codes, in gender roles – these over time do produce important and lasting changes in what schools do. Reforms that are consistent with other important changes in society are much more likely to have lasting impacts than those that arise and are sustained only within the education system. For example, the treatment of students with disabilities has changed permanently in schools because it has fit with a general change in the way people have seen and responded to the disabled, as well as with changing legal requirements, the development of new advocacy groups, and related changes in institutions outside the schools.

This does not mean that schools have to be blind adherents to the latest social theory. The social context of education is always complex, and at any given moment embodies a large number of developments pulling in all kinds of different – and sometimes entirely inconsistent – directions. Trends towards greater homogeneity and greater diversity, or greater tolerance and greater intolerance, can and do co-exist. Schools do have some autonomy of action and some ability to try to embody enduring educational values. Part of the purpose of education is surely to push against conventional thinking and to challenge the shibboleths of the moment. At the same time, schools cannot be isolated from the main social issues that a community or society confronts.

Focus on what makes a difference for student outcomes

The reforms described in this book were largely about governance, structures and system rules. They rested on a belief, sometimes articulated and sometimes not, that changing institutional arrangements would lead to better educational outcomes. Yet education happens very much in individual schools and classrooms, and the link between structural arrangements and school practices is not necessarily a very close one. All the evidence suggests that these structures do not have much effect on students' learning. Education policy would be better if it focused on what might really make a difference to learners (Hopkins and Levin, 2000).

This focus would likely pull us in two directions. First, we would focus on those things within the school that might really affect student outcomes. Second, we would pay more attention to schools' relationships with some of the critical contextual factors that shaped students' lives. Reform programs that helped schools improve their internal capacities for teaching and learning, and also helped them improve the community context in which they operated, would appear on present evidence to have the best chance of making a lasting impact. A formulation developed for the Annenberg Challenge program in urban communities in the United States includes five elements – school leadership, professional community, high-quality instruction, student-centered learning, and strong parent and community involvement (Smylie and Bryk, 2000).

While there is no magic formula or recipe for improving learner outcomes, there is good reason to think that there are some important things that could be done within schools. They could include improving teaching skills, providing better supports to learners, and strengthening connections with parents and communities. A focus on early success for students, so that they do not fall too far behind at the outset, has been another element of growing importance in some reform programs.

At the same time, changes in the social context mean that schools cannot simply take shelter in their curricular and instructional tasks. Readiness for school and hence initial success is deeply affected by children's family conditions, so schools will have to be more engaged with family education, with early childhood programs, with education of and support for young parents. Some schools are doing very exciting things in regard to assisting the overall economic and social development of their communities (Driscoll and Kerchner, 1999; Hunter, 2000).

Attention to effective use

Given the size and importance of the reforms discussed in this book, it is striking how little attention was given to issues of implementation and adaptation. Governments simply did not invest much time or energy in the work needed to move their policies into practice effectively.

In part the difficulty is technical, in the sense that governments did not pay attention to what is known about supporting implementation. The most common implementation vehicles for these reforms involved compulsion. Yet we know that effective support for implementation involves both pressure and support, using a range of policy levers. Even a brief consideration of the research evidence would have shown anyone interested in knowing that complex reforms cannot be successful without investments in building understanding and skills. The range of policy levers described in Chapter 6 provide a starting point for thinking about the various ways in which ambitious reforms can be supported. Mandates alone are not enough. Inducements, opinion mobilization and especially capacity-building are critical elements in ensuring that reforms take root and that they make a difference. The appropriate allocation and use of resources is a particularly neglected feature in many cases. More money may not always be necessary, but the shifting of time, attention and funds to new areas of endeavor is an essential requirement for any lasting change.

At the same time, any reform program conceived entirely as a top-down imposition on an unwilling system is inevitably going to run into difficulties and fall short of expectations. Whatever governments might think about educators, their assistance is essential to at least some degree in any significant program of change. This means that the goals of reform cannot be achieved unless reasonable allowance is made for adaptation as change proceeds. Given the complexity of education systems and practices, it is impossible to anticipate all the ramifications of a significant policy measure. People need to be encouraged to adapt policy to their own local circumstances and to take account of unanticipated elements.

These facts do raise political problems for some governments. If reform is rooted in strong critique of the existing system, it is hard to accept that the support of that system must be necessary for change. Governments have difficulty with the long time horizons implied by a strategy of systemic change based on capacity-building; the "goods" cannot be delivered in twelve or eighteen months. This is a fundamental political dilemma that may eventually lead to some changes in political rhetoric. Although it is common wisdom that voters are swayed by short-term commitments, one might wonder whether in fact people believe that large systems can actually be changed quickly. In some policy areas, such as taxation or debt reduction, political parties are talking increasingly in terms of longer-term commitments, even extending beyond a full electoral mandate. Perhaps we may eventually see the same kind of discussion about education, so that the public debate can be a more realistic one.

Reform as a learning experience

The reality is that we do not know how to solve the educational and social problems we face. Success is not a matter of simply implementing someone's nostrum. The problems are deep-seated and multi-faceted. In such a situation the only way forward is to focus on experimenting and learning. Education reform needs to take the best evidence we have, to try a variety of strategies that seem to have some empirical or conceptual support, to assess their results, and to make changes accordingly. Given complex systems, limited understanding and multiple intervening factors, it is vital to pursue reform with a strong set of commitments but a relatively open mind as to how they can best be fulfilled. All parties – politicians, civil servants, lobbyists, educators, parents, students and researchers – can both contribute to and benefit from a process that focuses on informed discussion about education, irrespective of one's starting position and values.

> For leaders to claim they are educative means they must be able to develop and maintain a climate that promotes inquiry, values problem solving, welcomes criticism, and encourages participation and learning about organizations. Openness to criticism and an ability to learn from mistakes becomes the basis for more valuable leadership action and cycles of reflection and decision-making.
>
> (Macpherson, 1996, p. 103)

Could this be done in political environments that are highly partisan? Clearly it will not be easy. Yet efforts are being made in this direction in a number of policy fields, with health care a particularly good example. Moreover, the partisan process can potentially contribute to learning, as it forces re-examination of the conventional wisdom and pushes people to consider very different points of view (Lindblom, 1990). A learning strategy does not require the elimination of partisan positions, but the use of these approaches, among others, as part of the way in which a society looks at what it has done and considers what it might do next.

The role of research and evidence

Much of the debate about reform generates more heat than light. Claims are often made with little or no supporting evidence. Of course, a brand new practice can never be justified on the basis of evidence, since it has not been tried before. However, it does seem desirable to have more cautious claims coupled with more efforts to ascertain outcomes.

It is interesting to compare the place of research in education policy with its role in health policy. Both areas are politically important and both generate a great deal of controversy. Yet in health care nobody would seriously advocate an important policy change without giving at least some attention to the available evidence. Health policy research has grown rapidly in many countries. The idea of evidence-based decision-making is now very popular in health policy circles. Compare this with education, a field in which there is very little policy research, while both policy-makers and practitioners are often disdainful of research and dismiss it as having little potential value.

Yet evidence can play a powerful role in education. The evidence about reforms efforts, for example, could help everyone involved in education focus on those things that really do make a difference for students. In individual schools, evidence can also change beliefs as to what needs to be done (Levin, 2000).

Evidence both contributes to and derives from clarity about purposes and intended outcomes. The more specific we can be about the intentions behind reforms, the more likely it is that good evidence can help us see how to move forward – and where to retreat. An investment in research would seem to be a useful part of any reform strategy, yet is largely absent from most.

Suggestions for Research

The conceptual framework

Much of the literature on education reform does not work from an explicit framework. This absence creates a danger that the researcher will conflate what ought to be considered separately: that, for example, the statements of advocates (or, for that matter, opponents) will be taken as an accurate description of the true purposes or even the actual results of a reform.

This book conceptualized reform as having four phases that, while conceptually distinct, were in practice overlapping and interactive. These phases were origins, adoption, implementation and outcomes. This way of framing the issues is quite useful. It provides a way of distinguishing between elements that have different dynamics while not losing sight of the degree to which various aspects of reform loop back on each other. At the same time, it is important to remember that the phases are an analytic device. The phases not only overlap, but there is considerable feedback from implementation and outcomes back to intentions, so that intentions can change in the face of events.

The point is not to advocate one framework over another, but to emphasize the importance of having an articulated frame as the basis for any analysis. Other models with merit have been mentioned earlier in the book. Each will have its own emphases and omissions, just as any map points out some features and ignores others. The frame used in this book, while borrowing in some ways from a technical approach to reform, actually gives considerable emphasis to the political and the contingent. In reality the process is never as linear or clear-cut as a stage framework implies, and the categories used should not be taken as suggesting that reform should or does proceed in a planned and orderly way.

A key consideration to keep in mind is the enormous complexity of change in large education systems, and the concomitant inability to predict, let alone plan, the precise trajectory of any proposal. The complication of complexity and chance – Dror's "high probability of low probability events" (1986, p. 168) – makes it dangerous to assume clear lines between one thing and another. Whatever the origins of a reform program, for example, its working out in practice will have a life of its own, dependent on a set of institutional, personal and other contextual factors that are generally far too complicated to be built into planning. At every stage, new contextual elements will emerge to affect the way the process unfolds, and this unfolding will itself have compounding implications for later stages. For example, lack of attention to implementation in initial phases of a reform can lead to growing cynicism about the whole program that might result in less effective implementation in later stages, even when additional resources have been provided. Even more unpredictably, the attitude or behavior of a small number of people can change the way a given reform develops. Researchers have to be open to this ambiguity and unpredictability.

Comparative analysis

Looking at reforms across jurisdictions can be an important exercise. On the one hand, it draws our attention to important trends and similarities in policy approaches. It is important to be aware that all the jurisdictions in this study took up issues of increased assessment, school choice or parental involvement. It is worth noting that reform advocates tended to advance quite similar rationales for their proposals in the various settings. The existence of commonalities in rhetoric and in policy across countries with quite different circumstances does suggest important international trends. It draws our attention to the factors that support such trends, including international institutions, international media, international political links, as well as a general move to more travel and exchange of ideas.

At the same time, comparative work makes us aware of the degree to which things unfold differently in each setting whatever the commonalities in rhetoric or general approach. Looking across jurisdictions in a more detailed way is a reminder that culture, history and institutional arrangements differ substantially, and that these differences have powerful consequences for what happens. Ideas that look similar on the surface end up looking very different when filtered through the beliefs, practices and political systems of any given jurisdiction.

The question is not whether education reform is an international phenomenon or not. In some ways clearly it is, and in other ways clearly it is not. Looking internationally allows us to think in more sophisticated ways about each individual setting as well as the broader sweep of events.

Comparative work carries some important caveats, as well. This study looks only at five industrialized, English-speaking jurisdictions. This is hardly a world sample. Indeed, it may give a false picture of international trends just because it is so focused on countries that share many characteristics. While English-speaking countries have been focusing on ideas of choice or assessment, continental European countries and Asian countries have been moving in some quite different directions. Moreover, even in Canada and the United States there have been great variations in reform patterns across provinces and states. Generalizations about international trends should be made with great caution, and are likely to be wrong more than they are right.

Original evidence

Because education reform is so highly charged politically and raises such strong feelings, it is important for researchers to try to look at original material and empirical evidence. Many claims are made for and against reforms. The claims may misrepresent the positions and views of those they criticize, and they may certainly misrepresent the actual effects of any reform.

It is not easy to assess either intentions or outcomes, as earlier discussion has shown. But a careful look at what people actually said, what they actually did, and what the real changes on the ground have been is always a salutary exercise and usually one that softens conclusions. High standards for the use of evidence would help produce more valuable research.

Contribution to public debate

A point made several times in this book is that the public debate about education reform is often polarized and is more like a yelling match than a debate. Political realities are an important factor in this situation, of course. Making a loud noise may get more attention than having an informed view. Surely one of the responsibilities of researchers, though, is to try to contribute this informed view.

In many cases researchers have discharged this responsibility well. Many of the studies cited in this book were also offered as contributions to public debate through interviews with the media, articles in mass circulation publications, and dissemination in other ways to educators, parents and others. Such contributions can help make the public discussion more thoughtful, less acrimonious and better informed. The kinds of vehicles for influencing public debate that were discussed in Chapter 5 provide new opportunities for researchers to take an active role, not necessarily in promoting a particular policy (though each of us has a right to do this as well) but in trying to bring evidence and thoughtfulness into a vital public policy arena. Although research has not been an important influence on education policy in many cases, there are indications that this situation is changing. As people are better educated they are increasingly interested in evidence. Efforts to improve the quality and impact of education research are under way in a number of countries. In other policy areas, such as the environment, agriculture, labor markets and social welfare, the contributions of research are increasing in quality and impact. The efforts of researchers will certainly not in themselves reshape political debate, but they can be part of the wider effort to do so, and there are grounds for feeling optimistic about what might be possible in this regard.

Conclusion

Education reform will remain on the political agenda for the foreseeable future. Public interest in education remains high, fed partly by continuing discussion of the importance of lifelong learning and the essential role of education in economic welfare. Governments will continue to be concerned with improving education, and will continue to put forward a variety of ideas for doing so. Some of these ideas may be well justified and others not. In a world in which ideas do move across borders and in which large-scale reform can unfold with startling rapidity and unknown consequences, there will be a continuing need to study the policy process carefully and thoroughly. I hope that this book will help with that agenda.

Appendix 1

Guide to the Literature

Documents

Although the secondary literature has been invaluable in putting together this study, there is no substitute for looking at the original documents, especially in cases when the debate around reforms is so highly charged. Several main kinds of documents were used in this study. Only the most important are cited in the reference list.

1   Parliamentary debates. I reviewed *Hansard* in the four parliamentary jurisdictions for the critical periods of reform. In England this meant primarily the debate on the Education Reform Act in 1987 and 1988. In New Zealand *Hansard* was reviewed not only for the Labour reforms in 1988, but for the main National reforms in 1991 and after. (The only print copy of the New Zealand *Hansard* in North America is in Washington DC; my excellent research assistant James Aryee was able to locate it through a web-based information provider who allowed us to download the relevant portions for a very reasonable fee.) In Manitoba the review covered the period from early 1994 through 1996, and in Alberta it involved the debate and passage of the reforms in early 1994. The value of *Hansard* is in giving a first-hand impression of the issues that legislators felt it important to raise publicly.

   Unfortunately there is no printed public record of debate in the Minnesota legislature. The records are only on tape, and require the researcher to specify the dates requested and then listen to the tapes. This was simply too unwieldy an activity for the scope of this project.

2   Government documents. Each of the governments involved put out a number of documents around their reforms. Finding these documents is not necessarily easy, though it has been made much easier recently by the World Wide Web, where increasingly both parliamentary debates and many government documents can be found.

   In Britain, important examples were the white papers put out by the Conservatives in 1987 prior to the ERA, and the paper on *Choice and Diversity* in 1993. A number of other policy circulars and official reports shed light on the kinds of rationales for reform that the government wanted to put in the public view. Organizations such as Ofsted and the various incarnations of the curriculum and testing agency also produced a variety of reports that were of interest. In New Zealand, key documents were *Administering for Excellence* (the Picot Report); *Tomorrow's Schools* (the government's response to Picot); the Treasury briefs to the incoming government in 1984, 1987 and 1990; and *Today's Schools: a review of the education reform implementation* (the Lough Committee Report) issued in 1990. Several reports issued by the ERO were also consulted. In Manitoba, there were two key *New Directions* documents issued in 1994 – one outlining the overall plan and the second called *The Action Plan*. These were followed by a large number of other documents covering various elements of *New Directions*. In Alberta, three-year business plans were produced by the Department of Education under the broad headings of *Achieving the Vision* and *Meeting the Challenge*. There were also several documents prepared for or resulting from the various consultation activities in 1993 and 1994. In Minnesota, several relevant documents were issued by the State Department of Education, such as the Minnesota Educational Effectiveness Plan.

3   Non-government documents. Many groups and organizations other than government produced documents of various kinds on the reforms. These are even harder to locate since one does not know very well what might be there to be found.

Documents consulted included those put out by some of the main interest groups. Examples include newsletters, reports and position papers by teacher unions in New Zealand, Canada and Minnesota; local authority associations in Britain; business groups in Minnesota and New Zealand; parent groups in Britain; and a variety of others.

A very limited effort was made to look at media coverage of the reforms, particularly in Alberta, Manitoba and Minnesota, where other sources were least available. A full treatment of media coverage would itself warrant a book.

Secondary Literature

Of the five jurisdictions studied here, England has produced the largest amount of academic work, probably because it has the largest population and hence the greatest number of academics. (It may also ironically be the case that market pressures to do more research in universities, introduced by the Conservatives, led to more work on the impact of education reform.) Considering its small population, New Zealand has produced a substantial amount of academic research on education reform, including several recent books looking back at the reforms after a decade. The literature on Minnesota is limited but of good quality. There is very little published work on reform in Alberta or Manitoba. A fairly extensive comparative literature looks at reform across more than one of these settings.

England

Thatcherite education policy in England and Wales attracted substantial academic interest from the outset. Work that looks at the Conservative period in a longer-term perspective includes Dale (1989), Jones (1989), Knight (1990) and Lawton (1992, 1994). Bottery (1996, 1998) has looked at education reform in comparison with other public sectors such as health care.

In regard to specific policies, initially much of the work was speculative, but over time a strong body of empirical evidence has been accumulated on the impacts and outcomes of various reforms. Studies exist of most of the major Conservative education efforts, including the Assisted Places Scheme (Edwards *et al.*, 1989), the City Technology College initiative (Whitty *et al.*, 1993), the development of grant-maintained schools (Fitz *et al.*, 1993), local management of schools (Levačić, 1995; Thomas and Martin, 1996), the role of school governors (Deem *et al.*, 1995), the role of parents (Vincent, 1996) and the development of inspection (Wilcox and Gray, 1996). The development of open enrolment and parent choice has been a particularly strong focus of research (e.g. Gewirtz *et al.*, 1995; Walford, 1994; Woods *et al.*, 1998). A group of researchers including John Fitz, Sharon Gewirtz, David Halpin, Sally Power and Geoff Whitty have been involved in a number of these studies and among them have written extensively and perceptively on many aspects of British education policy. Stephen Ball and colleagues have produced several important books and many articles on various aspects of the reforms with an emphasis on the ERA and school choice. In addition to books, the British literature also includes a large number of journal articles by quite a large number of researchers.

In addition to academic work, there are some accounts by the actors themselves. Ribbins and Sherratt (1997) have published a collection of interviews with all the Conservative Secretaries of State for Education that gives some insight into their motives and actions. A number of key Conservatives, including Margaret Thatcher and Kenneth Baker, have published autobiographies that have something to say about education policy.

New Zealand

As in Britain, the New Zealand reforms have been the subject of intensive academic interest, although the size of the academic community and therefore its output is much smaller than in Britain. New Zealand materials are also often harder to get in North America or Europe. The wider context for the New Zealand public sector reforms is very important and is described in several works of quite varying political stripes, such as Boston *et al.* (1996), Jesson (1989) and Kelsey (1997). In the last few years, several volumes have reviewed the reforms in education in some detail. A quasi-official history, by Butterworth and Butterworth (1998), provides a great deal of detail about the origins and implementation process, albeit from a point of view that generally supports the reforms. Smelt (1998), a staff member of the Treasury during the reforms, has also produced a brief account. Edited volumes by Olssen and Matthews (1997) and Thrupp (1999) provide a more critical analysis.

Three sets of studies reported on the reforms as they proceeded. Work by David Mitchell and colleagues was reported under the general heading of *Monitoring Tomorrow's Schools* (1993), and looked at a variety of aspects of implementation in the first year or so of the reforms. Hugh Lauder and colleagues (Lauder *et al.*, 1999) conducted what became known as the Smithfield Studies, looking at the impact of school choice on the social composition of schools. The New Zealand Council for Educational Research also produced a series of studies of the impact of the reforms on schools which included surveys of school principals, teachers, parents and members of school boards. The last two of these reports (Wylie, 1997 and 1999) are cited in the references, but there are a number of other publications by Wylie that are also relevant.

There are fewer volumes of memoirs than in Britain. Those of McQueen (1991), an advisor to David Lange, show the relatively small role education played in the overall agenda of the Labour government. Richardson (1995) provides a perspective from the National Party side.

Canada

An overview of the structure and politics of Canadian education can be found in Young and Levin (1998). Barlow and Robertson (1994) provide a strong critique of recent education policies across the country. Taylor (1996) provides extensive documentation of the reform process in Alberta. There are very few published sources on the specific reforms in Alberta or Manitoba, although a new edited book (Harrison and Kachur, 1999) does look at a number of aspects of the reforms in education.

Minnesota

The published literature on Minnesota is not extensive, but is fortunately of high quality. Tim Mazzoni tracked reform in Minnesota over more than twenty years and has written a number of insightful accounts (1991, 1993, 1994). A book by Roberts and King (1996) provides a very detailed discussion of the 1985–7 Perpich reforms as a case study of changing public policy. Joe Nathan, an advocate of both choice and charter schools, has described the politics around these developments in Minnesota in his account (1996).

Comparative work

Comparative work on education reform began to emerge with some regularity in the 1980s.

Edited volumes tend to be of uneven quality but usually do have some useful elements. Some of these include Beare and Boyd (1993), Carter and O'Neil (1995), Lingard *et al.* (1993) and Taylor *et al.* (1997). Glatter *et al.* (1997) is primarily English but does include some comparative work on school choice. Whitty (1997) and Whitty *et al.* (1998) focus primarily on England, Australia and some aspects of the United States. Dale and Ozga (1993) compare developments in England and New Zealand, while Davies and Guppy (1997) and Fowler (1994) look at several countries. Reports by the OECD (e.g. Hirsh, 1994) are also a source of useful comparative data and analysis with the advantage of including countries that are not English-speaking.

Appendix 2

Chronologies of Reform

England and Wales

1979   Election of the Conservatives under Margaret Thatcher.

1979   The Conservatives repeal Labour legislation requiring comprehensive secondary schools.

1980   Education Act; the Assisted Places Scheme (APS) subsidizes students to attend independent schools. More parents are added to school governing bodies. LEAs and governors are required to provide more information about the school for parents. Restrictions are placed on the ability of the LEA right to refuse places to those outside the school catchment area.

1980   The Employment Act makes strikes and secondary picketing more difficult for teachers and other workers.

1985   White Paper *Better Schools* published.

1986   Education (No. 2) Act. Additional powers are given to school governors over their schools' finances. Every school is now required to have a governing body with more parents; governors have to present annual reports to parents and hold meetings to discuss the reports.

1986   City Technology Colleges instituted.

1987   Teachers' Pay and Conditions Act effectively ends collective bargaining over teachers' pay and working conditions.

1988   Education Reform Act. Main provisions of the Act include open enrolment, local management of schools, and grant-maintained schools as well as creation of a National Curriculum and national assessment. The Act also abolishes the Inner London Education Authority.

1992   Education (Schools) Act, creates the Office for Standards in Education (Ofsted) and introduces a system of compulsory privatized inspection of all schools with public reporting of results.

1993   White Paper *Choice and Diversity*.

1993   Education Act eases provisions for schools to become grant-maintained and increased schools' scope to select students based on academic ability.

1993   Education Bill (Teacher Education) moves funding for teacher education from the Higher Education Funding Council to a Teacher Training Agency (TTA) directly appointed by the Education Secretary. Schools are required to play a much greater role in teacher education and concomitantly reduce the role of universities.

1997   Conservatives defeated by Labour in general election.

New Zealand

1984   Third Labour government elected with David Lange as prime minister; massive campaign of privatization begins.

1986   Royal Commission on Social Policy established.

1987, July	Taskforce to Review Education Administration (Picot Taskforce) appointed to investigate the education sector excluding the universities.
1987, August	Labour government returned to office. Prime Minister Lange also takes on the Education portfolio.
1987, November	*Government Management: Brief to the Incoming Government* published by the Treasury and lays out rationale for moving to a public agency approach to provision of social services.
1988, May	The Picot Report, *Administering for Excellence: Effective Administration in Education*, is released.
1988, August	Government response to Picot Report, entitled *Tomorrow's Schools*, is released.
1988, December	State Sector Amendment (No. 2) Act and Education Amendment Act, embodying the *Tomorrow's Schools* recommendations, are enacted.
1988, 1989	State Sector Act (1988) and Public Finance Act (1989) reduce the role of unions and put contract theory into legislation as a main vehicle for social services.
1989, May	First elections for boards of trustees for schools.
1989, August	David Lange resigns as prime minister. Phil Goff appointed minister of education.
1989, October	Education Act comes into force implementing most of *Tomorrow's Schools*,
1990, April	Lough Report (*Today's Schools*) issued.
1990, July	Education Amendment Act establishes further elements of reform.
1990, October	Labour government defeated; National government elected.
1991	Education Amendment Act 1991 passed, modifying some major provisions of the Labour legislation
1991	Employment Contracts Act largely eliminates the role of labor unions.

Minnesota

1985	DFL Governor Rudy Perpich introduces the *Access to Excellence* school reform plan. Learner outcomes, state tests and open enrollment across district boundaries are among his proposals.
1985	The Legislature enacts "post-secondary options;" Minnesota becomes the first state to permit high school juniors and seniors to take courses at local colleges for both high school and future higher education credit.
1986	State Board of Education includes Outcome-Based Education (OBE) demonstration sites among its strategic goals and also adopts the Education Department's proposal for a new student assessment system oriented to learner outcomes.
1985–7	The Governor's Discussion Group (created after the 1985 legislative session) includes open enrolment and a core curriculum with measurable outcomes in its dozen recommendations.
1987	Legislature approves open enrolment to be phased in over several years.
1988	Open enrollment made mandatory for all school districts, but two years are allowed for full implementation.
1988	Legislature creates Task Force on Education Organization; learner outcomes and assessment among areas to be studied. State Board of Education scraps traditional graduation standards approach (which it has been working on since 1987) to develop a new outcome-based rule.
1990–91	All school districts in Minnesota required to be open for interdistrict student transfers, i.e. open enrollment.
1990	Republican Arne Carlson elected governor.
1991	The Legislature passes legislation authorizing a small number of charter schools (first state to pass such legislation). The Legislature also indicates support for OBE; the term is defined in law.
1992	City Academy, the nation's first outcome-based charter school, opens in St Paul.
1993	Minnesota Legislature expands the number of available statewide charters from eight to twenty. Governor Carlson had urged authorization of an unrestricted number.

1994   Minnesota Legislature increases the number of charter schools allowed to thirty-five.

Alberta

1993   The government amalgamates thirty-five non-operating school districts (districts that do not have any schools) with adjacent, operating districts which, in most cases, were already providing educational services to the students from the non-operating boards.

1993, December   Ralph Klein, as new leader of the Alberta Conservative Party, wins re-election for his Conservative government.

1994, 17 January   Premier Klein announces a four-year reduction target for education of 12.4 per cent, the lowest of the major spending departments.

1994, 18 January   Education Minister Halvar Jonson announces plans for a major restructuring of the education system. The plan involves reducing the number of school districts, limiting the power of districts, and moving control over money to the provincial government.

1994, 24 February   A three-year education business plan, *Key Directions for Education in Alberta*, is released by the government confirming the January announcement. The plan also increases choice for parents in selecting schools and announces the piloting of charter schools.

1995, September   The first three charter schools open in Alberta.

Manitoba

1990, September   Conservative government of Gary Filmon is re-elected with a very narrow majority.

1993–7   Provincial funding for education is reduced or frozen for five years. Teachers are required to take days off without pay. Professional development time is reduced.

1993, Fall   Clayton Manness moves from finance minister to minister of education.

1994, July   *Renewing Education: New Directions – A Blueprint for Action* released, outlining a six-element program of education reform.

1994, November   Final report of the commission to review school district boundaries is released, but never implemented.

1995, January   *Renewing Education: New Directions – The Action Plan* released, outlining the reforms in more details. This document is followed by a considerable number of further publications over several years detailing various aspects of the plan.

1995, April   The Conservative government is re-elected with majority. Clayton Manness does not run; Linda McIntosh is appointed minister of education.

1996, Fall   Several pieces of legislation passed that increase substantially the powers of the minister, limit teacher rights in collective bargaining, provide for parent choice of schools, require schools to have public annual plans.

1999, September   The Conservative government is defeated by the New Democratic Party.

Formal interviews

Stephen Ball (British academic) – October 1998
John Bangs (British teacher union official) – April 1999
Reno Bosetti (Alberta Deputy Minister) – May 2000
Graham and Susan Butterworth (New Zealand historians) – February 2000
John Carlyle (Manitoba Deputy Minister) and Carolyn Loeppky (Assistant Deputy Minister)
     September 1997 and September 1998
David King (Alberta Public School Boards Association, former Education Minister) –
     October 1998
David Lange (New Zealand Prime Minister) – February 2000
Clayton Manness (Manitoba Education Minister) – September 1998
David Mitchell (New Zealand academic) – February 2000
Joe Nathan (Minnesota lobbyist) – October 1999
Frank Peters (Alberta academic) – October 1998
Peter Ramsay (member of Picot Taskforce, New Zealand) – February 2000
Marijke Robinson (New Zealand State Services Commission official) – February 2000
Martin Thrupp (New Zealand academic) – April 1999
Darrell Ward (New Zealand Educational Institute) – April 1999 and February 2000
Margaret Wilson (New Zealand Labour Party official) – February 2000

I also discussed the ideas and issues in this book with many other people in all the jurisdictions.

References

Alberta (1994) *Meeting the Challenge*. Edmonton, Alberta: Department of Education.

Aldrich, R. (1995) "Educational reform and curriculum implementation in England: an historical perspective," in D. Carter and M. O'Neil (eds) *International Perspectives on Educational Reform and Policy Implementation* (pp. 125–39). London: Falmer Press.

Allison, G. (1971) *Essence of Decision: explaining the Cuban missile crisis*. Boston: Little, Brown.

Apple, M. (1990) *Ideology and Curriculum*, 2nd edn. New York: Routledge.

——(1996) *Cultural Politics and Education*. New York: Teachers' College Press.

Argyris, C. and Schon, D. (1978) *Organization Learning: a theory of action perspective*. Reading, MA: Addison Wesley.

Aspin, D. and Chapman, J. (1994) *Quality Schooling*. London: Cassell.

Baker, K. (1993) *The Turbulent Years: my life in politics*. London: Faber.

Ball, S. (1990) *Politics and Policy Making in Education*. London: Routledge.

——(1997) "Policy sociology and critical social research: a personal review of recent education policy and policy research," *British Educational Research Journal* 23(3), 257–74.

——(1998) "Big policies/small world: an introduction to international perspectives in education policy," *Comparative Education* 34(2), 119–29.

Ball, S. and Vincent, C. (1998) "I heard in on the grapevine: 'hot' knowledge and school choice," *British Journal of Sociology of Education* 19(3), 377–400.

Barber, M. and Dann, R. (eds) (1996) *Raising Educational Standards in the Inner Cities*. London: Cassell.

Barlow, M. and Robertson, H-j. (1994) *Class Warfare*. Toronto: Key Porter.

Beare, H. and Boyd, W. (eds) (1993) *Restructuring Schools*. London: Falmer Press.

Bell, L., Halpin, D. and Neill, S. (1996) "Managing self-governing primary schools in the locally maintained, grant-maintained and private sectors,' *Educational Management and Administration* 24(3), 253–61.

Beniger, J. (1986) *The Control Revolution*. Cambridge, MA: Harvard University Press.

Berger, P. (1976) *Pyramids of Sacrifice*. New York: Doubleday Anchor.

Berliner, D. and Biddle, B. (1995) *The Manufactured Crisis: myth, fraud, and the attack on America's public schools*. New York: Addison Wesley.

Beyle, T. (1993) "Being governor," in C.E. van Horn (ed.) *The State of the States*, 2nd edn. Washington: CQ Press.

Billig, M., Condor, S., Edwards, D., Gane, M., Middleton, D. and Radley, A. (1990) *Ideological Dilemmas*. London: Sage.

Bishop, J. (1994) "Impact of curriculum-based examinations on learning in Canadian secondary schools." Working Paper 94–30, Center for Advanced Human Resource Studies, Cornell University.

Black, P. (1994) "Performance assessment and accountability: the experience in England and Wales," *Educational Evaluation and Policy Analysis* 16(2), 191–205.

Borman, K., Castenell, L. and Gallagher, K. (1993) "Business involvement in school reform: the rise of the Business Roundtable," in C. Marshall (ed.) *The New Politics of Race and Gender* (pp. 69–83). London: Falmer Press.

Boston, J, Martin, J., Pallot, J. and Walsh, P. (1996) *Public Management: the New Zealand model*. Auckland: Oxford University Press.

Bottery, M. (1996) "The challenge to professionals from the New Public Management: implications for the teaching profession," *Oxford Review of Education* 22(2), 179–97.

——(1998) *Professionals and Policy: management strategy in a competitive world*. London: Cassell.

Bovens, M. and t'Hart, P. (1994) *Understanding Policy Fiascoes*. New Brunswick, NJ: Transaction.

Bowe, R., Ball, S. and Gold, A. (1992) *Reforming Education and Changing Schools*. London: Routledge.

Boyd, W.L. (1999) "Paradoxes of educational policy and productivity," *Educational Policy* 13(2), 227–50.

Boyd, W.L., Lugg, C. and Zahorchak, G. (1996) "Social traditionalists, religious conservatives, and the politics of outcome-based education: Pennsylvania and beyond," *Education and Urban Society* 28(3), 347–65.

Brown, D. (1990) *Decentralization and School-based Management*. London: Falmer Press.

Busher, H. and Saran, R. (1995) *Teachers' Conditions of Employment*. London: Kogan Page.

Butterworth, G. and Butterworth, S. (1998). *Reforming Education: the New Zealand experience 1984–1996*. Palmerston: Dunmore Press.

Carroll, S. and Walford, G. (1997) "The child's voice in school choice," *Educational Management and Administration* 25(2), 169–80.

Carter, D. and O'Neil, M. (eds) (1995) *International Perspectives on Educational Reform and Policy Implementation*. London: Falmer Press.

Chubb, J. and Moe, T. (1992) *A Lesson in School Reform from Great Britain*. Washington: Brookings Institute.

Cibulka, J. (1991) "Educational accountability reforms: performance information and political power," in S. Fuhrman and B. Malen (eds) *The Politics of Curriculum and Testing* (pp. 181–201). London: Falmer Press.

——(1995) "The evolution of education reform in the United States: policy ideals or *Realpolitik?*" in D. Carter and M. O'Neil (eds) *International Perspectives on Educational Reform and Policy Implementation* (pp. 15–30). London: Falmer Press.

Citizens' Commission on Civil Rights (1997) *Difficult Choices: do magnet schools service children in need?* Washington: The Commission.

Cody, C., Woodward, A. and Elliott, D. (1993) "Race, ideology and the battle over curriculum," in C. Marshall (ed.) *The New Politics of Race and Gender* (pp. 48–57). London: Falmer Press.

Cohen, D. (1992) "Policy and practice: the relations between governance and instruction," *Review of Research in Education* 18, 3–49.

——(1995) "What is the system in systemic reform?" *Educational Researcher* 24(9), 11–17, 31.

Cohen, M., March, J. and Olson, J. (1972) "A garbage can model of organizational choice," *Administrative Science Quarterly* 17(1), 1–25.

Cox, T. (ed.) (2000) *Combating Educational Disadvantage*. London: Falmer Press.

Crowson, R., Boyd, W. and Mawhinney, H. (eds) (1996) *The Politics of Education and the New Institutionalism: reinventing the American school*. Washington: Falmer Press.

Cuttance, P. (1994) "Quality assurance in education systems," *Studies in Educational Evaluation* 20, 99–112.

Dale, R. (1989) *The State and Education Policy*. Milton Keynes: Open University Press.

Dale, R., and Jesson, J. (1992) "Mainstreaming education: the role of the State Services Commission," *New Zealand Annual Review of Education* 2, 7–34.

Dale, R. and Ozga, J. (1993) "Two hemispheres – both new right? 1980s education reform in New Zealand and England and Wales," in B. Lingard, J. Knight and P. Porter (eds) *Schooling Reform in Hard Times* (pp. 63–87). London: Falmer Press.

Davies, S. (1999) "From moral duty to cultural rights: a case study of political framing in education," *Sociology of Education* 72(1), 1–21.

Davies, S. and Guppy, N. (1997) "Globalization and educational reforms in Anglo-American democracies," *Comparative Education Review* 41(4), 435–59.

Deem, R., Brehony, K. and Heath, S. (1995) *Active Citizenship and the Governing of Schools*. Buckingham: Open University Press.

Dehli, K. (1996) "Travelling tales: education reform and parental 'choice' in postmodern times," *Journal of Education Policy* 11(1), 75–98.

DfE (1992) *Choice and Diversity: a new framework for schools*. London: HMSO.

Diamond, J. (1997) *Guns, Germs and Steel*. New York: W.W. Norton.

Donald, J. and Hall, S. (1986) *Politics and Ideology*. Milton Keynes: Open University Press.

Douglas, M. (1986) *How Institutions Think*. Syracuse, NY: Syracuse University Press.

Driscoll, M. and Kerchner, C. (1999) "The implications of social capital for schools, communities, and cities: educational administration as if a sense of place mattered," in J. Murphy and K.S. Louis (eds) *Handbook of Research on Educational Administration*, 2nd edn (pp. 385–404). San Francisco: Jossey-Bass.

Dror, Y. (1986) *Policymaking under Adversity*. New York: Transaction Books.

Edelman, M. (1964) *The Symbolic Uses of Politics*. Urbana: University of Illinois Press.

——(1988) *Constructing the Political Spectacle*. Chicago: University of Chicago Press.

Edwards, T. and Whitty, G. (1995) "Marketing quality: traditional and modern versions of educational excellence." Paper presented to the American Educational Research Association, San Francisco, April.

Edwards, T., Fitz, J. and Whitty, G. (1989) *The State and Private Education*. London: Falmer Press.

Elmore, R. (1987) "Reforming the finance and structure of US education in response to technological change," in G. Burke and R. Rumberger (eds) *The Future Impact of Technology on Work and Education* (pp. 158–75). London: Falmer Press.

——(1995) "Structural reform in educational practice," *Educational Researcher* 24(9), 23–6.

Epstein, J. (1995) "School/family/community partnerships: caring for the children we share," *Phi Delta Kappan* 76(9), 701–12.

Fidler, B., Earley, P., Ouston, J. and Davies, J. (1998) "Teacher gradings and Ofsted inspections." *School Leadership and Management* 18(2), 257–70.

Finegold, D., McFarland, L. and Richardson, W. (eds) (1993) *Something Borrowed, Something Learned? The transatlantic market in education and training reform*. Washington: Brookings Institute.

Fitz, J. and Halpin, D. (1991) "From a 'sketchy policy' to a 'workable scheme': the DES and grant-maintained schools," *International Studies in Sociology of Education* 1, 129–51.

——(1994) "Ministers and mandarins: educational research in elite settings," in G. Walford (ed.) *Researching the Powerful in Education* (pp. 32–50). London: UCL Press.

Fitz, J., Halpin, D. and Power, S. (1993) *Grant-maintained Schools: education in the market place*. London: Kogan Page.

Fowler, F. (1994) "The international arena: the global village," in J Scribner and D. Layton (eds) *The Study of Educational Politics* (pp. 89–102). London: Falmer Press.

Fullan, M. (1991) *The New Meaning of Educational Change*. New York: Teachers College Press/OISE Press.

——(1995) "The school as a learning organisation: distant dreams," *Theory into Practice* 34(4), 230–35.

Fuller, B., Elmore, R. and Orfield, G. (eds) (1996) *Who Chooses, Who Loses?* New York: Teachers' College Press.

Gewirtz, S., Ball, S. and Bowe, R. (1995) *Markets, Choice and Equity in Education*. Buckingham: Open University Press.

Giddens, A. (1994) *Beyond Left and Right*. Cambridge: Polity Press.

Ginsberg, R. and Plank, D. (eds) (1995) *Commissions, Reports, Reforms and Educational Policy*. Westport, CT: Praeger.

Gipps, C. (1995) "National Curriculum assessment in England and Wales," in D. Carter and M. O'Neil (eds) *International Perspectives on Educational Reform and Policy Implementation* (pp. 140–57). London: Falmer Press.

Glatter, R., Woods, P. and Bagley, C. (eds) (1997) *Choice and Diversity in Schooling: perspectives and prospects*. London: Routledge.

Goldring, E. (1997) "Parental involvement and school choice," in R. Glatter, P. Woods and C. Bagley (eds) *Choice and Diversity in Schooling* (pp. 86–101). London: Routledge.

Good, T. (1997) "Educational researchers comment on the Education Summit and other policy proclamations," *Educational Researcher* 25(8), 4–6.

Gorard, S. and Fitz, J. (1998) "The more things change … the missing impact of marketisation," *British Journal of Sociology of Education* 19(3), 365–76.

Gordon, L. (1999) "From nation-building to profit making: the past, present and future of schooling in New Zealand," in M. Thrupp (ed.) *A Decade of Reform in New Zealand Education: where to now?* Special Issue of *New Zealand Journal of Educational Studies* 34(1), 247–54.

Grace, G. (1995) *School Leadership*. London: Falmer Press.

Gramsci, A. (1992) *Prison Notebooks (Volume 1)*. New York: Columbia State University Press.

Grubb, N. (1998) "Opening classrooms and improving schools: lessons from inspection systems in England." Paper presented to the American Educational Research Association, San Diego, April.

Guthrie, J. (1996) "Evolving political economies and the implications for educational evaluation," in *Evaluating and Reforming Education Systems* (pp. 61–83). Paris: OECD.

Halpin, D. and Troyna, B. (1995) "The politics of education policy borrowing," *Comparative Education* 31(3), 303–10.

Halpin, D. Fitz, J. and Power, S. (1997) "Opting into the past? Grant-maintained schools and the reinvention of tradition," in R. Glatter, P. Woods and C. Bagley (eds) *Choice and Diversity in Schooling* (pp. 59–70). London: Routledge.

Hargreaves, A. (1994) *Changing Teachers, Changing Times*. New York: Teachers College Press.

Hargreaves, A., Lieberman, A., Fullan, M. and Hopkins, D. (eds) (1998) *International Handbook of Educational Change*. Dordrecht: Kluwer.

Harold, B., Hawksworth, L., Mansell, H. and Thrupp, M. (1999) "A decade of change and continuity: emerging themes from the front lines of school reform," in M. Thrupp (ed.) *A Decade of Reform in New Zealand Education: where to now?* Special Issue of *New Zealand Journal of Educational Studies* 34(1), 234–46.

Harrison, T. and Kachur, J. (eds) (1999) *Contested Classrooms: education, globalization and democracy in Alberta*. Edmonton: University of Alberta Press and Parkland Institute.

Hart, D. and Livingstone, D. (1998) "The 'crisis' of confidence in schools and the neoconservative agenda: diverging opinions of corporate executives and the general public," *Alberta Journal of Educational Research* 44(1), 1–19.

Herndon, J. (1972) *How to Survive in Your Native Land*. New York: Bantam.

Hirsh, D. (1994) *A Matter of Choice*. Paris: OECD.

——(1995) "Policies for school choice: what can Britain learn from abroad?" in R. Glatter, P. Woods and C. Bagley (eds) *Choice and Diversity in Schooling* (pp. 152–65). London: Routledge.

Holmes, M. (1998) *The Reformation of Canada's Schools: breaking the barriers to parental choice*. Montreal: McGill/Queen's University Press.

Hopkins, D. and Levin, B. (2000) "Government policy and school improvement," *School Leadership and Management* 20(1), 15–30.

Howlett, M. (1991) "Policy instruments, policy styles, and policy implementation: national approaches to theories of instrument choice," *Policy Studies Journal* 19(2), 1–21.

Howlett , M. and Ramesh,. M. (1995) *Studying Public Policy: policy cycles and policy subsystems*. Toronto: Oxford University Press.

Hunter, H. (2000) "In the face of poverty: what a community school can do," in J. Silver (ed.) *Solutions that Work: fighting poverty in Winnipeg* (pp. 111–25). Winnipeg: Canadian Centre for Policy Alternatives.

Ironside, M. and Seifert, R. (1995) *Industrial Relations in Schools*. London: Routledge.

Jenkins, P. (1988) *Mrs Thatcher's Revolution: the ending of the socialist era*. Cambridge, MA: Harvard University Press.

Jesson, B. (1989) *Fragments of Labour*. Auckland: Penguin.

Jesson, J. (1999) "Battling against the odds: the changing nature of the teacher unions," in M. Thrupp (ed.) *A Decade of Reform in New Zealand Education: where to now?* Special Issue of *New Zealand Journal of Educational Studies* 34(1), 122–43.

Jones, K. (1989) *Right Turn: the Conservative revolution in education*. London: Hutchinson.

Kallen, D. (1996) "New educational paradigms and new evaluation policies," in *Evaluating and Reforming Education Systems* (pp. 7–23). Paris: OECD.

Kaufman, H. (1985) *Time, Chance and Organizations: natural selection in a perilous environment*. Chatham, NJ: Chatham House.

Kelsey, J. (1997) *The New Zealand Experiment*. Auckland: Auckland University Press.

Kiesler, S. and Sproull, L. (1982) "Managerial response to changing environments: perspectives on problem sensing from social cognition," *Administrative Science Quarterly* 27(4), 548–70.

Kingdon, J. (1994) *Agendas, Alternatives and Public Policies*, 2nd edn. New York: Harper-Collins.

Knight, C. (1990) *The Making of Tory Education Policy in Post-war Britain, 1950–1986*. London: Falmer Press.

Krahn, H. (1996) "School-work transitions: changing patterns and research needs." Consultation paper for the Applied Research Branch of Human Resources Development Canada.

Lange, C. (1996) "Open enrolment and its impact on school districts: an in-depth study of eight Minnesota school districts." Paper presented to the American Educational Research Association, New York, April.

Lauder, H., Hughes, D., Watson, S., Waslander, S., Thrupp, M., Strathdee, R., Simiyu, I., Dupuis, A., McGlinn, J. and Hamlin, J. (1999) *Trading in Futures: why markets in education don't work*. Buckingham: Open University Press.

Lawton, D. (1992) *Education and Politics in the 1990s: conflict or consensus?* London: Falmer Press.

——(1994) *The Tory Mind on Education*. London: Falmer Press.

Levačić, R. (1995) *Local Management of Schools: analysis and practice*. Buckingham: Open University Press.

Levin, B. (1993) "School response to a changing environment," *Journal of Educational Administration* 31(2), 4–21.

——(1995) "Education and poverty," *Canadian Journal of Education* 20(2), 211–24.

——(1997) "The lessons of international educational reform," *Journal of Education Policy* 12(3), 253–66.

——(1998a) "An epidemic of education policy: (what) can we learn from each other?" *Comparative Education* 34(2), 131–41.

——(1998b) "Criticizing the schools: 1957 and 1997," *Educational Policy Analysis Archives* 16(6), August 20. Http://olam.ed.asu.edu./epaa.

——(2000) "Putting students at the centre in education reform," *Journal of Educational Change*, 1(2), 155–72.

References

Levin, B. and Riffel, J.A. (1997) *Schools and the Changing World: struggling toward the future.* London: Falmer Press.

Levin, H. (1998) "Educational performance standards and the economy," *Educational Researcher* 27(4), 4–10.

Lindblom, C. (1980) *The Policy-making Process,* 2nd edn. Englewood Cliffs, NJ: Prentice-Hall.

——(1990) *Inquiry and Change.* New Haven: Yale University Press.

Lingard, B., Knight, J. and Porter, P. (1993) *Schooling Reform in Hard Times* (pp. 63–87). London: Falmer Press.

Linn, R. (2000) "Assessments and accountability," *Educational Researcher* 29(2), 4–15.

Lisac, M. (1995) *The Klein Revolution.* Edmonton, Alberta: NeWest.

Livingstone, D. (1998) *The Education–Jobs Gap.* Toronto: Garamond.

Livingstone, D. and Hart, D. (1998) "Where the buck stops: class differences in support for education," *Journal of Education Policy* 13(3), 351–77.

Loveless, T. (1997) "The structure of public confidence in education," *American Journal of Education* 105(2), 127–59.

Lowe, G. (2000) *The Quality of Work.* Toronto: Oxford University Press.

McDonnell, L. and Elmore, R. (1987) "Getting the job done: alternative policy instruments," *Educational Evaluation and Policy Analysis,* 9(2), 133–52.

McEwen, N. (1995) "Accountability in education in Canada," *Canadian Journal of Education* 20(1), 1–17.

McGeorge, C. (1995) "Private and integrated schools in NZ: subsidizing the illusion of choice," *Journal of Education Policy* 10(3), 259–70.

McLaughlin, M. (1987) "Learning from experience: lessons from policy implementation," *Educational Evaluation and Policy Analysis* 9(2), 171–8.

Macpherson, R. (1989) "Radical administrative reforms in New Zealand education: the implications of the Picot Report for institutional managers," *Journal of Educational Administration* 27(1), 29–44.

——(1996) "Accountability: towards raising a 'politically incorrect' issue," *Educational Management and Administration* 23(4), 139–50.

——(1999) "Towards bicultural daughters of Picot: nation building through 'low politics' educative leadership," in M. Thrupp (ed.) *A Decade of Reform in New Zealand Education: where to now?* Special Issue of *New Zealand Journal of Educational Studies* 34(1), 222–33.

McQueen, H. (1991) *The Ninth Floor: inside the Prime Minister's Office.* Auckland: Penguin.

Majone, G. (1989) *Evidence, Argument and Persuasion in the Policy Process.* New Haven: Yale University Press.

Manzer, R. (1994) *Public Schools and Political Ideas.* Toronto: University of Toronto Press.

March, J. (1978) "American public school administration: a short analysis," *School Review* 86(2), 217–50.

——(1984) "How we talk and how we act: administrative theory and administrative life," in T. Sergiovanni and J. Corbally (eds) *Leadership and Organizational Culture* (pp. 18–35). Urbana, IL: University of Illinois Press.

——(1991) "Exploration and exploitation in education," *Organizational Science* 2(1), 71–87.

March, J. and Olsen, J. (1989) *Rediscovering Institutions.* New York: Free Press.

Mazzoni, T. (1991) "Analyzing state school policymaking: an arena model," *Educational Evaluation and Policy Analysis* 13(2), Summer, 115–38.

——(1993) "The changing politics of state education policy making: a 20-year Minnesota perspective," *Educational Evaluation and Policy Analysis* 15(4), 357–79.

——(1994) "State policymaking and school reform: influences and influentials," in J. Scribner and D. Layton (eds) *The Study of Educational Politics* (pp. 53–74). London: Falmer Press.

Mehrens, W. (1998) "Consequences of assessment: what is the evidence?" *Educational Policy Analysis Archives* 6(13). Http:\\olam.ed.asu.edu/epaa/v6n13.html.

Merson, M. (1995) "Political explanations for economic decline in Britain and their relationship to policies for education and training," *Journal of Education Policy* 10(3), 303–15.

Metz, M. (1990) "Real school: a universal drama mid disparate experiences," in D. Mitchell and M. Goertz (eds) *Education Politics for the New Century*. London: Falmer Press.

Meyer, J. and Rowan, B. (1977) "Institutionalized organizations: formal structure as myth and ceremony," *American Journal of Sociology* 83(2), 340–63.

Mintrom, M. (2000) *Policy Entrepreneurs and School Choice*. Washington: Georgetown University Press.

Mitchell, D., McGee, C., Moltzen, R. and Oliver, D. (1993) *Hear Our Voices. Final Report of Monitoring Today's Schools Research Project*. Hamilton: University of Waikato.

Morris, R., Reid, E. and Fowler, J. (1993) *Education Act 93: a critical guide*. London: Association of Metropolitan Authorities.

Munn, P. (1993) "Parents as school board members," in P.Munn (ed.) *Parents and Schools* (pp. 87–100). London: Routledge.

Nathan, J. (1996) *Charter Schools*. San Francisco: Jossey-Bass.

Nathan, J. and Ysseldyke, J. (1994) "What Minnesota has learned about school choice," *Phi Delta Kappan* 75(9), 682–8.

National Committee for Responsive Philanthropy (1997) *Moving a Public Policy Agenda: the strategic philanthropy of conservative foundations*. Washington: NCRP. See also ncrop.org.

New Zealand (1988) *Tomorrow's Schools*. Wellington: Government Publishing.

New Zealand Treasury (1987) *Government Management: Brief to the Incoming Government, 1987. Volume II: Education Issues*. Wellington: The Treasury.

Odden, A. and Busch, C. (1998) *Financing Schools for High Performance: strategies for improving the use of educational resources*. San Francisco: Jossey-Bass.

OECD (1993) *Education at a Glance*. Paris: CERI/OECD.

——(1995) *Decision-Making in 14 OECD Education Systems*. Paris: OECD.

——(1996) *Meeting of the Education Committee at Ministerial Level – Lifelong Learning for All. Report of the Secretariat*. Paris; OECD.

Olssen, M. and Matthews, K. (eds) (1997) *Education Policy in New Zealand: the 1990s and beyond*. Palmerston: Dunmore Press.

Ouston, J., Fidler, B. and Earley, P. (1998) "The educational accountability of schools in England and Wales," in R. Macpherson, J. Cibulka, D. Monk and K. Wong (eds) *The Politics of Accountability* (pp. 107–19). Thousand Oaks: Corwin Press.

Peters, F. (1999) "Deep and brutal: funding cuts to education in Alberta," in T. Harrison and J. Kachur (eds) *Contested Classrooms: Education, Globalization and Democracy in Alberta* (pp. 85–97). Edmonton, Alberta: University of Alberta Press and Parkland Institute.

Plank, D. and Boyd, W.L. (1994) "Antipolitics, education, and institutional choice: the flight from democracy," *American Educational Research Journal* 31(2), 263–81.

Power, S. (1992) "Researching the impact of education policy: difficulties and discontinuities," *Journal of Education Policy* 7(5), 493–500.

Prawat, R. and Peterson, P. (1999) "Social constructivist views of learning," in J. Murphy and K. Louis (eds) *Handbook of Research on Educational Administration*, 2nd edn (pp. 203–26). San Francisco: Jossey-Bass.

Pressman, J. and Wildavksy, A. (1973) *Implementation*. Berkeley: University of California Press.

Raab, C., Munn, P., McAvoy, L., Bailey, L., Arnott, M. and Adler, M. (1997) "Devolving the management of schools in Britain," *Educational Administration Quarterly* 33(2), April, 140–57.

Ramsay, P. (1993) "Picot – vision and reality in New Zealand schools: an insider's view," in B. Lingard, J. Knight and P. Porter (eds) *Schooling Reform in Hard Times* (pp. 261–83). London: Falmer Press.

Ranson, S. (1994) *Towards the Learning Society*. London: Cassell.

References

Ribbins, P. and Sherratt, B. (1997) *Radical Educational Policies and Conservative Secretaries of State*. London: Cassell.

Richardson, R. (1995) *Making a Difference*. Christchurch: Shoal Bay Press.

Riffel, J., Levin, B. and Young, J. (1996) "Diversity in Canadian education," *Journal of Education Policy* 11(1), 113–23.

Roberts, N. and King, P. (1996) *Transforming Public Policy*. San Francisco: Jossey-Bass.

Robertson, S. and Smaller, H. (eds) (1996) *Teacher Activism in the 1990s*. Toronto: James Lorimer.

Robertson, S., Dale, R., Thrupp, M., Vaughan, K. and Jacka, S. (1997) *A Review of ERO – Final Report for the PPTA*. Auckland, University of Auckland.

Rogers, E. (1983) *Diffusion of Innovations*, 3rd edn. New York: Free Press.

Rose, R. (1993) *Lesson Drawing in Public Policy*. Chatham, NJ: Chatham House.

Schon, D. (1971) *Beyond the Stable State*. New York: Norton.

Senge, P. (1990) *The Fifth Discipline*. New York: Doubleday.

Sexton, S. (1990) *New Zealand Schools: an evaluation of recent reforms and future directions*. Wellington: New Zealand Business Roundtable.

Silver, H. and Silver, P. (1991) *An Educational War on Poverty*. Cambridge: Cambridge University Press.

Smelt, S. (1998) *Today's Schools: governance and quality*. Wellington: Victoria University Institute of Policy Studies.

Smrekar, C. (1996) *The Impact of School Choice and Community*. Albany: State University of New York Press.

Smylie, M. and Bryk, A. (2000) "Processes and mechanisms of change in Chicago Annenberg schools." Paper presented to the American Educational Research Association, Chicago, April.

Sofer, A. (2000) "LEAs: the problem or the solution?" in T. Cox (ed.) *Combating Educational Disadvantage* (pp. 177–90). London: Falmer Press, 2000.

Staw, B. (1976) "'Knee-deep in the Big Muddy': a study of escalating commitment to a chosen course of action," *Organizational Behavior and Human Performance* 16(1), 27–44.

Stone, D. (1988) *Policy Paradox and Political Reason*. New York: HarperCollins.

Taylor, A. (1996) "Education for 'post-industrial' purposes: understanding the context of change in Alberta Schools." Unpublished Ed.D. dissertation, University of Alberta.

Taylor, S., Rizvi, F., Lingard, B. and Henry, M. (1997) *Educational Policy and the Politics of Change*. London and New York: Routledge.

Thomas, H. and Martin, J. (1996) *Managing Resources for School Improvement*. London: Routledge.

Thrupp, M. (1998) "Exploring the politics of blame: school inspection and its contestation in New Zealand and England," *Comparative Education* 34(2), 195–209.

——(1999) *Schools Making a Difference: let's be realistic*. Buckingham and Philadelphia: Open University Press.

Thrupp, M. and Smith R. (1999) "A decade of ERO," in M. Thrupp (ed.) *A Decade of Reform in New Zealand Education: where to now?* Special Issue of *New Zealand Journal of Educational Studies* 34(1), 186–98.

Tomlinson, S. (2000) "Ethnic minorities and education: new disadvantages," in T. Cox (ed.) *Combating Educational Disadvantage* (pp. 17–36). London: Falmer Press.

Tuchman, B. (1978) *A Distant Mirror*. New York: Ballantine.

Tyack, D. (1995) "Reinventing schooling," in D. Ravitch and M. Vinovskis (ed.) *Learning from the Past: what history teaches us about school reform* (pp. 191–216). Baltimore: Johns Hopkins University Press.

Tyack, D. and Tobin, W. (1994) "The grammar of schooling: why has it been so hard to change?" *American Educational Research Journal* 31(3), 453–79.

Vincent, C. (1996) *Parents and Teachers: power and participation*. London: Falmer Press.

Walberg, H. (1987) "Learning and life-course accomplishments," in C. School and K. Warner Schaie (eds) *Cognitive Functioning and Social Structure over the Life Course* (pp. 203–29). Norwood, NJ: Ablex.

Walford, G. (ed.) (1994) *Researching the Powerful in Education*. London: UCL Press.

Wallace, M. (1995) "The contribution of the mass media to the education policy process," *International Journal of Educational Reform* 4(2), 124–30.

——(1998) "Mutual parasitism and symbiosis: interaction between media professionals and sources with a stake in education policy." Paper presented to the American Educational Research Association, San Diego, April.

West, M. and Hopkins, D. (1995) "Reconceptualising school effectiveness and school improvement." Paper presented to the British Educational Research Association/ European Conference on Educational Research, Bath, September.

Whitty, G. (1989) "The New Right and the national curriculum: state control or market forces?" *Journal of Education Policy* 4(4), 329–41.

——(1997) "Creating quasi-markets in education: a review of recent research on parental choice and school autonomy in three countries," *Review of Research in Education* 22, 3–47.

Whitty, G. and Edwards, T. (1992) "School choice policies in Britain and the USA: their origins and significance." Paper presented to the American Educational Research Association, San Francisco, April.

——(1994) "Researching Thatcherite education policy," in G. Walford (ed.) *Researching the Powerful in Education* (pp. 14–31). London: UCL Press.

——(1998) "School choice policies in England and the United States: an exploration of their origins and significance," *Comparative Education* 34(2), 211–27.

Whitty, G., Edwards, T. and Gewirtz, S. (1993) *Specialisation and Choice in Urban Education*. London: Routledge.

Whitty, G., Power, S. and Halpin, D. (1998) *Devolution and Choice in Education*. Buckingham and Philadelphia: Open University Press.

Wideen, M., O'Shea, T., Pye, I. and Ivany, G. (1997) "High-stakes testing and the teaching of science," *Canadian Journal of Education* 22(4), 428–44.

Wilcox, B. and Gray, J. (1996) *Inspecting Schools*. Buckingham: Open University Press.

Wildavsky, A. (1973) "If planning is everything, maybe it's nothing," *Policy Sciences* 4(2), 127–53.

Willis, D. (1992) "Educational assessment and accountability: a New Zealand case study," *Journal of Education Policy* 7(2), 205–21.

Wilson, J. (1989) *Bureaucracy*. New York: Basic.

Wilson, S., Peterson, P., Ball, D. and Cohen, D. (1996) "Learning by all," *Phi Delta Kappan* 77(7), 468–76.

Woods, P., Bagley, C. and Glatter, R. (1998) *School Choice and Competition: markets in the public interest?*. London: Routledge.

Wylie, C. (1997) *Self-managing Schools Seven Years On: what have we learned?* Wellington: New Zealand Council for Educational Research.

——(1999) *Ten Years On: how schools view educational reform*. Wellington: New Zealand Council on Educational Research.

Young, J. and Levin, B. (1998) *Understanding Canadian Schools: an introduction to educational administration*. Toronto: Harcourt Brace.

——(2000) "Education in transition: Canada," in D. Coulby, R. Cowen and C. Jones (eds) *World Yearbook of Education, 2000: Education in Times of Transition* (pp. 50–62). London: Kogan Page.

Index

2578 014

WITHDRAWAL